団体向け
テストプログラム

はじめて受ける
TOEFL ITP® TEST
総合対策【改訂版】

埼玉県立大学名誉教授
島崎美登里
順天堂大学国際教養学部教授
ポール・ワーデン
株式会社リンクグローバルソリューション プリンシパル
ロバート・ヒルキ

語研

本書は，弊社刊『はじめて受ける TOEFL® ITP TEST 総合対策』を TOEFL ITP® TEST の出題形式，出題傾向に即して改訂し，加筆修正したものです。

はじめに

TOEFL® (Test of English as a Foreign Language) は世界中で受験されている英語運用能力テストです。そのなかで TOEFL ITP® (Institutional Testing Program) は，団体向けテストプログラムであり，世界では 50 カ国以上で使用され，日本では 500 以上の教育機関や企業などの団体で利用されています。受験目的には大学のクラス分け，単位認定，実力診断，大学院入試，留学者選抜試験などがあります。

本書は，この TOEFL ITP® で高スコアを達成していただくための受験対策書です。まだ受けたことがない方，受験したことはあるものの，なかなかスコアが上がらずに苦労している方，そして受験日が迫って短期間での対策が必要な方に，本書が必ず役に立つと確信しています。一定以上のスコアを獲得するためには，Listening Comprehension，Structure and Written Expression，そして Reading Comprehension の 3 セクションのすべてについて，効果的な受験ストラテジーを身につける必要があります。本書は，初めて受験する方や，短期間でスコアを上げたいという皆さんを対象に，最も重要かつ効率のよい受験ストラテジーをまとめています。効果的な受験対策を行うためには，単に攻略法を知るだけでなく，TOEFL ITP® を忠実に反映した教材で学ぶ必要があります。本書は，過去の問題を詳細に分析し，問題傾向の推移を把握したうえで作成したものです。

- ● 効果の高い攻略ストラテジーとわかりやすい解説
- ● 本物に限りなく近い出題傾向とコンテンツ
- ● ハイクオリティの音声データ

本書のこれらの要素が，皆さんのスコアアップ，ひいては大学生活，留学生活を成功させる一助となることを心より願っています。

2023 年 1 月

著　者

目 次

I　Section 1　Listening Comprehension　攻略ストラテジー＋練習問題

Part A　*Short Conversations*
Part B　*Long Conversations*

Part C　*Talks*

本書の構成と使い方

本書の構成

本書は，セクション別攻略ストラテジー＋練習問題（Strategies），セクション別集中練習問題（Bursts），および本試験1回分の総合模試（Practice Test）により構成されています。

I	Section 1 Listening Comprehension 攻略ストラテジー＋練習問題
II	Section 2 Structure and Written Expression 攻略ストラテジー＋練習問題
III	Section 3 Reading Comprehension 攻略ストラテジー＋練習問題
IV	総合模試

攻略ストラテジー＋練習問題（Strategies）

各セクションを攻略するために，頻出設問パターンとその対策を学びます。まずはここでどのような設問が出題されるのか，それらの設問にどう対処すればよいのかといった基本事項を理解します。それぞれのストラテジーには，出題傾向に沿った練習問題が付属します。1問ずつ解答し，確実に攻略法を身につけてください。

集中練習問題（Bursts）

攻略ストラテジーの後半には数セットの集中練習問題を用意してあります。ここでは解答を確認しながら1問ずつ解くのではなく，1セットごとにまとめて解いたうえで，解答を確認するようにしてください。Burst とは本来は「集中射撃」という意味です。まとまった数の問題を一気に解くことで，試験のための集中力と解答のペースを身につけましょう。

総合模試（Practice Test）

各セクションの対策を終えたら，最後の仕上げとして模試にチャレンジしましょう。解き終わったら解説を読み，間違えた問題を中心に復習します。一度だけでなく何度も繰り返して解くことで，着実に実力をつけることができます。

◉ 本書の音声は無料でダウンロードできます。下記の URL または QR コードの【無料音声ダウンロードはこちら】から本書紹介ページにアクセスしてご利用ください（通信費が発生する場合があります）。

https://www.goken-net.co.jp/catalog/card.html?isbn=978-4-87615-368-8

◉ 音声は全 111 ファイルです。［Ⅰ Section1 Listening Comprehension 攻略ストラテジー＋練習問題］および［Ⅳ 総合模試］の Section1 Listening Comprehension で使用するすべての音声が収録されています。トラック番号はアイコン（🔊 001 〜）で示しています。

◉ 音声ファイルを利用して，ディクテーションやシャドウイングなど様々な学習方法に取り組んでみましょう。再生速度を変更して行うトレーニングもおすすめです。

⚠ **注意事項** ⚠

- ダウンロードで提供する音声は，複数のファイル・フォルダを ZIP 形式で 1 ファイルにまとめています。ダウンロード後に復元してご利用ください。ダウンロード後に，ZIP 形式に対応した復元アプリを必要とする場合があります。
- 音声ファイルは MP3 形式です。モバイル端末，パソコンともに，MP3 ファイルを再生可能なアプリ，ソフトを利用して聞くことができます。
- インターネット環境によってダウンロードできない場合や，ご使用の機器によって再生できない場合があります。
- 本書の音声ファイルは，一般家庭での私的使用の範囲内で使用する目的で頒布するものです。それ以外の目的で本書の音声ファイルの複製・改変・放送・送信などを行いたい場合には，著作権法の定めにより，著作権者等に申し出て事前に許諾を受ける必要があります。

【装丁】 山田 英春

【音声吹き込み】 Edith Kayumi
　　　　　　　　 Josh Keller
　　　　　　　　 Jack Merluzzi
　　　　　　　　 Carolyn Miller

TOEFL ITP® TESTについて

TOEFL（Test of English as a Foreign Language）は米国，カナダの大学，大学院への留学を希望する，英語を母国語としない人々に課される英語能力評価テストです。アメリカの標準化テスト開発機関 ETS（Educational Testing Service）が問題を作成し，日本での運営は ETS Japan 合同会社が行っています。

TOEFL は本来，留学希望者の英語能力を評価する目的で作成されているため，その内容もキャンパスでの会話，大学でのディスカッション，アメリカ史や地学などの大学での講義内容を素材として，アカデミズム指向の強い試験となっています。

TOEFLはこれまで，PBT（Paper-Based Test），CBT（Computer-Based Test），iBT（internet-Based Test）とさまざまな形式を取り入れてきましたが，2006 年以降は，留学希望者に対しては TOEFL iBT のみの受験が義務付けられています。

TOEFL ITP（Test of English as a Foreign Language Institutional Testing Program）は団体受験に限って実施されているテストで，マークシート方式のペーパー版と，インターネット接続できるコンピュータを使用したデジタル版があります。2020 年から導入されたデジタル版は，問題数およびスコアスケールがペーパー版と同一です。TOEFL ITP は，主に大学，短期大学，語学学校でのクラス分けや大学院入試のために活用されています。受験結果は公式の TOEFL スコアとしては認定されないため，留学志望先に提出することはできません（TOEFL iBT のスコアを提出する必要があります）。しかし，過去のペーパーテスト版TOEFL（PBT）の問題を再利用し，採点方法なども TOEFL iBT に準じているため，TOEFL iBT のスコアと高い相関関係があるとされています。そのため，現在 500 以上の教育機関（高校・大学・大学院など）や団体，企業で実施されています。生徒や社員の英語力の測定，交換留学の選抜試験，社員の研修，クラス分けのために利用されています。また，TOEFL iBT に比べ，受験料も安くて受験しやすいため，TOEFL iBT の受験準備にも多く利用されています。TOEFL ITP は団体受験限定ですので，受験申し込みについては所属している団体や教育機関にご確認ください。

　TOEFL ITP は Listening Comprehension，Structure and Written Expression，Reading Comprehension の 3 つのセクションで構成されています。TOEFL ITP には Level 1 と Level 2 があり，Level 1 は過去の PBT 問題をそのまま利用し，Level 2 は内容をやさしめに作られています。本書では Level 1 を対象としています。

Section 1	Listening Comprehension（解答時間：約 35 分　問題数：50 問）
Part A	短い会話を聞き，その内容についての設問に答える。（約 15 分　30 問）
Part B	長めの会話を聞き，その内容についての設問に答える。 （約 7 分　8 問または 9 問，会話は 2 題）
Part C	講義，学術的なトークなどを聞き，その内容についての設問に答える。 （約 12 分　12 問または 11 問，トークは 3 題）

Section 2	Structure and Written Expression（解答時間：25 分　問題数：40 問）
Structure	空所補充問題（15 問）
Written Expression	誤文訂正問題（25 問）

Section 3	Reading Comprehension（解答時間：55 分　問題数：50 問）
パッセージ（250 〜 350 語程度）を読み，その内容あるいは語彙についての設問に答える。 （50 問，パッセージは 5 題または 6 題）	

　試験時間は約 2 時間，問題は全部で 140 問あります。試験官の指示に従い，最初に Listening Comprehension を解き，その後に Structure and Written Expression と Reading Comprehension に移ります。試験監督官の指示に従って，指定されたセクションだけを解かなければなりません。他のセクションを無断で解いていると判断された場合にはスコアが無効になる可能性があります。

　なお，減点法は採用されていませんので，必ず全問を解くように心がけてください。どうしても正答がわからない場合は，必ず選択肢のひとつにマークしてから次の問題に進みます。その際は常に特定の選択肢にマークしても，そのつどマークする選択肢を変えても，それが偶然に正答になる確率は変わりません。

TOEFL ITP の問題冊子（test book）では，Section 1-3 の各最初のページに例題と，それ
に基づく解答方法が Test Directions として英文で説明されています。Test Directions の著
作権は ETS（Educational Testing Service）が有しているため，本書では掲載することがで
きません。そこで，出題形式と解答方法を簡単に説明しておきます。受験前に出題形式と解
答方法を知っておけば，受験の際に Test Directions を読む必要はありません。なお，3 セクショ
ンとも 4 つの選択肢から正解ひとつを選ぶ 4 択式問題です。(A)(B)(C)(D) の選択肢のうちか
ら正解ひとつを選んで，解答用紙の該当するマークを鉛筆で塗りつぶすマークシート形式で
す。くれぐれも問題番号を間違えないようにしてください。なお，ペーパー版の試験では問
題冊子への書き込みが可となり，デジタル版の試験では自分で用意した紙にメモをとること
が許可されています。また，途中休憩はありません。

Section 1 *Listening Comprehension*

会話，講義を聞いて理解する能力を評価します。話者が述べた内容，あるいは言葉で明確
に述べていなくても示唆している内容に基づいて正解を選びます。

Part A: Short Conversations

2 人の短い会話を聞きます。設問と選択肢が，問題冊子に記載されています。会話が終わ
ると，その内容に関して設問が読まれます。会話，設問ともに一度だけ読まれます。問題冊
子にある 4 つの選択肢から正解と思われるものひとつを選んで，解答用紙のマークを塗りつ
ぶします。会話および問題数は 30 問です。

Sample Answer
● Ⓑ Ⓒ Ⓓ

What does the man mean?

(A)　He was not able to make the deadline.
(B)　He did not know when the assignment was due.
(C)　He was not able to find the reference book.
(D)　He did not discuss with the professor.

Part B: Long Conversations

2人の長めの会話を聞きます。設問と選択肢が，問題冊子に記載されています。会話が終わると，その内容に関して4つの設問が読まれます。会話，設問ともに一度だけ読まれます。問題冊子にある4つの選択肢から正解と思われるものひとつを選んで，解答用紙のマークを塗りつぶします。会話は2つ，問題数は計8問または9問です。

Sample Answer

Ⓐ ● Ⓒ Ⓓ

What are the man and woman discussing?

(A) Job opportunities

(B) Course requirements

(C) Class schedules

(D) Faculty members

Part C: Talks

ひとりの話者による講義などのトークを聞きます。設問と選択肢が，問題冊子に記載されています。トークが終わると，その内容に関して3~5つの設問が読まれます。トーク，設問ともに一度だけ読まれます。問題冊子にある4つの選択肢から正解と思われるものひとつを選んで，解答用紙のマークを塗りつぶします。トークは3つ，問題数は計12問または11問です。

Sample Answer

Ⓐ ● Ⓒ Ⓓ

What is the main point of this lecture?

(A) Global warming

(B) Endangered species

(C) Tidal waves

(D) Deforestation

標準的な書き言葉の英語を理解する能力を評価します。Structure（空所補充問題）と Written Expression（誤文訂正問題）の2種類の問題があります。

Structure

文の一部が空所になっています。その空所を構文，あるいは文法的に正しく補う語句を，4 つの選択肢からひとつ選びます。15問あります。

Sample Answer

(A) ● (C) (D)

A librarian can help you ------- the books you need.

(A) finds

(B) find

(C) found

(D) having found

Written Expression

文中の4つの語句に下線が引かれています。文法的な誤りを含む語句をひとつ選びます。 25問あります。

Sample Answer

(A) (B) ● (D)

Computers <u>can facilitate</u> self-paced <u>learning</u>, while <u>to give</u>
          A   B   C

immediate reinforcement <u>and</u> feedback.
                          D

Section 3 *Reading Comprehension*

　大学の授業で読むアカデミックな内容のパッセージを読んで理解する能力を評価します。パッセージの後に 10 問前後の設問と，それぞれ 4 つの選択肢が用意されています。設問に対する解答として正しいものをひとつ選びます。パッセージで述べられている内容，あるいは言葉で明確に述べられていなくても示唆している内容に基づいて正解を選びます。パッセージは 5 つまたは 6 つ，問題数は計 50 問です。

Sample Answer

Ⓐ Ⓑ Ⓒ ●

What does the passage mainly discuss?

(A) Media literacy

(B) Religious beliefs

(C) Mass communication

(D) Interpersonal skills

	TOEFL ITP		TOEFL iBT	
	問題数	解答時間	問題数	解答時間
Listening (Comprehension)	50 問	約 35 分	28 問 講義：3 題（各 6 問） 会話：2 題（各 5 問）	36 分
Structure and Written Expression	40 問	25 分		
Reading (Comprehension)	50 問	55 分	20 問 2 パッセージ（各 10 問）	35 分
Speaking			4 問 Independent task 1 問 Integrated tasks 3 問	16 分
Writing			2 問 Integrated task 1 問 Academic Discussion task 1 問	29 分
合計	140 問	約 115 分	54 問	約 2 時間

 TOEFL ITP は Listening Comprehension, Structure and Written Expression, Reading Comprehension の 3 部構成です。TOEFL iBT には Structure and Written Expression はなく，Reading, Listening, Speaking, Writing の 4 セクションがあります。

スコアについて

　スコアレポートは 1 〜 2 週間で発送されます。スコアは Listening Comprehension と Structure and Written Expression が 31 〜 68 点，Reading Comprehension が 31 〜 67 点で計算されます。合計点の算出方法は，

$$\text{(Listening + Structure + Reading)} \times 10 \div 3$$

という計算式で，最低 310 点，最高 677 点になります。

　一般的に，大学での交換留学に必要な最低基準は 500 点，アメリカやカナダの大学への正規留学には最低 500 〜 550 点，大学院への留学では最低 550 〜 600 点が必要となります。

TOEFL ITP デジタル版に関する注意点

　デジタル版の受験は要件を満たしたパソコンのみ使用が認められています。タブレットやスマホを使って受験することはできません。

　問題数，スコアスケール，スコアの見方はペーパー版と同じです。ただし，Structure and Written Expression と Reading Comprehension のセクションでは受験者が時間内に解答を終えれば，次のセクションに進んだり，試験を終了したりすることができるため，所定の解答時間より早く終わることがあります。

　Listening Comprehension のセクションについては，本書は主としてペーパー版試験の解法を示しています。デジタル版については，各会話やトークが始まるときに設問と選択肢が一緒に表示される形式へ切り替えられてきています。その形式の場合，設問を先読みする時間はほとんどありませんが，それでも設問の最初の疑問詞，主語，動詞などに素早く目を通し，設問の答えに関連する情報を聞き取るように努めるとよいでしょう。

I

Section 1
Listening Comprehension
攻略ストラテジー＋練習問題

Section 1 　　Part A/B（会話問題）の概要

Listening Comprehension セクションは以下の構成になっている。本節では，Short Conversations と Long Conversations を攻略する（赤色の部分）。

Listening Comprehension（50問：約35分）

Part A（30問）	Part B（8または9問）	Part C（12または11問）
Short Conversations	Long Conversations	Talks

> **主な特徴**
>
> ◆ 全問とも四肢択一形式。
>
> ◆ 音声に合わせて試験が進行するため，解答時間を自分で配分することができない。
>
> ◆ 問題用紙に設問と選択肢が印刷されている。

Short Conversations

2人の人物が交わす短い会話30編を聞き，その内容についての設問に答える出題形式。ひとつの会話につき1問が出題される。解答は4つの選択肢からひとつを選ぶ四肢択一形式。

Long Conversations

同様に2人の人物の会話を聞き，その内容についての設問に答える出題形式だが，Short Conversations に比べ会話は長めである。会話は2つあり，ひとつの会話につき約4問出題される。4つの選択肢からひとつを選ぶ四肢択一形式。

Short Conversations，Long Conversations のいずれも，学生同士，学生と教官，あるいは学生と大学職員などによりキャンパス内で展開される会話がほとんどである。また，会話の話題も授業，アルバイト，課外活動など，大学生活になじみの深いものが多い。

Section Ⅰ Part A/B

Section Ⅰ Part C

Section 2

Section 3

総合模試

総合模試 解答・解説

▰◀ Listening Comprehension PartA/B のストラテジー

　本節では，会話問題で共通して使える［総合的なストラテジー］と，頻出の設問形式やヒントとなる表現に的を絞った［特有のストラテジー］の2種類に分けて学習を進める。基本的なストラテジーはShort Conversationsで学習し，「4. Long Conversationsへの応用1」「10. Long Conversations への応用2」で Part B への応用を学ぶ。

▰◀ 総合的なストラテジー

1.　話の核となる「キーワード」を聞き取る
2.　「設問を先読み」して答えに関する情報を聞き取る
3.　「繰り返される情報」に注意する
4.　Long Conversations への応用1

▰◀ 特有のストラテジー

5.　「出来事」と「行動」を理解する
6.　「問題点」と「解決策」を把握する
7.　「示唆」と「意図」を推測する
8.　「賛成」と「反対」に注意する
9.　「イントネーション」と「皮肉表現」に注意する
10.　Long Conversations への応用2

1. 話の核となる「キーワード」を聞き取る

最重要ストラテジー ▶▶▶

◆ はっきりと発音される「キーワード」に注意して会話を聞くことで，話の内容と解答のヒントをつかむことができる。

◆ 「キーワード」がそのまま使われている選択肢は誤答の可能性が高い。正解にはキーワードの言い換え表現が用いられることが多い。

　会話の内容を理解するには，まず話の核となる「キーワード」を聞き取る必要がある。ここで言う「キーワード」とは，具体的な意味を持つ内容語（名詞や動詞など）のことである。話者は相手にメッセージを伝えようとするため，内容語は機能語（前置詞や助動詞など）に比べ，よりはっきりと発音される。また，特に重要な語は声の大きさ，発音の長さ，イントネーションなどで強調されるため，認識しやすい。こうしたキーワードの聞き取りは，会話のポイントをつかんで内容を理解するうえで大きなヒントとなる。

例えば次のような会話を考えてみよう。

> W: Have you ever **received financial aid** from the **college**?
> M: No, this is my **first time**.

　この会話の場合，最も強調して発音されるのは太字の received，financial aid，college，first time である。これらの語を聞き取るだけでも，大学の奨学金申請に関するやりとりであることがつかめる。特にリスニングを苦手とする学習者の場合，まずはこうした内容語の聞き取りに集中し，会話の中心になっている話題を把握する練習から始めるのがよい。学習の過程で繰り返し会話を聞き，徐々に耳を慣らして機能語，文全体，会話全体の理解へと進めていく学習法が有効である。

　ただし，聞き取れた「単語そのもの」にとらわれることは危険である。TOEFL ITP では，誤答選択肢中に会話で使われた語句をそのまま使い，正答ではキーワードを言い換え，別の表現で表すことが多い。はっきり聞こえた語がそのままの形で使われている選択肢には注意する必要がある。重要なのは，キーワードの表す「内容」であって，単語そのものではない。

練習問題　▶▶▶　☞ はっきりと聞き取れる「キーワード」に注意して会話を聞き，解答しなさい。

◀)) 001　**1.** What does the man plan to do?

(A) See the professor later today

(B) Drop the professor's class

(C) Visit the professor tomorrow

(D) Contact the professor at home　Ⓐ Ⓑ Ⓒ Ⓓ

◀)) 002　**2.** What is the woman's problem?

(A) Her advisor is leaving the university.

(B) She cannot take a required class.

(C) She does not want to major in psychology.

(D) A professor would not let her enroll in his class.　Ⓐ Ⓑ Ⓒ Ⓓ

◀)) 003　**3.** What will the man probably do?

(A) Read the world news next

(B) Order what the woman suggested

(C) Continue making a plan

(D) Ask the server to bring a menu　Ⓐ Ⓑ Ⓒ Ⓓ

1.

🔊 001 **M:** Professor Johnson, I have class next period, but I really need to talk to you. Could I drop by your office this afternoon?

W: Sure, I have an office hour today from three to four. I'll look forward to seeing you then.

Q: What does the man plan to do?

M: ジョンソン先生，次の時限にクラスがあるのですが，どうしてもお話ししたいことがあります。今日の午後オフィスにうかがってよろしいでしょうか。

W: いいですよ，今日は3時から4時までがオフィスアワーです。その時間にお会いするのを楽しみにしています。

設問訳 男性は何をするつもりですか。

(A) 今日のちほど教授に会う
(B) 教授のクラスの受講をやめる
(C) 明日教授を訪ねる
(D) 自宅にいる教授に連絡する

解法 設問を先読みしてから会話を聞き，会話内で男性が今後行うことを聞き取る。強くはっきりと話されるキーワードを聞き取ることで，会話の内容と問題を解くヒントが得られる。この会話のキーワードは professor，talk，drop by，office hour，today などで，男性が教授と会う約束をしている会話であることがわかる。設問は男性の今後の行動について問うもので，今日の3時から4時のオフィスアワーの間に会うと教授に言われていることから，正解は (A)。

重要語
- **drop by ...**「~に立ち寄る」
- **office hour**「オフィスアワー」
  *教官がオフィスにいて学生の対応をする時間

2.

🔊 002 **W:** I just found out I can't register for a psychology course I need for my major. It's full. And Dr. Fredericks is on leave next semester, so I can't take it then, either.

M: Wow, I guess that means you'll have to postpone graduation. That's one of the problems with course requirements.

Q: What is the woman's problem?

W: 専攻にとって必要な心理学を履修できないことがわかったところなのよ。もう定員なの。次の学期にはフレデリクス先生は休暇を取るので，そのときも履修できないわ。

M: あれ，それじゃ卒業を延ばさなきゃならないってことだと思うよ。必修科目に起こるような問題のひとつだね。

設問訳 女性の問題は何ですか。

(A) 彼女の指導教官が大学を去る。

(B) 彼女は必修のクラスを取れない。

(C) 彼女は心理学を専攻したくない。

(D) 教授は彼女が自分のクラスに履修登録するのを許してくれない。

解法 設問を先読みしてから会話を聞き，会話内で女性の問題点を聞き取る。この会話のキーワードは can't register，psychology course，need などであり，必修科目である心理学の履修登録について話していることがわかる。女性の問題は心理学を履修できないことであり，正解は (B)。(A) の leaving「辞める」と会話中の on leave「休暇中」の違いに注意。

重要語
- □ **register for ...** 「~に登録する」
- □ **psychology**「心理学」
- □ **major**「専攻」
- □ **postpone**「~を延期する」

3.

解答：B

W: A lot of the items on this menu look interesting, but I know the meatball spaghetti and the garlic bread are out of this world.

M: Well, that sounds like a plan, then.

Q: What will the man probably do?

W: このメニューの多くの料理には興味をそそられるけど，ミートボールスパゲティとガーリックブレッドが絶品だってことはわかっているの。

M: じゃあ，それがよさそうだね。

設問訳 男性はおそらく何をしますか。

(A) 次に世界のニュースを読む

(B) 女性の提案したものを注文する

(C) 計画を練り続ける

(D) メニューを持ってくるように給仕人に頼む

解法 設問を先読みしてから会話を聞き，会話内で男性がおそらく行うことを聞き取る。menu，meatball spaghetti などから，レストランの注文に関する会話であることがわかる。男性は Well, that sounds like a plan, then. と述べ，彼は女性が勧めるものを注文すると予測できるので，正解は (B)。(A) の world，(C) の plan，(D) の menu は会話中に登場する語だが，正解ではない。受験者を惑わすために用いられている。正解の (B) に会話内の単語は使われておらず，内容を言い換える表現になっていることに注意。

重要語
- □ **out of this world** 「絶品の」
- □ **That sounds like a plan.** 「よさそうですね」

2. 「設問を先読み」して答えに関する情報を聞き取る

最重要ストラテジー ▶▶▶

◆ 漠然と会話を聞いていては要点や解答のポイントをつかみにくい。会話を聞く前に設問を素早く読み，その答えに関する情報を聞き取るようにする。

　流れてくる会話を漠然と聞いていると，解答のポイントを逃してしまいがちになる。これを避けるため，受験者は常に会話を聞く前に設問をさっと読み，会話内の何にフォーカスして聞けばよいかを知っておき，その情報を聞き取るようにする必要がある。

　会話問題の代表的な設問には次のようなものがある。

設問例

🦎 **現在の出来事，今後の行動，過去の思い込みを問う設問**

　　□ What is the man doing?

　　□ What will the man probably do?

🦎 **会話で述べている問題点やトラブル，問題点に対する解決策を問う設問**

　　□ What is the man's problem?

　　□ What does the man suggest?

🦎 **会話で示唆されている内容，話者の意図を問う設問**

　　□ What can be inferred from this conversation?

　　□ What does the woman imply?

🦎 **話者の賛否を問う設問**

　　□ What does the man mean?

🦎 **話者の感情や皮肉を読み取る設問**

　　□ How does the man feel?

Section Ⅰ Part A/B

Section Ⅰ Part C

Section 2

Section 3

総合模試

総合模試 解答・解説

それぞれの設問タイプについては Part A 特有のストラテジー（38 ページ以降）で再び学習する。本項では聞く前に設問を読み，会話内の聞き取るべきポイントを把握したうえで会話を聞く練習を行う。

練習問題 ▶▶▶　　☞ 設問を素早く読んでから会話を聞き，解答しなさい。

🔊 004　　**4.** What does the professor suggest that the man do?

　　(A)　Hand in his paper on time

　　(B)　Better focus the topic of his essay

　　(C)　Consider moving out of the dorm

　　(D)　Get more involved in class activities　　Ⓐ Ⓑ Ⓒ Ⓓ

🔊 005　　**5.** What is the man planning to do?

　　(A)　Eat lunch at the cafeteria

　　(B)　Pick up books at the bookstore

　　(C)　See an exhibit of student art

　　(D)　Meet an admissions officer　　Ⓐ Ⓑ Ⓒ Ⓓ

🔊 006　　**6.** What does the woman want to do?

　　(A)　Purchase a motorcycle

　　(B)　Sell her old bike

　　(C)　Buy a bicycle

　　(D)　Go biking with the man　　Ⓐ Ⓑ Ⓒ Ⓓ

4.

🔊 004 **M:** Professor Richards, our dorm is holding a festival this week and I was wondering if I could get an extension on the due date for my essay.

W: Jack, we all have competing interests and activities in our lives, but I'm going to have to insist that you try to meet the deadline. It wouldn't be fair to the other students if I gave you special treatment.

Q: What does the professor suggest that the man do?

　M: リチャーズ先生，寮で今週フェスティバルがあって，レポートの提出期限を延ばしていただけないかと思っていました。

　W: ジャック，だれもが生活の中で，両立できないような興味や活動を経験しますが，締め切りに間に合うようにがんばってみなさい。あなたを特別扱いしたら，ほかの学生に公平ではありませんから。

設問訳 教授は男性に何をするよう提案していますか。

(A) レポートを期日どおりに提出する
(B) レポートのトピックをさらに絞る
(C) 寮から出ることを検討する
(D) クラス活動にもっと積極的に参加する

解法 設問を先読みしてから会話を聞き，会話内で教授が提案していることを聞き取る。男性は I was wondering if I could get an extension ... とレポート提出期限の延長を頼んでおり，教授が対応している。男性の問題点に対する教授の提案として，締め切りに間に合わせるためにがんばるよう男性に言っているので，正解は (A)。

重要語
☐ **due date**「締め切り日」
☐ **meet the deadline**「締め切りを守る」

5.

🔊 005 **M:** Excuse me, do you know where the senior art exhibit is being held?

W: Yes, it's over there at the Fine Arts Center. That's the red brick building just behind the cafeteria and right between the Admissions Office and the College Bookstore.

Q: What is the man planning to do?

　M: すみません，4年生の美術展がどこで開かれているかご存じですか。

　W: はい，あちらのファインアーツセンターです。カフェテリアの裏で，入学事務室と大学書店の間にある赤いレンガの建物です。

Section I Part A/B　Section I Part C　Section 2　Section 3　総合模試　総合模試 解答・解説

設問訳 男性は何をするつもりですか。

(A) カフェテリアで昼食をとる
(B) 書店で本を買う
(C) 学生の美術展を見る
(D) 入学課の職員に会う

解法 設問を先読みしてから会話を聞き，会話内で男性が今後行うことを聞き取る。男性は，do you know where ...?「どこ」，art exhibit「美術展」という表現を使って場所を尋ねていて，これから美術展に行くつもりであることがわかるので，正解は (C)。

重要語
□ **senior**「大学 4 年生」
□ **Admissions Office**「入学事務室」

6. 　解答：C

◀)) 006　**W:** The campus is so big and it's hard to get from one class to another. I'd really like to get a bicycle, but they're so expensive.

M: In that case, why don't you check the ads in the student newspaper? People advertise used bikes there all the time.

Q: What does the woman want to do?

　W: キャンパスがとても広くて，ひとつの授業から次の授業に行くのがたいへんだわ。自転車が本当にほしいけど，とても高いのよね。

　M: だったら学生新聞の広告を見てみたらどうかな。いつも中古自転車の広告が出ているよ。

設問訳 女性は何をしたいのですか。

(A) オートバイを買う
(B) 古い自転車を売る
(C) 自転車を買う
(D) 男性とサイクリングに行く

解法 設問を先読みしてから会話を聞き，会話内で女性がしたいことを聞き取る。会話中に get a bicycle，advertise used bikes と出てくるので，自転車の購入について話していることがわかり，正解は (C)。

重要語
□ **why don't you ...**「〜してはどうですか」
□ **bike**「自転車」(= bicycle)
□ **motorcycle**「オートバイ」

３. 「繰り返される情報」に注意する

最重要ストラテジー ▶▶▶

◆ 会話の中で繰り返し述べられる事実や情報が正答と結びつきやすい。

◆ 繰り返される情報は同意語や言い換え表現が使われる。選択肢に同じ語が使われている場合は，受験者を惑わすことを目的としている可能性が高いので注意が必要。

　TOEFL ITP では，会話の中で特定の情報，事実などが何度も繰り返し述べられることが多い。これらは重要な情報で，しばしば正答を導き出すポイントとなる。したがって，これらの繰り返される情報から正答を得られる可能性があることを受験者は覚えておくべきである。

　情報の繰り返しには同じ語句がそのまま使われることは少なく，多くの場合同意語や異なった文構成を用いて言い換えられる。このため単に単語レベルの聞き取りではなく，内容をしっかりと把握する力が必要となる。「1. 話の核となるキーワードを聞き取る」の項で解説したように，同じ単語を用いた選択肢は受験者を惑わすために使われる可能性が高いので注意が必要である。

次の会話を見てみよう。

> W: I remember you told me you wanted to work with young kids after <u>you got your teaching certification</u>. Are you still <u>enrolled in the teacher education program</u>?
>
> M: I am. In fact, **I'm on my way to a local elementary school right now. I work there two days a week, and three days a week I do volunteer teaching in a kindergarten.**
>
> Q: What do we learn about the man from this conversation?
>
> A: He is preparing to become a teacher.

　上記の例では，教職課程をとっていることが下線部で，そのためにしている活動について太字部分でそれぞれ何度か述べられている。これらから，設問の解答に結びつく「男性は教師になる準備をしている」ことがわかる。

練習問題 ▶▶▶　☞ 会話の中で繰り返される情報に注意して解答しなさい。

◀)) 007　**7.** What does the man say about the reading assignment?

(A) He did not have time to go over it yet.

(B) He does not think it is so interesting.

(C) He could not understand it.

(D) He was not able to find his copy.　Ⓐ Ⓑ Ⓒ Ⓓ

◀)) 008　**8.** What will the woman probably do?

(A) Loan the man some money

(B) Return home to change her clothes

(C) Join the man for dinner

(D) Make another cup of coffee　Ⓐ Ⓑ Ⓒ Ⓓ

◀)) 009　**9.** What do the man and woman say about Professor Callahan?

(A) Her lectures could be better organized.

(B) She did not make enough handouts for her lecture.

(C) Her examples are not very relevant.

(D) She is an outstanding lecturer.　Ⓐ Ⓑ Ⓒ Ⓓ

7.

◀))） 007

W: I read the article Professor Allison assigned us but couldn't make heads or tails out of it. What about you?

M: The same. Why don't we go over to see her during her office hour this afternoon? I'm glad to hear I'm not the only one who couldn't figure it out.

Q: What does the man say about the reading assignment?

　　W: アリソン先生が課題にした論文を読んだけど，さっぱりわからなかったわ。あなたはどう？

　　M: 同じだよ。今日の午後，先生のオフィスアワーに会いに行ってみようか。理解できなかったのが僕だけではなくてほっとしたよ。

設問訳 男性はリーディングの課題について何と言っていますか。

(A) まだ読む時間が取れなかった。
(B) それほど興味を持てなかった。
(C) 理解できなかった。
(D) プリントが見つからなかった。

解法 設問を先読みしてから会話を聞き，会話内で男性が課題について言っていることを聞き取る。男性が課題を理解できなかったことは"couldn't make heads or tails out of it.""The same.""I'm glad to hear I'm not the only one who couldn't figure it out."という発言からわかる。正解は (C)。

重要語
□ **assign**「～を割り当てる，課題として出す」
□ **can't make heads or tails**「さっぱりわからない」
□ **figure out**「～を理解する」

8.

◀))） 008

M: Jo Anne, is there any way I could borrow a dollar to get another cup of coffee?

W: I guess I could spare some change, as long as you promise to pay me back.

Q: What will the woman probably do?

　　M: ジョアン，コーヒーをお代わりしたいんだけど，1ドル借りられないかな。

　　W: 返すと約束してくれるなら，いくらか貸してあげられるけど。

設問訳 女性はおそらく何をしますか。

 (A) 男性にお金を貸す

 (B) 着替えるために帰宅する

 (C) 男性の夕食につきあう

 (D) コーヒーをもう一杯いれる

解法 設問を先読みしてから会話を聞き，会話内で女性がおそらく行うことを聞き取る。borrow a dollar，spare some change，pay me back のようにお金の貸し借りについての情報が繰り返し出てくる点に注意。正解は (A)。

重要語

□ **spare some change**「いくらか貸す」

□ **pay back**「返済する」

9.　　　　　　　　　　　　　　　　　　　　　　　　　　　　　解答：D

🔊 009

M: Professor Callahan has got to be one of the best lecturers at the school. Her talk today was so well organized and easy to follow. She even gave us that handout that outlined what she was going to cover.

W: Best of all are her examples. Since they're from her own experience, they are really interesting and really support the points she's making.

Q: What do the man and woman say about Professor Callahan?

 M: キャラハン教授は，間違いなくこの学校で最高の講師のひとりだよ。今日の話はよく組み立てられていて理解しやすかった。押さえておきたいことを概説したプリントまでくれたしね。

 W: 何より先生の挙げる例がいいわよ。自分の経験に基づいているから，本当におもしろいし，先生の主張を支えているわね。

設問訳 男性と女性はキャラハン教授について何と言っていますか。

 (A) 彼女の講義はもっとよい構成にできる。

 (B) 彼女が講義のために作ったプリントは数が足りなかった。

 (C) 彼女の挙げる例はあまり適切ではない。

 (D) 彼女はすばらしい講師である。

解法 設問を先読みしてから会話を聞き，会話内で男性と女性が教授について言っていることを聞き取る。キャラハン教授がすばらしい講師（one of the best lecturers at the school）であることを，2人は次のように複数の理由を挙げて説明している。正解は (D)。

 》 Her talk today was so well organized and easy to follow.

 》 Best of all are her examples.

 》 they are really interesting and really support the points she's making

重要語

□ **handout**「プリント」

□ **outline**「～を概説する」

4.　Long Conversations への応用 1

最重要ストラテジー ▶▶▶

◆ 話の核となる「キーワード」を聞き取る

◆ 「設問を先読み」して答えに関する情報を聞き取る

◆ 「繰り返される情報」に注意する

　これまでに学習してきた Part A の総合的なストラテジーは，Part B にも応用することができる。ただし，Part A に比べて会話が長く，ひとつの会話に対して複数の設問があるため，さらに高度なリスニング力が求められる。

これまでに学んだストラテジーを応用し，以下のことを心がけよう。

◈ 話の核となる「キーワード」を聞き取り，会話の内容を把握する。

◈ 漠然と会話を聞かず，「設問を先読み」してから答えに関する情報を聞き取る。

◈ 会話の中で「繰り返される情報」に注意する。

　Part B では「いつ」「どこで」「だれが(と)」「何を」「どのように」などの会話内の情報を問う問題が，Part A より多く見受けられる。基本的な話の流れや，会話で述べる数字や日付などの具体的な情報に留意して，整理しながらリスニングを行おう。

練習問題　▶▶▶　☞ 設問を素早く読み，キーワード，繰り返される情報に注意しながら会話を聞いて，解答しなさい。

10. At what time of the year is this conversation probably taking place?

 (A) During spring vacation

 (B) At the beginning of spring term

 (C) Toward the end of spring term

 (D) At the start of summer vacation   Ⓐ Ⓑ Ⓒ Ⓓ

11. What kind of job will the woman have this summer?

 (A) Lifeguard

 (B) Part-time teacher

 (C) Food server

 (D) Sales clerk   Ⓐ Ⓑ Ⓒ Ⓓ

12. What field is the woman studying?

 (A) Psychology

 (B) Nutrition

 (C) Business

 (D) Ecology   Ⓐ Ⓑ Ⓒ Ⓓ

13. With whom will the man probably live this summer?

 (A) His mother and father

 (B) His sister

 (C) His friends

 (D) His dorm roommate   Ⓐ Ⓑ Ⓒ Ⓓ

◀)) 010　Listen to the following conversation between two students at school.

M: So, Julie, only two more weeks to go until the end of spring term. Have you got anything lined up for summer vacation?

W: I do as a matter of fact. I'm going to stay around here. One of the great things about living off-campus is that you don't have to move out when classes end.

M: You can say that again. In my case, I either have to get summer housing or move back in with my parents.

W: Anyway, at the moment, I've got a part-time job working as a waitress in a restaurant—in the evenings, that is—and during the day I'm going to help out in the research institute in the psychology department. I won't get paid much for that, but I figure I'll get to know some of the psychology professors better, and I'll also get some valuable experience related to my major. How about you, Jim?

M: Believe it or not, I'm still not sure. I'll probably head back to my hometown and stay with my folks, when I move out of the dorm. My father can always use an extra hand in our family business. Of course, it's not easy working for your dad, but it's better than nothing.

W: I see your point. At least you can probably save some money by living at home. For now, let's just do our best to get through the last few weeks of the term.

　学校で2人の学生が交わす次の会話を聞きなさい。

M:　ジュリー，春学期が終わるまであと2週間だね。夏休みに何か計画してる？

W:　実のところ計画しているわよ。私はこのあたりに残るわ。キャンパスの外に住むことのよいところは，授業が終わっても出ていかなくてすむことね。

M:　まったくだ。僕の場合は夏の間住むところを見つけるか，親元に戻らなければいけないけど。

W:　とにかく，今のところレストランでウェイトレスのアルバイト，これは夜だけど。昼間は心理学部の研究所で助手をするつもりよ。それほどお金にはならないけど，心理学の教授をもっと知ることができると思うし，私の専攻に関する貴重な体験ができる。あなたはどうするの，ジム。

M:　信じられないかもしれないけど，まだ確定していないよ。寮を出たら，たぶん実家に帰って家族と過ごすよ。父は家業で人が増えても，いつでも使いこなせるんだ。もちろん父親の下で働くのは楽ではないけど，何もないよりはましさ。

W:　わかるわ。少なくとも実家にいれば多少お金を節約できるもの。まあ今は，学期最後の数週間を乗り越えるようがんばろうね。

◈ 設問を素早く先読みしてから会話を聞き，次の点を聞き取る。

10. 会話の時期，　**11.** 女性の夏の仕事，　**12.** 女性の専攻，　**13.** 男性がおそらく一緒に住む人

Section Ⅰ Part A/B　Section Ⅰ Part C　Section 2　Section 3　総合模試　総合模試 解答・解説

10.
解答：C

🔊 011　**設問訳** この会話は一年のどの時期のものと思われますか。

(A) 春休み中　　　　　　　　(C) 春学期の終わりごろ
(B) 春学期の始め　　　　　　(D) 夏休みの始め

解法 会話の時期を問う問題。冒頭の only two more weeks to go until the end of spring term から，春学期が終わるまであと 2 週間であるとわかるので，正解は (C)。

11.
解答：C

🔊 011　**設問訳** 女性はこの夏何の仕事をする予定ですか。

(A) 監視員　　　　　　　　　(C) 給仕人
(B) パートタイムの教員　　　(D) 店員

解法 女性の夏の仕事を問う問題。基本的な設問のひとつ「何を」が用いられている。I've got a part-time job working as a waitress in a restaurant 以下でわかるように，女性はレストランのウェイトレスと心理学部の研究所の助手をする予定であり，正解は (C)。

12.
解答：A

🔊 011　**設問訳** 女性は何の分野を勉強していますか。

(A) 心理学　　　　　　　　　(C) ビジネス
(B) 栄養学　　　　　　　　　(D) 環境学

解法 女性の専攻を問う問題。基本的な質問のひとつ「何を」が用いられている。女性は，夏のアルバイトとして心理学部の研究所の助手をする予定で，自分の専攻に関する貴重な体験ができると話している。よって専攻は心理学であることがわかり，正解は (A)。

13.
解答：A

🔊 011　**設問訳** この夏男性はおそらくだれと一緒に住みますか。

(A) 彼の両親　　　　　　　　(C) 彼の友人
(B) 彼の姉　　　　　　　　　(D) 寮のルームメイト

解法 男性がおそらく一緒に住む人を問う問題。基本的な質問のひとつ「だれ」が用いられている。move back in with my parents, stay with my folks, my father can always use と繰り返し述べられていることから，親と住むことがわかる。my folks は家族や両親を指す。正解は (A)。

重要語
□ ... to go「残り〜」
□ **You can say that again.**「まったくだ，そのとおり」
□ **folks**「家族，両親」
□ **dorm**「寮」(< dormitory)
□ **I see your point.**「(言いたいことが) わかります」

37

5. 「出来事」と「行動」を理解する

最重要ストラテジー ▶▶▶

◆ 現在の出来事「男性は何をしていますか」「彼らは何について話していますか」

◆ 今後の行動「会話の後，彼らは何をするでしょうか」

◆ 過去の思い込み「男性はどのように思い込んでいましたか」

　これらは Part A 頻出の設問である。これらの設問を念頭に置き，会話内の出来事や行動を理解するよう心がけよう。

　Part A の設問ポイントとして，「会話の中で何が起きているか」「この会話の後で何が起こるか」を問われることは多い。この設問形式は大きく次の 3 つに分類できる。

設問例

🐾 現在の出来事を問う設問

話者の状況や会話内の出来事

☐ What is the man doing?

☐ What has happened to the speakers?

☐ What does the woman ask the man to do?

☐ What are they discussing?

🐾 今後の行動を問う設問

会話後の行動を推測する

☐ What will the man probably do?

☐ What will the woman do next?

☐ What are the speakers planning to do?

🐾 過去の思い込みを問う設問

会話の前に話者が抱いていた「考え」

☐ What had the man assumed?

　　これらの設問に答えられるように，まずは現在の出来事を表すキーワードを聞き取り，会話の状況を把握しよう。そのうえで，I will〔won't〕...，I'm going to ...，Let's ...，Why not ...? などの未来を表す表現，I thought ...，I knew ... など過去の考えを表す表現も聞き取り，今後の行動，過去の思い込みや考えを把握することが大切である。

練習問題 ▶▶▶　　☞ 会話内の「出来事」に注意しながら解答しなさい。

🔊 012　**14.** What is the woman doing?

(A) Transferring to a different dormitory

(B) Looking for an inexpensive motel

(C) Taking some time off from school

(D) Going to nearby accommodations　　Ⓐ Ⓑ Ⓒ Ⓓ

🔊 013　**15.** What will the man and woman probably do?

(A) Visit the man's brother

(B) Attend the event together

(C) Make airplane reservations

(D) Try to sell their tickets　　Ⓐ Ⓑ Ⓒ Ⓓ

🔊 014　**16.** What had the woman assumed?

(A) The man was not accepted into a graduate program.

(B) The man decided not to apply to graduate school.

(C) The man had only applied to one graduate program.

(D) The man had already enrolled in a graduate school.

Ⓐ Ⓑ Ⓒ Ⓓ

14.

解答：D

🔊 012

M: Where are you going with that suitcase? Taking a vacation in the middle of the term?

W: A water pipe in our dorm broke last night, and it's going to take them a week to fix the damage. I'm going to stay in a cheap motel room close to campus.

Q: What is the woman doing?

M: そんなスーツケースを持ってどこへ行くの。学期の途中に休みを取るつもり？

W: 昨夜，寮の水道管が破裂して，直すのに1週間かかるのよ。キャンパスの近くの安いモーテルの部屋に泊まるわ。

設問訳 女性は何をしているところですか。

(A) 別の寮へ引っ越している

(B) 安いモーテルを探している

(C) 学校をしばらく休んでいる

(D) 近くの宿泊施設に向かっている

解法 設問を先読みしてから会話を聞き，会話内で女性がしていることを聞き取る。寮の水道管が破裂して，直すのに1週間かかるので，女性はスーツケースを持って，キャンパス近くの安いモーテルに泊まりに行こうとしている。stay, motel room などのキーワードを聞き取る必要がある。正解は (D)。

15.

解答：B

🔊 013

M: Sarah, would you like to go to the folk music festival with me this weekend? My brother was going to go but can't. I've got two tickets.

W: Wow. I won't pass up an opportunity like this. Thanks.

Q: What will the man and woman probably do?

M: サラ，今週末一緒にフォークミュージック・フェスティバルに行かない？　弟が行く予定だったけど行けなくなったんだ。チケットが2枚あるよ。

W: まあ。こんなチャンスは逃せないわね。ありがとう。

設問訳 男性と女性はおそらく何をしますか。

(A) 男性の弟に会いに行く

(B) 一緒にイベントに参加する

(C) 飛行機の予約をする

(D) チケットを売ろうとする

解法　設問を先読みしてから会話を聞き，会話内で男性と女性が今後行うことを聞き取る。男性がイベントに誘うと，女性は I won't pass up an opportunity like this. と受けているので，これからの行動は，一緒にフェスティバルに行くことであるとわかる。正解は (B)。

重要語
□ **pass up ...**「～を逃す」

16.　　解答：C

🔊 014
M: I'm really nervous. I haven't heard from any of the five graduate programs I applied to.

W: Five! I only knew about your application to State Tech.

Q: What had the woman assumed?

M:　とても不安な気持ちだよ。出願した大学院 5 校のどこからも連絡がないんだ。

W:　5 校！　私は州立工科大学に出願したことしか知らなかったわ。

設問訳　女性はどのように思っていましたか。

(A) 男性は大学院に受からなかった。
(B) 男性は大学院に出願しないことにした。
(C) 男性はひとつの大学院だけに出願した。
(D) 男性はすでに大学院に入学した。

解法　設問を先読みしてから会話を聞き，会話内で女性が思っていたことを聞き取る。女性は I only knew about your application to State Tech. と述べているので，男性が 1 校だけに願書を出したと思っていた。正解は (C)。

重要語
□ **apply**「申し込む」
□ **State Tech**「州立工科大学」

6. 「問題点」と「解決策」を把握する

最重要ストラテジー ▶▶▶

◆ 会話で述べている問題点やトラブル「男性の問題は何ですか」

◆ 問題点に対する解決策——話者の提案「女性は何を提案していますか」

　TOEFL ITP 頻出の設問に「会話で述べている問題点やトラブル」と「その解決策」を問うものがある。そのような設問の場合，会話内の問題点やトラブル，解決策に注意して会話を聞くよう心がけよう。

　問題点，解決策を問う代表的な設問には次のようなものがある。

**　設問例**

🐾 会話で述べている問題点やトラブルを問う設問

☐ What is the man's problem?

☐ What is the woman concerned about?

🐾 問題点に対する解決策を問う設問

☐ What does the man suggest?

☐ What will the woman do?

☐ What is the man going to do?

☐ What does the woman plan to do?

☐ What is the woman's advice?

　また，解決策には，Why don't you ...? / I suggest [recommend] ... / You'd better *do* ... など，提案を表す定型表現がヒントとなる。

練習問題 ▶▶▶　　☞ 会話で述べている「問題点」や「解決策」に注意しながら聞き，解答しなさい。

◀) 015　**17.** What is the man's problem?

 (A) He neglected to declare his minor.

 (B) He cannot find a summer job.

 (C) He has to go to summer school.

 (D) He registered for the wrong course. Ⓐ Ⓑ Ⓒ Ⓓ

◀) 016　**18.** What will the man do?

 (A) Turn off his music

 (B) Study for the test

 (C) Plan ahead for his assignments

 (D) Listen to the stereo with headphones Ⓐ Ⓑ Ⓒ Ⓓ

◀) 017　**19.** What is the woman concerned about?

 (A) An increase in their rent

 (B) An unexpected illness in her family

 (C) An expensive phone bill

 (D) A telephone call from her father Ⓐ Ⓑ Ⓒ Ⓓ

17.

🔊 015

M: I really wanted to take the summer off and work part time, but I guess I'll have to take summer session.

W: It's too bad you didn't notice earlier that you had two more required courses to complete your minor.

Q: What is the man's problem?

M: 夏は，本当は休暇をとってアルバイトしたかったけど，夏期講座をとらなきゃならないようだ。

W: 副専攻課程を修了するには必修科目が2つ残っているということに，もう少し前に気がつかなくて残念だったわね。

設問訳 男性の問題は何ですか。

(A) 副専攻を申告するのを怠った。
(B) 夏休みの仕事が見つからない。
(C) 夏期講座に通わなければならない。
(D) 間違った科目を登録した。

解法 設問を先読みしてから会話を聞き，会話内で男性の問題点を聞き取る。男性の問題は，副専攻課程修了に必要な2科目をとっていなかったため，夏期講座をとらなければならないことである。正解は (C)。

重要語
□ **summer session**
「夏期講座」
□ **minor**「副専攻」

18.

🔊 016

W: Oliver, would you mind turning down your stereo, please? I've got a test tomorrow and I'm trying to study.

M: Oh, sorry. I didn't realize the music was bothering you. Why don't I just put on my headphones?

Q: What will the man do?

W: オリバー，ステレオの音量を下げてもらえない？　明日テストがあって勉強したいのよ。

M: おっと，ごめん。迷惑かけているとは思わなかったよ。ヘッドホンをつけるよ。

設問訳 男性は何をしますか。

(A) 音楽の再生を切る

(B) 試験勉強をする

(C) 課題の事前準備をする

(D) ヘッドホンでステレオを聴く

解法 設問を先読みしてから会話を聞き，会話内で男性の解決策を聞き取る。会話内の問題はステレオの音量が大きいことで，男性は Why don't I just put on my headphones? とヘッドホンをすることを申し出ている。正解は (D)。

重要語
- □ **Would you mind ...?**
「～してもらえますか」
- □ **bother**「～に迷惑をかける」
- □ **put on ...**「～をつける，着る」

19.　　　　　　　　　　　　　　　　　　　　　　　　　解答：C

◀)) 017

W: Leonard, did you see this month's phone bill? It's almost 200 dollars!

M: I guess that's because I called my family so many times. You did know my dad was in the hospital. He's doing fine now, though.

Q: What is the woman concerned about?

W: レナード，今月の電話代の請求書を見た？　200ドル近いわよ！

M: きっと家族によく電話したからだろうな。僕の父親が入院していたことは知っていたよね。今は元気だけどね。

設問訳 女性は何を気にしていますか。

(A) 家賃の値上げ

(B) 自分の家族に不意に病人が出たこと

(C) 高額な電話代の請求書

(D) 自分の父親からの電話

解法 設問を先読みしてから会話を聞き，会話内で女性の問題点を聞き取る。女性は電話代の請求書を見たかどうか男性に尋ね，200ドル近いと言っている。彼女はこの請求書を気にかけ，問題視しているので，正解は (C)。

重要語
- □ **phone bill**
「電話代の請求書」

7. 「示唆」と「意図」を推測する

最重要ストラテジー ▶▶▶

◆ 会話で示唆されている内容「この会話から何が推測できますか」

◆ 話者の意図「男性は何が言いたいのですか」

TOEFL ITP では，会話で示唆されている内容や話者の意図を推測したり理解したりする問題が出題される。

示唆，意図を問う代表的な設問には次のようなものがある。

設問例

🐒 会話で示唆されている内容を問う設問

☐ What can be inferred from this conversation?

☐ What can be inferred about the man?

🐒 話者の意図を問う設問

☐ What does the woman imply?

☐ What does the man mean?

解答は会話の中で直接には述べられず，答えるために必要なヒントが示されている。ひとりの話者の行動や発言にもうひとりの話者がどのように答え，どのような反応を示しているかがこの種の問題のキーポイントとなる。また，話者の意図を問う問題では，話者の語調やイントネーションがヒントとなることもある。

練習問題 ▶▶▶　　☞ 状況を想像しながら会話を聞き，解答しなさい。

🔊 018　**20.** What can be inferred from this conversation?

　　(A)　There are only ten people in the history class.

　　(B)　Dr. Tomlin's class requires a lot of reading.

　　(C)　The woman may have to wait to read the book.

　　(D)　The book is no longer being kept on reserve.　　Ⓐ Ⓑ Ⓒ Ⓓ

🔊 019　**21.** What can be inferred about the man?

　　(A)　He has not taken many chemistry courses.

　　(B)　He missed the chemistry lab. this afternoon.

　　(C)　He has already decided to major in chemistry.

　　(D)　He is taking the same chemistry course as the woman.

　　　　　　　　　　　　　　　　　　　　　　　　　　　Ⓐ Ⓑ Ⓒ Ⓓ

🔊 020　**22.** What does the professor imply the woman should do?

　　(A)　Go ahead and register for his economics seminar

　　(B)　Analyze her reasons for taking his class

　　(C)　Take all of the required classes before signing up for his course

　　(D)　Bring him the correct form in order to get a recommendation

　　　　　　　　　　　　　　　　　　　　　　　　　　　Ⓐ Ⓑ Ⓒ Ⓓ

20. 解答：C

◀)) 018 **W:** I'm supposed to read a book on Simon Fraser for my Canadian history class. But I don't see it in the reserve book section.

M: Oh, Dr. Tomlin's History 344 class, right? You're probably the tenth person who came in to ask about that book. If it's not on the shelf, someone else is reading it now.

Q: What can be inferred from this conversation?

　　W: カナダ史の授業でサイモン・フレイザーの本を読むことになっています。でも予約指定図書コーナーに見当たりません。

　　M: ああ，トムリン先生の歴史 344 の授業ですね？　その本のことを聞きにきたのはあなたがたぶん 10 人目ですよ。もし棚になければ，ほかの人が今読んでいますね。

設問訳 この会話から何が推測できますか。

　　(A) その歴史のクラスには 10 人しかいない。
　　(B) トムリン先生の授業ではたくさん本を読まなければならない。
　　(C) 女性はその本を読むのに待たなければならないかもしれない。
　　(D) その本はもう予約指定図書として置かれていない。

解法 設問を先読みしてから会話を聞き，会話から推測できることを聞き取る。男性の発言によれば，女性が読まなければならない本はほかの人が読んでいる可能性がある。彼女は待たなければならないかもしれないことが推測できる。正解は (C)。

重要語
□ **reserve book**
　「予約指定図書」

21. 解答：A

◀)) 019 **M:** I just spent six hours in the chem. lab., and according to the schedule it's supposed to last only from 1:30 to 3:30.

W: Hmm, first time you took a chemistry course, is it?

Q: What can be inferred about the man?

　　M: 化学の実験室に 6 時間もいたんだよ。予定表では 1 時半から 3 時半までしかかからないことになっているのに。

　　W: ふうん，化学を取ったのは初めてでしょう？

設問訳 男性について何が推測できますか。

(A) 彼はあまり化学の科目を取ったことがない。

(B) 彼は今日の午後の化学実験に出席しなかった。

(C) 彼はすでに化学を専攻することに決めた。

(D) 彼は女性と同じ化学の授業を受けている。

解法	設問を先読みしてから会話を聞き，会話から男性について推測できることを聞き取る。予定をかなり越えて長時間化学の実験室にいたことに不満気な男性は，女性から「ふうん，化学を取ったのは初めてでしょう？」と言われた。女性は，化学の授業ではそれくらい当たり前だと考えていると思われる。男性には化学受講の経験があまりないことが推測できるので，正解は (A)。	**重要語** □ **chem.=chemistry** 　「化学」 □ **lab.=laboratory** 　「実験室」 □ **last**「続く」

22.　　　　　　　　　　　　　　　　　　　　　　　　　　　　　　解答：C

🔊 020 **W:** Professor Carleton, I'd really like to take your seminar in theories of economics, but I haven't taken all of the prerequisites, such as quantitative analysis.

M: I'd like to say go ahead and register for the seminar. But I honestly think you need the quantitative analysis class under your belt to really participate fully in the seminar. So, I think you understand what my recommendation is.

Q: What does the professor imply the woman should do?

W: カールトン先生，先生の経済論のゼミにぜひ参加したいのですが，数量分析のような前もって履修するべき科目のすべてを取ってはいません。

M: ゼミの登録をどうぞしなさいと言いたいところです。しかし，正直なところ，ゼミに十分に参加するためには，数量分析のクラスの経験が必要だと思います。私が何を勧めているかおわかりだと思います。

設問訳 教授は女性に何をするべきだと示唆していますか。

(A) 経済学のゼミに登録する

(B) 教授のクラスを取る自分なりの理由を分析する

(C) 教授の科目を履修する前に必要なクラスをすべて取る

(D) 推薦状を書いてもらうために正しい用紙を教授に持ってくる

解法	設問を先読みしてから会話を聞き，会話内で教授が女性に示唆したことを聞き取る。教授は，ゼミに十分に参加するには数量分析のクラスの経験が必要だと述べているので，教授のゼミを取る前に，必要なクラスをすべて取ることを勧めている。正解は (C)。	**重要語** □ **quantitative analysis** 　「数量分析」 □ **under** *one's* **belt** 　「経験して」

8. 「賛成」と「反対」に注意する

最重要ストラテジー ▶▶▶

　話者がある事柄に関して賛成なのか反対なのかを判断しなければならない問題が，会話問題ではしばしば見受けられる。Part A および Part B の会話には日常口語表現がよく使われるため，Yes/No や agree/disagree 以外にも，よく用いられる賛成，反対を表す口語表現を知っておく必要がある。

　賛成，反対の表現がカギとなる問題の代表的な設問には次のようなものがある。

設問例

話者の賛否を問う設問

□ What does the man mean?

TOEFL によく登場する賛成，反対の表現を確認しておこう。

✹ 賛成を表す表現 ✹	✹ 反対を表す表現 ✹
Absolutely.	Give me a break.
You can say that again.	No way.
You said it.	You've got to be kidding.
You bet.	No kidding.
You can bet on it.	You really think so?
Isn't it ever?	That's out of the question.
Isn't it, though?	Not on your life.
I couldn't agree more.	I've seen [had/heard] better.
No doubt about it.	Cut it out.
You took the words right out of my mouth.	Knock it off.
	Over my dead body.

練習問題　▶▶▶　　☞ 賛成，反対を表す表現に注意しながら会話を聞き，解答しなさい。

◀) 021　**23.** What does the man mean?

(A)　He thought the lecture was dull.

(B)　He did not hear what the woman said.

(C)　He would like to hear the lecture again.

(D)　He also did not get a seat for the lecture.　　Ⓐ Ⓑ Ⓒ Ⓓ

◀) 022　**24.** What does the woman mean?

(A)　She does not know the way to the Sports Center.

(B)　There is no way to get the tickets at the Sports Center.

(C)　She does not have a way to get to the Sports Center.

(D)　She will not try to get tickets tonight at the Sports Center.　　Ⓐ Ⓑ Ⓒ Ⓓ

◀) 023　**25.** What does the woman mean?

(A)　She is feeling the same as the man.

(B)　She wants to tell the man something.

(C)　She disagrees with the man.

(D)　She already said the same thing.　　Ⓐ Ⓑ Ⓒ Ⓓ

23. 解答：A

🔊 021　**W:** That lecture lasted more than two hours. And it's got to have been one of the most boring ones I've ever sat through.

M: You can say that again!

Q: What does the man mean?

　　W: あの講義，2時間以上もあったわよ。それに今まで受けた授業の中で間違いなく最も退屈な部類に入るわね。

　　M: まったくだ！

設問訳 男性は何を言いたいのですか。

(A) 彼はその講義がつまらないと思った。

(B) 彼は女性の言ったことが聞こえなかった。

(C) 彼はその講義をもう一度受けたいと思っている。

(D) その講義では彼にも席がなかった。

| **解法** 設問を先読みしてから会話を聞き，会話内で男性が言いたいことを聞き取る。男性の言った You can say that again! は「まったくだ」という意味で，女性に同意している。正解は (A)。boring と dull は同意語。 | **重要語** □ **sit through ...** 「～を終わりまで聞く」 □ **You can say that again.** 「まったくだ，そのとおり」 |

24. 解答：D

🔊 022　**M:** Peggy, I heard you went to the Sports Center last night and stood in line for four hours trying to get playoff tickets. So, are you going to go back tonight?

W: No way.

Q: What does the woman mean?

　　M: ペギー，ゆうべスポーツセンターに行って決勝戦のチケットのために4時間も並んだって？今夜も並ぶつもりなのかい？

　　W: まさか。

設問訳 女性は何を言いたいのですか。

(A) 彼女はスポーツセンターまでの行き方を知らない。

(B) スポーツセンターでチケットを手に入れる方法はない。

(C) 彼女はスポーツセンターに行く手段がない。

(D) 彼女は今夜スポーツセンターでチケットを手に入れようとはしない。

| **解法** 設問を先読みしてから会話を聞き，会話内で女性が言いたいことを聞き取る。女性が言った No way. は「まさか」の意味で，並ぶつもりがないことがわかる。正解は (D)。 | **重要語** □ **playoff** 「決勝戦，延長戦」 □ **No way.** 「まさか」 |

25.　　　　　　　　　　　　　　　　　　　　　　　　　　　　　　　　　　解答：A

◀) 023　**M:** That was our last final exam, Carla. No more tests this term and two weeks of vacation—
　　　　it's got to be one of the best feelings in the world.

　　W: Hal, you took the words right out of my mouth.

　　Q: What does the woman mean?

　　　　M:　あれで期末試験も終わりだね，カーラ。今学期はもう試験もないし，2週間の休みで，もう最
　　　　　　高の気分だね。

　　　　W:　ハル，私が言おうと思ったことを先に言ったわね。

設問訳　女性は何を言いたいのですか。

　　　(A) 彼女は男性と同じ気持ちでいる。
　　　(B) 彼女は男性に何かを伝えたい。
　　　(C) 彼女は男性には賛成できない。
　　　(D) 彼女はもうすでに同じことを言った。

解法　設問を先読みしてから会話を聞き，会話内で女性が言いたいことを聞き取る。女性は男性に同
　　　意して，Hal, you took the words right out of my mouth. 「ハル，私が言おうと思ったことを
　　　先に言ったわね」と述べている。正解は (A)。

9.「イントネーション」と「皮肉表現」に注意する

最重要ストラテジー ▶▶▶

　会話問題では話者の声の抑揚や話し方が重要なポイントになる問題がある。日本語の日常会話と同様に英語でも，同じ Yes にも言い方によって肯定，驚き，無関心，皮肉など，いろいろなニュアンスがある。単語の表面上の意味だけではなく，会話の状況と言い方を理解して判断しなければならない。感情や皮肉を読みとらなければならない問題は難しい部類に入るが，この手法は「7. 示唆と意図を推測する」「8. 賛成と反対に注意する」にも応用し，解答のヒントとすることができる。

　イントネーション，皮肉表現がカギとなる問題の代表的な設問には次のようなものがある。

設問例

話者の感情や皮肉を読み取る設問

　　□ How does the man feel?

　　□ What does the woman imply?

　　□ What does the man mean?

　上記以外にも，リスニングセクション全般を通して，話者の声の調子や話し方は解答するうえでのヒントとなることを覚えておこう。前項まででも見てきたように，ただ単に聞こえてきた「音そのもの」「単語や表現そのもの」を問うのではなく，その「内容」や「会話の状況」を問う問題が多いことを認識しておくべきである。

練習問題　▶▶▶　☞ イントネーションや声の調子に注意し，会話の状況を想像しながら解答しなさい。

◀))024　**26.** What does the woman imply?

    (A)　She thinks no one else knows about Tony.

    (B)　She already knows Tony is a poor student.

    (C)　She would like to know what was on the news.

    (D)　She does not believe what the man said.　　Ⓐ Ⓑ Ⓒ Ⓓ

◀))025　**27.** What does the woman mean?

    (A)　Tom did not become the professor's assistant.

    (B)　Professor Condon did not hire an assistant.

    (C)　She thinks that Tom quit his new position.

    (D)　She is surprised that Tom got the job.　　Ⓐ Ⓑ Ⓒ Ⓓ

◀))026　**28.** How does the woman feel?

    (A)　Frustrated

    (B)　Relieved

    (C)　Pleased

    (D)　Relaxed　　Ⓐ Ⓑ Ⓒ Ⓓ

26.　　　　　　　　　　　　　　　　　　　　　　　　　解答：B

🔊 024
M: Did you hear that Tony is on academic probation? He's getting D's in all of his classes.

W: So what else is new?

Q: What does the woman imply?

　　M: トニーが仮及第期間に入ったって聞いた？　全部の授業がDだよ。

　　W: それで，ほかに何か新しい話題はないの？

設問訳 女性は何を示唆していますか。

(A) 彼女はトニーのことをほかのだれも知らないと思っている。

(B) 彼女はトニーが出来の悪い学生だとすでに知っている。

(C) 彼女はニュースの中身を知りたがっている。

(D) 彼女は男性の言ったことを信じていない。

解法 設問を先読みしてから会話を聞き，会話内で女性が示唆していることを聞き取る。イントネーションがキーポイントとなる問題。So what else is new? のイントネーションから，トニーが出来の悪い学生だと女性はすでに知っていて，その話にはうんざりしていることがわかる。正解は (B)。

重要語
□ **academic probation**
「仮及第期間」

27.　　　　　　　　　　　　　　　　　　　　　　　　　解答：D

🔊 025
M: Did you hear that Tom got hired as Professor Condon's new research assistant?

W: No, he didn't!

Q: What does the woman mean?

　　M: トムがコンドン教授の新しい研究助手に採用されたって聞いた？

　　W: そんなはずないわ！

設問訳 女性は何を言いたいのですか。

(A) トムは教授の助手にならなかった。

(B) コンドン教授は助手を雇わなかった。

(C) 彼女はトムが新しい職を辞めたと思っている。

(D) 彼女はトムがその職に就いたことに驚いている。

解法 設問を先読みしてから会話を聞き，会話内で女性が言いたいことを聞き取る。イントネーションがキーポイントとなる問題。女性の No, he didn't! の言い方は，男性が言ったことを否定しているというよりむしろ，その事実に驚きを示している。正解は (D)。

28.

解答：A

◀)) 026

M: I'll do my best to make your copies, but it's going to take a few minutes for the machine to warm up. I just turned it on.

W: Great. That's just what I need right now. My class starts in five minutes.

Q: How does the woman feel?

M: コピーをとるよう最善を尽くしますが，機械のウォームアップに数分かかります。今電源を入れたばかりですから。

W: すごいわね。今必要なことはそれね。授業はあと5分で始まるわ。

設問訳 女性はどのように感じていますか。

(A) いらいらしている
(B) 安心している
(C) 喜んでいる
(D) くつろいでいる

解法 設問を先読みしてから会話を聞き，会話内で女性がどのように感じているかを聞き取る。皮肉表現がキーポイントとなる問題。女性が言っている Great. That's just what I need right now. は，男性に本当にすばらしいと言っているのではなく，時間がないのに，男性が今ごろ電源を入れたことにいらいらして皮肉を言っていることが，状況と女性の声の調子からわかる。正解は (A)。

10. Long Conversations への応用 2

最重要ストラテジー ▶▶▶

これまでに学んだ Part A 特有のストラテジーも，Part B に応用することができる。特に「出来事と行動」「問題点と解決策」は，Part B にも頻出の設問ポイントである。

練習問題 ▶▶▶ ☞ 出来事，行動，問題点，解決策に注意しながら会話を聞き，解答しなさい。

◁》027 028

29. Where does this conversation probably take place?

(A) In a counseling center

(B) In a language laboratory

(C) In a college classroom

(D) In a professor's office (A) (B) (C) (D)

30. According to the professor, why is the student having a problem following the lectures?

(A) He did not take the prerequisite courses.

(B) He is not a native speaker of English.

(C) He is not familiar with academic vocabulary.

(D) He does not know how to take notes in class. (A) (B) (C) (D)

31. What advice does the professor give to the student?

(A) Find someone to tutor him privately

(B) Read the assigned textbook carefully

(C) Focus on grasping the main points

(D) Enroll in an intensive reading course (A) (B) (C) (D)

32. What does the student hope to do after graduation?

(A) Attend a graduate program

(B) Work for the government

(C) Travel with his family

(D) Start his own company (A) (B) (C) (D)

練習問題　解答・解説 ▶▶▶

29.-32.　　　　　　　　　　　　　　　　　　　　　Long Conversation

🔊 027　Listen to the following conversation between a professor and a student.

M: Good afternoon, Professor Sanders. Do you have a moment to talk with me now?

W: Certainly, Fernando. That's what my office hours are for. Please sit down. What can I do for you?

M: I'm a bit embarrassed to say this, but I am having a very difficult time understanding what you say in class.

W: Perhaps it's a problem of background knowledge. Have you taken all the prerequisite courses?

M: Yes, I took a couple of similar math courses before when I was a high school student in Nicaragua.

W: In Nicaragua? You're not a native speaker of English?

M: Well, I suppose I am. I was born here and went to elementary school in Canada, but my family moved to Nicaragua when I was 12, so I went to junior high and high school there.

W: Oh, I see. Then probably the reason you're having a hard time following along is that you aren't familiar with the academic vocabulary we use at universities in North America. I wouldn't worry so much about that. This is just your first semester, right? You'll pick it up quickly enough.

M: I hope so, but in the meantime, what should I do? Do you think I should hire a private tutor or something?

W: You know, the most important thing for you to do is to just listen for the main points I present in class. Don't worry about understanding everything perfectly. With your background in math, all of this should start making sense pretty quickly, I imagine. By the way, Fernando, why did you decide to transfer to college here in the United States?

M: I've always had a dream of working as a diplomat. I figured I'd have a better chance of doing that if I graduated from an American university. Anyway, thanks for your time, Professor Sanders. I'll do my best to follow what you say in class.

W: Oh, and Fernando. Don't hesitate to stop by again if you have any questions or concerns. My door is always open.

教授と学生が交わす次の会話を聞きなさい。

M: こんにちは，サンダース先生。今ちょっとお話する時間はありますか。

W: ええ，フェルナンド。そのためのオフィスアワーです。どうぞ座ってください。どうしました？

M: ちょっと申し上げるのが恥ずかしいのですが，先生が授業でおっしゃっていることを理解するのがとても難しいのです。

W: たぶんそれは基礎知識の問題ですね。先修条件科目は全部取りましたか。

M: はい。類似した数学科目を2つ，ニカラグアの高校で取りました。

W: ニカラグアで？　あなたの母語は英語ではないのですか。

M: 英語と言ってもよいと思います。僕はここで生まれ，カナダの小学校に通いました。でも僕が12歳のとき家族がニカラグアに引っ越したので，そこの中学校と高校に通ったのです。

W: わかりました。それならついていくのが難しいというのはたぶん，北米の大学で使われている学術用語に慣れていないせいでしょうね。それならばあまり心配はいりません。今が最初の学期でしょう？　すぐに理解できるようになりますよ。

M: そうだとよいのですけど，それまでのあいだ僕は何をするべきでしょうか。家庭教師か何か頼むべきだと思いますか。

W: そうね，一番大事なことは，私が授業で言う要点を聞き取ることですね。何もかも完璧に理解しようと考えないこと。あなたに数学の基礎知識があれば，きっとすぐにわかるようになるはずです。ところでフェルナンド，なぜアメリカの大学に入ることに決めたのですか。

M: 僕はずっと外交官として働くのが夢でした。アメリカの大学を卒業したほうが可能性はあると考えたわけです。ともかく，ありがとうございました，サンダース先生。先生が授業でおっしゃることについていけるようがんばります。

W: あっ，それからフェルナンド。もし質問や気がかりなことがあったら，また遠慮なく立ち寄ってください。ドアはいつも開いていますよ。

◈ 設問を素早く先読みしてから会話を聞き，次の点を聞き取る。
29. 会話の場所，　**30.** 学生の問題点，　**31.** 教授のアドバイス，　**32.** 学生がしたいこと

29.
解答：D

◀)) 028　**設問訳** この会話はおそらくどこで行われていますか。

(A) カウンセリングセンターで　　　(C) 大学の教室で
(B) ＬＬ教室で　　　　　　　　　　(D) 教授の研究室で

解法 会話が行われている場所を推測する問題。教授は「そのためのオフィスアワーです。どうぞ座ってください」「また遠慮なく立ち寄ってください」と言っているため，教授の研究室で話していることがわかる。正解は (D)。

30.
解答：C

◀)) 028　**設問訳** 教授によれば，なぜ学生は講義についていくのに問題があるのですか。

(A) 先修条件科目を受講しなかった。　　(C) 学術用語に慣れていない。
(B) 英語のネイティブスピーカーではない。(D) 授業でノートを取る方法を知らない。

解法 問題点を問う問題。授業についていくのが難しいという学生の問題は，おそらく北米の大学で使われている学術用語に慣れていないせいだと教授は述べている。正解は (C)。会話で述べられた問題点とその解決法は，Long Conversations でも重要な出題ポイントとなるので注意しよう。

31.
解答：C

◀)) 028　**設問訳** 教授は学生にどんなアドバイスをしていますか。

(A) 個人指導してくれる家庭教師を探す　(C) 要点をつかむことに集中する
(B) 課題のテキストを注意して読む　　　(D) 精読のクラスに登録する

解法 問題の解決策を問う問題。教授は，授業についていくのに一番大事なことは，授業の要点を聞き取ることであるとアドバイスしている。正解は (C)。会話内の listen for the main points は，正解の選択肢では focus on grasping the main points と言い換えられている。

32.
解答：B

◀)) 028　**設問訳** 学生は卒業後何をしたいと思っていますか。

(A) 大学院に行く　　　　　　(C) 家族と旅行をする
(B) 政府機関で働く　　　　　(D) 自分の会社を興す

解法 学生が卒業後にしたいことを問う問題。学生は外交官として働くのが夢なので，正解は (B)。会話内の work as a diplomat は，正解の選択肢では work for the government と言い換えられている。

重要語
□ **background knowledge**「基礎知識，背景知識」
□ **prerequisite course**「先修条件科目，履修前提科目」
□ **academic vocabulary**「学術語彙」
□ **pick up ...**「〜を理解する」
□ **in the meantime**「その間」
□ **tutor**「家庭教師，個別指導教師」

61

集中練習問題 ❶ Part A 形式 12 問＋ Part B 形式 1 題 4 問

BURST ONE

Part A Short Conversations

◀) 029

1. What does the woman mean?

    (A) The concert was not very good.

    (B) The band has not done its best yet.

    (C) The band performed its last concert.

    (D) The man's opinion is correct.   Ⓐ Ⓑ Ⓒ Ⓓ

◀) 030

2. What will the man probably do?

    (A) Help the woman rewrite her essay

    (B) Try to repair the broken computer

    (C) Find the file that the woman needs

    (D) Give the woman some new software   Ⓐ Ⓑ Ⓒ Ⓓ

◀) 031

3. When is the pool open on Saturdays?

    (A) From 9 a.m. to 6:30 p.m.

    (B) From 9 a.m. to 7 p.m.

    (C) From 10 a.m. to 6:30 p.m.

    (D) From 10 a.m. to 7 p.m.   Ⓐ Ⓑ Ⓒ Ⓓ

◀) 032

4. What had the woman assumed about the information session?

    (A) It was not likely to start on schedule.

    (B) More faculty members would be available for consultation.

    (C) Representatives from the various programs would be present.

    (D) Attending it would not be a good use of her time.   Ⓐ Ⓑ Ⓒ Ⓓ

◀) 033

5. What does the man mean?

    (A) He is afraid he cannot graduate on time.

    (B) He will go on an ocean cruise after graduation.

    (C) He is having a tough time finding a job.

    (D) He hopes to find a position in marketing.   Ⓐ Ⓑ Ⓒ Ⓓ

🔊 034　**6.** What does the woman imply?

    (A)　She forgot to mail an important letter.

    (B)　She needs to buy some airmail stamps.

    (C)　She rarely buys airmail stamps.

    (D)　She will come with the man to mail the letter.　　Ⓐ Ⓑ Ⓒ Ⓓ

🔊 035　**7.** What will the man probably do?

    (A)　Vote in the election

    (B)　Take a walk with the woman

    (C)　Have lunch in the student center

    (D)　Return the notes tomorrow　　Ⓐ Ⓑ Ⓒ Ⓓ

🔊 036　**8.** What will the woman probably do?

    (A)　Try to adjust the thermostat

    (B)　Put on some extra clothing

    (C)　Wait until other students arrive for class

    (D)　Unlock the door herself　　Ⓐ Ⓑ Ⓒ Ⓓ

🔊 037　**9.** What does the man imply?

    (A)　He is satisfied with Dr. Hanson's class.

    (B)　He will take the course next semester.

    (C)　He is not very interested in physics.

    (D)　He is hoping to major in physics.　　Ⓐ Ⓑ Ⓒ Ⓓ

🔊 038　**10.** What will the woman probably do?

    (A)　Go to the university computer center

    (B)　Use the copy machine on campus

    (C)　Buy an ink cartridge for the printer

    (D)　Pick up the book at the library herself　　Ⓐ Ⓑ Ⓒ Ⓓ

🔊 039　**11.** What do we learn from this conversation?

    (A)　The professor will permit the woman to join the class.

    (B)　The woman should have worked harder on her essay.

    (C)　The professor is impressed with the woman's writing.

    (D)　The woman submitted her assignment after the deadline.

                                        Ⓐ Ⓑ Ⓒ Ⓓ

Section Ⅰ Part A/B　Section Ⅰ Part C　Section 2　Section 3　総合模試　総合模試 解答・解説

◀)) 040 **12.** What does the man say about the members of his presentation group?

    (A) They ought to change their presentation topic.

    (B) They will probably have access to appropriate information.

    (C) They intend to go on a dolphin watching cruise.

    (D) They need to communicate with each other better.   Ⓐ Ⓑ Ⓒ Ⓓ

Part B Long Conversation

◀)) 041 042 **13.** What type of course is the student taking from the professor?

    (A) Research methods

    (B) Independent study

    (C) History

    (D) Composition

14. What aspect of the research paper is the student having difficulty with?

    (A) Organization

    (B) Sources

    (C) Subject

    (D) Conclusion

15. What advice does the professor give the student?

    (A) Conduct research together with a classmate

    (B) Locate key information in the library

    (C) Compose an outline before writing

    (D) Choose a topic closely related to the course   Ⓐ Ⓑ Ⓒ Ⓓ

16. When does this conversation probably take place?

    (A) At the beginning of the term

    (B) Midway through the term

    (C) Towards the end of the term

    (D) During final examinations   Ⓐ Ⓑ Ⓒ Ⓓ

集中練習問題 ❶　解答・解説

1.　　　　　　　　　　　　　　　　　　　　　　　　　　　　　　　　　　　　　　　解答：D

🔊 029　**M:** Irene, that band concert last night was the best yet.

　　W: Wasn't it, though?

　　　M:　アイリーン，昨夜のバンドコンサートは今までで最高だったよ。

　　　W:　そうでしょう？

What does the woman mean?	女性は何を言いたいのですか。
(A) The concert was not very good.	(A) コンサートはそれほどよくなかった。
(B) The band has not done its best yet.	(B) そのバンドはまだベストの演奏をしていない。
(C) The band performed its last concert.	(C) そのバンドは最終公演をした。
(D) The man's opinion is correct.	(D) 男性の意見は正しい。

> **解法**　設問を先読みしてから会話を聞き，会話内で女性が言いたいことを聞き取る。同意表現がポイントとなる問題。女性は男性の意見について，Wasn't it, though? と言っている。これは Wasn't it the best? の意味で，男性に同意している。though は「けれども」ではなく，強調の「やはり，もっとも」を意味する。正解は (D)。

2.　　　　　　　　　　　　　　　　　　　　　　　　　　　　　　　　　　　　　　　解答：C

🔊 030　**W:** Oh, no! This computer just erased the file I was working on. I can't find the work that I thought I'd saved.

　　M: Don't panic. I think this software has a program that automatically makes back-up files, so we may be able to find what you've written after all.

　　　W:　あら，いやだ！　作業していたファイルをこのコンピュータが消しちゃった。保存しておいたと思ったファイルが見つからないわ。

　　　M:　落ち着いて。このソフトウェアには自動的にバックアップを取るプログラムが組み込まれていると思うから，きみの書いたものは探し出せるかもしれないよ。

What will the man probably do?	男性はおそらく何をしますか。
(A) Help the woman rewrite her essay	(A) 女性が書いたレポートの書き直しを手伝う
(B) Try to repair the broken computer	(B) 壊れたコンピュータを直そうとする
(C) Find the file that the woman needs	(C) 女性の必要としているファイルを探し出す
(D) Give the woman some new software	(D) 女性にいくつか新しいソフトウェアをあげる

> **解法**　設問を先読みしてから会話を聞き，会話内で男性がおそらく行うことを聞き取る。問題の解決策を問う問題。女性の問題は，作業ファイルをコンピュータが消し，保存ファイルが見つからないことである。男性はファイルを探し出せるかもしれないと言っているので，正解は (C)。

65

3.

🔊 031 **W:** Do you know what time the swimming pool is open on Saturdays?

M: Let's see. It's open on weekdays from 10 a.m. until 6:30 p.m. and on weekends from 9 until 7.

W: 土曜日にプールが開いている時間帯がわかるかしら。

M: ええと。平日は午前 10 時から午後 6 時半まで，週末は 9 時から 7 時までだね。

When is the pool open on Saturdays?	土曜日にプールが開いているのはいつですか。
(A) From 9 a.m. to 6:30 p.m.	(A) 午前 9 時から午後 6 時半まで
(B) From 9 a.m. to 7 p.m.	(B) 午前 9 時から午後 7 時まで
(C) From 10 a.m. to 6:30 p.m.	(C) 午前 10 時から午後 6 時半まで
(D) From 10 a.m. to 7 p.m.	(D) 午前 10 時から午後 7 時まで

解法 設問を先読みしてから会話を聞き，会話内でプールが土曜日に開いている時間帯を聞き取る。会話内の情報を問う問題。登場する数字を聞き逃さないようにする。土曜日にプールが開いている時間帯について，男性は on weekends from 9 until 7 と言っているので，正解は (B)。

4.

🔊 032 **M:** Aren't you going to the grad school information session? The faculty are going to talk about the strengths and weaknesses of various graduate programs. And also, there will be university catalogs and information pamphlets available.

W: No kidding. I had absolutely no idea it might be so worthwhile.

M: 大学院情報セミナーに行かないの？ 教授がいろいろな大学院プログラムの長所と短所について意見を言ってくれるんだ。それに大学のカタログや，情報の載ったパンフレットももらえるよ。

W: ほんとう？ そんなに充実しているとは全然思ってもみなかったわ。

What had the woman assumed about the information session?	女性は情報セミナーについてどのように思っていましたか。
(A) It was not likely to start on schedule.	(A) 予定どおりの時刻には始まりそうもない。
(B) More faculty members would be available for consultation.	(B) 相談のためにもっと多くの教授が参加するだろう。
(C) Representatives from the various programs would be present.	(C) いろいろなプログラムの代表が参加するだろう。
(D) Attending it would not be a good use of her time.	(D) 時間を割いて参加するほどのものではないだろう。

解法 設問を先読みしてから会話を聞き，会話内で女性が思っていたことを聞き取る。女性が思い込んでいた事柄に関する問題。女性は I had absolutely no idea it might be so worthwhile.「そんなに充実しているとは全然思ってもみなかった」と言っているので，正解は (D)。

重要語
- **grad school**「大学院」
- **faculty**「教授陣，学部」

5.　　　　　　　　　　　　　　　　　　　　　　　　　　　　　　解答：C

🔊 033　**W:** With the job market being like it is right now, I have no idea what I'll do in June after I graduate. What about you?

M: We're pretty much in the same boat, I'm afraid. I haven't been able to find anything yet, either.

W: 労働市場が今みたいな状態だったら，卒業後 6 月に何をしているかわからないわ。あなたは？

M: 残念ながら同じ状況だよ。僕もまだ何も見つかっていないよ。

What does the man mean? 男性は何を言いたいのですか。

(A) He is afraid he cannot graduate on time.

(B) He will go on an ocean cruise after graduation.

(C) He is having a tough time finding a job.

(D) He hopes to find a position in marketing.

(A) 予定どおりには卒業できないかもしれないと思っている。

(B) 卒業したらクルージングに行く予定である。

(C) 仕事を探すのに苦労している。

(D) マーケティングに職を見つけることを望んでいる。

解法 設問を先読みしてから会話を聞き，会話内で男性が言いたいことを聞き取る。同意表現がポイントとなる問題。男性のWe're pretty much in the same boat は「私たちは同じ状況だ」という表現。男性も女性も就職先を見つけるのが難しいという状況がわかるため，正解は (C)。

重要語
- **job market**「労働市場」
- **be in the same boat**「同じ境遇にある」

6.　　　　　　　　　　　　　　　　　　　　　　　　　　　　　　解答：C

🔊 034　**M:** I'm going to run over to the post office to mail a letter. You need any airmail stamps or anything?

W: You know, I can't remember the last time I actually wrote a letter and mailed it. I do all my correspondence by e-mail these days.

M: 手紙を出しに郵便局へ行くけど。エアメール用の切手か何か必要なものはある？

W: あのね，最後に手紙を書いて出したのがいつかも覚えていないくらいだわ。最近はすべて電子メールでやりとりしているから。

What does the woman imply? 女性は何を示唆していますか。

(A) She forgot to mail an important letter.

(B) She needs to buy some airmail stamps.

(C) She rarely buys airmail stamps.

(D) She will come with the man to mail the letter.

(A) 彼女は大事な手紙を出すのを忘れた。

(B) 彼女はエアメール用の切手を何枚か買う必要がある。

(C) 彼女はエアメール用の切手を買うことはほとんどない。

(D) 彼女は手紙を出しに男性と一緒に出かける。

解法 設問を先読みしてから会話を聞き，会話内で女性が示唆していることを聞き取る。女性の発言の意図を問う問題。いつ最後に手紙を書いて出したかも覚えていないし，最近はすべて電子メールでやりとりしているということは，エアメール用の切手を買うことはほとんどないことを示している。正解は (C)。

重要語
- **correspondence**「通信」

7.

🔊 035

W: Is tomorrow the last day to vote in the student government election?

M: No. Today is. Thanks for reminding me. I need to walk over to the student center right now and cast my ballot.

W: 明日は学生自治会選挙の投票最終日かしら？

M: いや。今日だよ。思い出させてくれてありがとう。今すぐ学生会館まで歩いていって，投票しなきゃ。

What will the man probably do?	男性はおそらく何をしますか。
(A) Vote in the election	(A) 選挙の投票をする
(B) Take a walk with the woman	(B) 女性と散歩する
(C) Have lunch in the student center	(C) 学生会館で昼食をとる
(D) Return the notes tomorrow	(D) 明日記録を返却する

解法 設問を先読みしてから会話を聞き，会話内で男性がおそらく行うことを聞き取る。男性の行動を推測する問題。election, cast my ballot と言っているので，選挙の投票に行くことがわかる。正解は (A)。

重要語
□ **cast a ballot**「投票する」

8.

🔊 036

M: Brr. Do you know how to turn up the heat? There is a thermostat on the wall, but they've locked it so we can't adjust it.

W: Maybe it'll warm up when everyone gets here. I sure hope so, anyway.

M: うーっ。暖房を強くするにはどうすればよいかわかる？　壁に温度調節器があるけど，ロックされているから調節できないよ。

W: たぶん，みんなが来たら暖かくなるわね。とにかく，そうなることを望むわ。

What will the woman probably do?	女性はおそらく何をしますか。
(A) Try to adjust the thermostat	(A) 温度調節器を調節しようとする
(B) Put on some extra clothing	(B) 洋服を着込む
(C) Wait until other students arrive for class	(C) 他の学生が授業に来るまで待つ
(D) Unlock the door herself	(D) 自分でドアの錠を開ける

解法 設問を先読みしてから会話を聞き，会話内で女性がおそらく行うことを聞き取る。問題の解決策を問う問題。問題点は教室がとても寒いことであり，女性は，みんなが来たら暖かくなるだろうし，そうなることを望むと述べている。彼女は特に対策をとらず，他の学生が来るのを待つことが推測されるので，正解は (C)。

重要語
□ **thermostat**「温度調節器」
□ **adjust**「～を調節する」

9.

解答：A

🔊 037

M: My physics class couldn't be better. Dr. Hanson is one of the most talented lecturers I've ever met, and the subject matter is something I'm very interested in.

W: I know what you mean. I took the same course last year myself.

M: 物理学の授業はとてもいいね。ハンソン先生は今まで会った中で最も才能のある講師のひとりだし，題材もとても興味深いよ。

W: わかるわ。私も去年同じコースをとったから。

What does the man imply?	男性は何を示唆していますか。
(A) He is satisfied with Dr. Hanson's class.	(A) ハンソン先生の授業に満足している。
(B) He will take the course next semester.	(B) 来学期そのコースをとるつもりである。
(C) He is not very interested in physics.	(C) 物理学にはあまり興味がない。
(D) He is hoping to major in physics.	(D) 物理学を専攻したいと考えている。

解法 設問を先読みしてから会話を聞き，会話内で男性が示唆していることを聞き取る。男性の発言の意図を問う問題。男性は冒頭で，My physics class couldn't be better.「物理学の授業はとてもいいね」と述べている。続けてハンソン先生を称賛しているので，彼はハンソン先生の物理学の授業に満足していることがわかる。正解は (A)。

重要語
- □ **couldn't be better**
  「とてもよい，最高だ」
- □ **subject matter**
  「題材，内容」

10.

解答：C

🔊 038

W: Oh, no! Not again! The printer's out of ink.

M: Why don't you just run over to the campus bookstore and pick up another cartridge? It's still open for another hour.

W: ああ！ またなんて！ プリンターのインク切れだわ。

M: 大学の書店に走って行って，インクカートリッジを買ってきたらどう？ まだあと1時間は開いているよ。

What will the woman probably do?	女性はおそらく何をしますか。
(A) Go to the university computer center	(A) 大学のコンピュータセンターに行く
(B) Use the copy machine on campus	(B) キャンパスにあるコピー機を使う
(C) Buy an ink cartridge for the printer	(C) プリンターのインクカートリッジを買う
(D) Pick up the book at the library herself	(D) 図書館で本を自分で選ぶ

解法 設問を先読みしてから会話を聞き，会話内で女性がおそらく行うことを聞き取る。女性の行動を推測する問題。男性は，大学の書店に走って行って，インクカートリッジを買ってきたらどうかと勧めているので，正解は (C)。

重要語
- □ **be out of ...**
  「～が切れている」

11.

🔊 039

W: Dr. Neville, you wanted to talk with me about my essay? Is there some problem with it? I really worked hard on it, you know.

M: Actually, your effort is certainly apparent. In fact, the reason I wanted to see you is to ask your permission to use your essay as a model for other students to follow.

W: ネビル先生，私のレポートについてお話がおありですか。何か問題がありましたか。私は本当に一生懸命取り組みましたが。

M: 実際，あなたが努力したことは明らかですよ。実はお会いしたかったのは，あなたのレポートを他の学生にお手本として示す許可をもらいたかったからです。

What do we learn from this conversation? / この会話から何がわかりますか。

(A) The professor will permit the woman to join the class.
(B) The woman should have worked harder on her essay.
(C) The professor is impressed with the woman's writing.
(D) The woman submitted her assignment after the deadline.

(A) 教授は女性が授業に出ることを許可するだろう。
(B) 女性はレポートにもっと力を注ぐべきだった。
(C) 教授は女性の書いたものに感心している。
(D) 女性は締め切りを過ぎてから宿題を提出した。

| **解法** | 設問を先読みしてから会話を聞き，会話内で会話から推測できることを聞き取る。会話の内容を把握し，その背景を推測する問題。教授は，女性がレポートにとても力を注いだことを認め，そのレポートを他の学生にお手本として示したいと考えている。つまり，教授はそれを大いに評価していることが推測されるので，正解は (C)。 |

重要語
□ **apparent**「明らかな」

12.

🔊 040

W: Have you decided the topic of your group project presentation yet?

M: We're thinking about dolphin communication systems. Jerry found a couple of great sources in the library. And Ralph knows some Internet sites that should be useful.

W: グループ研究発表のトピックはもう決めた？

M: イルカのコミュニケーション方法を考えているよ。ジェリーが図書館でいくつかいい資料を見つけたんだ。ラルフも役に立つホームページをいくつか知っているしね。

Section 1 Part A/B　Section 1 Part C　Section 2　Section 3　総合模試　総合模試 解答・解説

What does the man say about the members of his presentation group?

(A) They ought to change their presentation topic.

(B) They will probably have access to appropriate information.

(C) They intend to go on a dolphin watching cruise.

(D) They need to communicate with each other better.

男性は自分の発表グループのメンバーについて何と言っていますか。

(A) 発表するトピックを変えるべきである。

(B) おそらく適切な情報を得るだろう。

(C) イルカ見学のクルーズに行くつもりである。

(D) もっとお互いの意志疎通をうまくやる必要がある。

解法 設問を先読みしてから会話を聞き，会話内で男性がメンバーについて言っていることを聞き取る。男性の発言の意図を問う問題。男性は研究発表の資料があることを Jerry found a couple of great sources と Ralph knows some Internet sites のように述べている。これらから適切な情報を得られるだろうと考えられるので，正解は (B)。

13.-16.　Long Conversation

🔊 041 Listen to the following conversation between a professor and a student.

M: Professor Harris, I'm sorry to bother you but I wonder if you have a moment.

W: Sure, Justin. How can I help you?

M: Well, it's my research essay. I'm having a hard time finding a topic. I like your class a lot, but it's my first history course at university, so I'm a little unsure of myself.

W: OK. But please don't worry about it too much. Finding a good topic is hard for all students—and even scholars sometimes. One thing you've already done right is to get on top of this at the mid-point of the term. If you wait until later in the course to find your topic and begin your research, you can really be in trouble. Let me give you some practical tips.

M: Great. I'm all ears.

W: To begin, browse through our readings in the course. Skim through our history textbook and look at what's caught your interest. What period are you most interested in? Second, look over your class notes and your lecture notes. What strikes your curiosity? What do you agree with or disagree with? What needs further exploration or explanation?

M: That's an interesting approach. I thought the essay had to be on something totally different from what we covered in the course. You know, like independent research.

W: No, not at all. The best research essays often pursue an issue, or focus on a subject, that's been addressed in a class but not treated in sufficient depth. Above all, my advice is to follow your curiosity and intellectual excitement.

教授と学生が交わす次の会話を聞きなさい。

M: ハリス教授，おじゃましてすみません。ちょっとよろしいですか。

W: もちろんですよ，ジャスティン。どうしたのですか。

M: 実は，研究レポートのことなんです。なかなかトピックが見つからなくて。教授の授業はとても好きですが，大学で初めての歴史のコースなので，どうしたらいいのかよくわからないのです。

W: わかりました。でも，あまり心配しないでください。よいトピックを見つけるのはどの学生にとっても難しいことです——学者でさえそんなときがあるくらいですからね。あなたがすでに正しく行っているのは，学期半ばでこの問題に取り組んでいることです。もしトピックを見つけてリサーチを始めるのをコースの後半まで待ったりしたら，本当にたいへんなことになりかねませんからね。いくつか実際的なヒントをあげましょう。

M: 助かります。ぜひ聞かせてください。

W: まず，授業の読書課題に目を通すことです。歴史のテキストにざっと目を通して，興味を引いたものから調べてみるといいですね。どの時代に最も興味がありますか。次に，クラスノートとレクチャーノートに目を通します。自分の興味に訴えかけるものは何か。自分が賛成するもの，反対するものは何なのか。さらに調査や説明が必要なのは何なのかというように。

M: 興味深いアプローチですね。レポートは授業で学んだものとはまったく別のことについて書くべきなのかと思っていました。自由研究のように。

W: いいえ，そんなことはありません。とてもよく書けた研究レポートは，授業で触れたにもかかわらず十分に掘り下げられなかったことを調べ上げたり，絞り込んで研究したりしているものなんです。とにかく，私のアドバイスは好奇心と知的興奮を追求することですね。

◆ 設問を素早く先読みしてから会話を聞き，次の点を聞き取る。

13. 学生の履修科目，　　　　　　　　　　**15.** 教授のアドバイス，

14. 学生の研究レポートに関する問題点，　　**16.** 会話の時期

13. 　　　　　　　　　　　　　　　　　　　　　　　　　　　　　　　解答：C

042　What type of course is the student taking from the professor?　　　学生は教授のどのタイプの科目を取っていますか。

(A) Research methods　　　　　　　　(A) 研究方法

(B) Independent study　　　　　　　　(B) 自由研究

(C) History　　　　　　　　　　　　(C) 歴史

(D) Composition　　　　　　　　　　(D) 作文

解法 繰り返される情報を問う問題。it's my first history course および our history textbook と述べている。正解は (C)。

14.

解答：C

🔊 042　What aspect of the research paper is the student having difficulty with?

(A) Organization
(B) Sources
(C) Subject
(D) Conclusion

学生は研究レポートのどの段階でつまずいていますか。

(A) 構成
(B) 文献
(C) トピック
(D) 結論

> **解法** 問題点を問う問題。男性は I'm having a hard time finding a topic と述べ，トピックが見つからない件で教授に相談している。正解は (C)。

15.

解答：D

🔊 042　What advice does the professor give the student?

(A) Conduct research together with a classmate
(B) Locate key information in the library
(C) Compose an outline before writing
(D) Choose a topic closely related to the course

教授が学生に与えたアドバイスは何ですか。

(A) クラスメートと一緒にリサーチする
(B) 図書館で核となる情報を見つける
(C) 書く前に大筋を決める
(D) 授業内容に関連したトピックを選ぶ

> **解法** 問題の解決策を問う問題。教授は Let me give you some practical tips「実際的なヒントをあげましょう」と前置きしたうえで，授業の読書課題やテキストの中からトピックを探すことを勧めている。これを言い換えた (D) が正解となる。

16.

解答：B

🔊 042　When does this conversation probably take place?

(A) At the beginning of the term
(B) Midway through the term
(C) Towards the end of the term
(D) During final examinations

この会話が交わされているのはおそらくいつですか。

(A) 学期初頭
(B) 学期半ば
(C) 学期の終盤
(D) 期末試験の期間中

> **解法** 会話の時期を問う問題。教授は会話中で at the mid-point of the term「学期半ばで」と述べている。正解は (B)。

重要語
- □ **have a hard time** *doing*「〜するのに苦労する」
- □ **tip**「ヒント，助言」
- □ **be all ears**「一心に耳を傾ける」
- □ **browse**「〜にざっと目を通す」
- □ **skim**「〜にざっと目を通す」
- □ **exploration**「探究」

集中練習問題 ② Part A 形式 12 問 + Part B 形式 1 題 4 問

BURST TWO

Part A Short Conversations

◀)) 043

1. What will the woman probably do tomorrow?

(A) See a movie

(B) Attend a football game

(C) Go on a picnic

(D) Study at the library

Ⓐ Ⓑ Ⓒ Ⓓ

◀)) 044

2. What does the man mean?

(A) He has to go to the doctor.

(B) He needs to talk to his professor.

(C) He would like to join the woman.

(D) He is not supposed to drink coffee.

Ⓐ Ⓑ Ⓒ Ⓓ

◀)) 045

3. What can be inferred about the woman from this conversation?

(A) She seldom goes to biology class.

(B) She plans to contact Cathie.

(C) She intends to lend the man her notebook.

(D) She will ask the man for his notes later.

Ⓐ Ⓑ Ⓒ Ⓓ

◀)) 046

4. What will the woman probably do during spring break?

(A) Work on her assignments

(B) Find a part-time job

(C) Go on a trip with her parents

(D) Visit her hometown

Ⓐ Ⓑ Ⓒ Ⓓ

◀)) 047

5. Why is the man at the student health center?

(A) To pick up some X-rays

(B) To take an annual physical

(C) To consult with a physician

(D) To renew his health card

Ⓐ Ⓑ Ⓒ Ⓓ

Go on to the next page ➡

◀⦚ 048　**6.** What does the man imply about the woman?

    (A)　She should have asked him earlier.

    (B)　She should not skip so many classes.

    (C)　She will likely do better than she expects.

    (D)　She will not be able to drop the class.　Ⓐ Ⓑ Ⓒ Ⓓ

◀⦚ 049　**7.** What does the woman mean?

    (A)　She missed her sociology class.

    (B)　She feels the man's question is too personal.

    (C)　She did not know the exam was canceled.

    (D)　She thinks she did poorly on the test.　Ⓐ Ⓑ Ⓒ Ⓓ

◀⦚ 050　**8.** What does the man imply about the woman?

    (A)　She ought to look for a different job.

    (B)　She should have worn a more formal dress.

    (C)　She usually dresses more casually.

    (D)　She has never visited Vancouver before.　Ⓐ Ⓑ Ⓒ Ⓓ

◀⦚ 051　**9.** What does the woman mean?

    (A)　She enjoyed the ceremony very much.

    (B)　The ceremony could have been better organized.

    (C)　The ceremony was shorter than she expected.

    (D)　She arrived late to the ceremony.　Ⓐ Ⓑ Ⓒ Ⓓ

◀⦚ 052　**10.** What does the man plan to do later in the day?

    (A)　Go to the airport

    (B)　Help the woman move

    (C)　Visit his friend's apartment

    (D)　Have dinner with the woman　Ⓐ Ⓑ Ⓒ Ⓓ

◀⦚ 053　**11.** What does the man suggest to the woman?

    (A)　She should not read so many books.

    (B)　She should weigh her backpack.

    (C)　She ought to carry a lighter backpack.

    (D)　She ought to exercise to strengthen her back.　Ⓐ Ⓑ Ⓒ Ⓓ

12. What is the woman's problem?

- (A) She does not know where the security office is.
- (B) She missed her humanities class.
- (C) She got lost walking around campus.
- (D) She left her glasses in a classroom. Ⓐ Ⓑ Ⓒ Ⓓ

Part B Long Conversation

13. Why is the man tired?

- (A) He just finished taking a test.
- (B) He has a part-time job at night.
- (C) He has been studying a lot.
- (D) He is preparing grad school applications. Ⓐ Ⓑ Ⓒ Ⓓ

14. How many mid-term exams does the man have?

- (A) Two
- (B) Three
- (C) Four
- (D) Five Ⓐ Ⓑ Ⓒ Ⓓ

15. What does the man regret about his first few years at the university?

- (A) He received rather low grades.
- (B) He chose the wrong major.
- (C) He spent too much time working.
- (D) He did not know what he wanted to study. Ⓐ Ⓑ Ⓒ Ⓓ

16. What field is the man majoring in?

- (A) Math
- (B) Business
- (C) Accounting
- (D) Computer science Ⓐ Ⓑ Ⓒ Ⓓ

Section 1　PartA/B

集中練習問題 ❷　解答・解説

Section Ⅰ Part A/B

Section Ⅰ Part C

Section 2

Section 3

総合模試

総合模試 解答・解説

1.

解答：B

◀)) 043　**W:** Have you heard the forecast for tomorrow? I'm trying to decide whether to go to the football game or maybe take in a movie.

M: As far as I know, it's supposed to be really nice—sunny and warm, a good day to be outside in a stadium rather than inside studying.

W: 明日の天気予報は聞いた？　フットボールの試合に行くか，映画にでも行くか決めようと思っているけど。

M: 僕の知っている限りでは，とてもいい天気で，晴天で暖かい日らしいよ。屋内で勉強するよりスタジアムのような屋外にいるのがぴったりの日のようだね。

What will the woman probably do tomorrow?	女性は明日おそらく何をしますか。
(A) See a movie	(A) 映画を見る
(B) Attend a football game	(B) フットボールの試合に行く
(C) Go on a picnic	(C) ピクニックに行く
(D) Study at the library	(D) 図書館で勉強する

解法　設問を先読みしてから会話を聞き，会話内で女性がおそらく行うことを聞き取る。女性の行動を推測する問題。tomorrow, sunny, warm, good day, outside などのキーワードを聞き取ると，明日は天気がよく屋外にいるのがぴったりの日であると言っていることがわかる。正解は (B)。

重要語
□ **be supposed to** *do*
「～することになっている」

2.

解答：C

◀)) 044　**W:** I don't know about you, but I've had a long afternoon of classes. What do you say to a cup of coffee at the student union?

M: I think that's just what the doctor ordered.

W: あなたはどうだったかわからないけど，私は午後ずっと授業で長かったわ。学生会館でコーヒーでも飲まない？

M: ちょうど飲みたいと思っていたよ。

What does the man mean?	男性は何を言いたいのですか。
(A) He has to go to the doctor.	(A) 医者に行かねばならない。
(B) He needs to talk to his professor.	(B) 教授と話す必要がある。
(C) He would like to join the woman.	(C) 女性に同行したい。
(D) He is not supposed to drink coffee.	(D) コーヒーを飲んではいけないことになっている。

重要語
☐ **What do you say to ...?**
「〜はどうですか」
(= Why not ...?)
☐ **just what the doctor ordered** 「ちょうどほしいと思っていたもの」

3. 解答：B

045 W: Charlie, I've got a favor to ask. I missed Professor Kent's biology lecture this afternoon and I wonder if I could borrow your notes.

M: You could if I had them, but I already lent them to Cathie. Why don't you check with her to see if she's finished going over them? Please give them back to me as soon as you're done with them.

W: チャーリー，お願いがあるの。今日の午後，ケント先生の生物学の授業に出られなかったので，ノートを貸してもらえないかしら。

M: 手元にあったら貸してあげられるけど，もうすでにキャシーに貸してしまったよ。彼女に使い終わったかどうか聞いてみたらどう？　終わったらすぐに僕に返してね。

What can be inferred about the woman from this conversation?

(A) She seldom goes to biology class.
(B) She plans to contact Cathie.
(C) She intends to lend the man her notebook.
(D) She will ask the man for his notes later.

この会話から女性について何が推測できますか。

(A) 彼女はめったに生物学の授業に出席しない。
(B) 彼女はキャシーに連絡するつもりだ。
(C) 彼女は男性に自分のノートを貸そうとしている。
(D) 彼女は男性にノートを貸してくれるよう後で頼むだろう。

解法 設問を先読みしてから会話を聞き，会話内で女性の行動について考えられることを聞き取る。推測に関する問題。borrow, lent, Cathie, check などから，女性がノートを借りたがっていること，女性がキャシーにノートを使い終わったかどうか聞くであろうことがわかる。正解は (B)。

重要語
☐ **biology**「生物学」

4.

解答：A

🔊 046　**M:** Are you still planning to visit your family during spring break?

W: Originally, I was. But my dad has to go to Canada on business and he decided to take my mom with him. It doesn't matter, though. I've got plenty of schoolwork here to keep me busy.

M: 春休みに家族のところへ行く予定に変わりはない？

W: そのつもりだったけど。でも，父は仕事でカナダに行かなければならなくて，母も連れていくことにしたの。かまわないんだけどね。私もここでする勉強がたくさんあって忙しいから。

What will the woman probably do during spring break?　女性は春休みにおそらく何をしますか。

(A) Work on her assignments

(B) Find a part-time job

(C) Go on a trip with her parents

(D) Visit her hometown

(A) 課題に取り組む

(B) アルバイトを探す

(C) 両親と旅行に行く

(D) 故郷を訪ねる

解法 設問を先読みしてから会話を聞き，会話内で女性が春休みにおそらく行うことを聞き取る。女性の行動を推測する問題。女性は春休みに家族のところへ行く予定だったが，父の仕事の関係で取りやめ，勉強で忙しいと述べている。そこから推測すると，正解は(A)。

5.

解答：D

🔊 047　**W:** What are you doing here at the health center? You're not sick again, are you?

M: Not at all. I had my annual check-up last week and now I just need to get my student health card updated.

W: 保健センターで何をしているの。また病気ということではないわよね。

M: 違う，違う。年に一度の健康診断を先週受けて，今回学生保健カードを更新する必要があるのさ。

Why is the man at the student health center?　男性はなぜ学生保健センターにいるのですか。

(A) To pick up some X-rays

(B) To take an annual physical

(C) To consult with a physician

(D) To renew his health card

(A) X線写真を受け取るため

(B) 年次健康診断を受けるため

(C) 医者にかかるため

(D) 保健カードを更新するため

解法 設問を先読みしてから会話を聞き，会話内で男性が学生保健センターにいる理由を聞き取る。会話の内容を問う問題。health center, student health card, updated などのキーワードから，男性は，今回学生保健カードを更新するために保健センターにいることがわかる。正解は(D)。

重要語
- **check-up**「健康診断」（= physical〔examination〕）
- **physician**「医者」

6.

W: Dr. Lawrence, would you mind signing this add card for me? I need to take it over to the registrar's office today before three.

M: Cutting it a little close, aren't we? It's already 2:30 and you're just coming to see me now?

W: ローレンス先生，この追加科目のカードにサインをしていただけますか。今日の3時までに学籍係のオフィスへ持って行かなくてはならないのです。

M: ちょっとぎりぎりに見積もっていないですか。もう2時半で，あなたは今になって私のところに来ているのですよ。

What does the man imply about the woman?	男性は女性について何を示唆していますか。
(A) She should have asked him earlier.	(A) 彼女はもっと早く自分に頼むべきだった。
(B) She should not skip so many classes.	(B) 彼女は授業をそんなに欠席すべきではない。
(C) She will likely do better than she expects.	(C) 彼女は自分で思っているよりうまくいくだろう。
(D) She will not be able to drop the class.	(D) 彼女は授業を落とすことはできない。

解法 設問を先読みしてから会話を聞き，会話内で男性が示唆していることを聞き取る。男性の発言の意図を問う問題。女性は締め切りぎりぎりになって男性のところに来たので，彼は少し皮肉っぽくそれをたしなめて，もっと早く頼むべきだったと示唆している。正解は (A)。男性の声の調子もヒントになる。

重要語
- □ **add card**「追加科目のカード」
- □ **registrar**「学籍係」
- □ **cut it close**「ぎりぎりに切り詰める」

7.

M: Hey, Sara. I heard your sociology test had a lot of difficult questions. How did you do on it?

W: Don't ask!

M: やあ, サラ。社会学の試験に難しい問題が多かったって聞いたよ。どうだったの。

W: 聞かないで！

What does the woman mean?	女性は何を言いたいのですか。
(A) She missed her sociology class.	(A) 社会学の授業を受けなかった。
(B) She feels the man's question is too personal.	(B) 男性の質問は個人的すぎると感じている。
(C) She did not know the exam was canceled.	(C) 試験がキャンセルされたことを知らなかった。
(D) She thinks she did poorly on the test.	(D) 自分の試験の出来は悪かったと考えている。

解法 設問を先読みしてから会話を聞き，会話内で女性が言いたいことを聞き取る。女性の発言の意図を問う問題。試験には難しい問題が多かったこと，彼女は試験の結果を「聞かないで」と言っていることから，彼女は自分の試験の出来は悪かったと考えていることが推測できる。正解は (D)。

重要語
- □ **sociology**「社会学」

8.

解答：C

🔊 050　W:　I've got an interview with a consulting firm from Vancouver—I sure hope I get the job.

M:　No wonder you're so dressed up. I don't think I've ever seen you in a suit before.

W:　バンクーバーから来たコンサルティング会社の人と面接があるの。職を得られれば本当にいいのだけど。

M:　どおりできちんとした服装をしているわけだね。君がスーツを着ているのを見たことはこれまでないと思うよ。

What does the man imply about the woman?

(A) She ought to look for a different job.

(B) She should have worn a more formal dress.

(C) She usually dresses more casually.

(D) She has never visited Vancouver before.

男性は女性について何を示唆していますか。

(A) 彼女は別の仕事を探すべきだ。

(B) 彼女はもっとフォーマルなドレスを着るべきだった。

(C) 彼女はふだんもっとカジュアルな服装をしている。

(D) 彼女はバンクーバーを訪れたことがない。

解法　設問を先読みしてから会話を聞き，会話内で男性が示唆していることを聞き取る。推測に関する問題。男性は，女性がスーツを着ているのを見たことはこれまでないと思うと言っている。普段彼女はもっとカジュアルな服装をしていることが推測できるので，正解は (C)。

重要語
□ **interview**「面接」

9.

解答：A

🔊 051　M:　So, you had a good time at the awards ceremony you attended last night?

W:　You said it. It was nothing short of perfect.

M:　それで昨晩出席した表彰式は楽しかった？

W:　そうなのよ。もう完璧だったわ。

What does the woman mean?

(A) She enjoyed the ceremony very much.

(B) The ceremony could have been better organized.

(C) The ceremony was shorter than she expected.

(D) She arrived late to the ceremony.

女性は何を言いたいのですか。

(A) 彼女は式典をとても楽しんだ。

(B) 式典はもっとうまく構成することができた。

(C) 式典は思ったより短かった。

(D) 彼女は式典に遅刻した。

解法　設問を先読みしてから会話を聞き，会話内で女性が言いたいことを聞き取る。同意表現がポイントとなる問題。女性は同意の表現 You said it. を使って「そうなのよ」と答えている。式典を楽しんだことを示しているので，正解は (A)。

重要語
□ **You said it.**「そのとおり」
□ **nothing short of ...**「〜そのもの」

10.

🔊 052　**W:** Could you give me a hand later this afternoon? I've decided to move to an apartment off-campus. A bunch of my friends are coming by to help, and I'm going to cook for everyone at my new place when we're done.

M: You know I would if I could, but I'm flying over to visit my folks in San Francisco and need to get out of here right after third period finishes.

　　　W: 今日の午後，手を貸してもらえるかしら。キャンパスの外のアパートに引っ越すことにしたのよ。友人連中が手伝いに来てくれるの。終わったら新居でみんなに料理を作るつもりよ。

　　　M: 可能だったら行くところだけど，サンフランシスコの両親のところに飛行機で行くので，3 限が終わったらすぐにここを出なきゃならないんだ。

What does the man plan to do later in the day?	男性はその日，後で何をする予定ですか。
(A) Go to the airport	(A) 空港へ行く
(B) Help the woman move	(B) 女性の引っ越しを手伝う
(C) Visit his friend's apartment	(C) 友人のアパートを訪ねる
(D) Have dinner with the woman	(D) 女性と夕食をとる

解法 設問を先読みしてから会話を聞き，会話内で男性が予定していることを聞き取る。今後の行動を問う問題。男性はサンフランシスコの両親のところに飛行機で行く予定だと述べている。正解は (A)。

重要語
- ☐ **my folks**「両親，家族」
- ☐ **period**「(学校の) 時限」

11.

🔊 053　**W:** My back is really bothering me. My backpack weighs a ton with all these books in it.

M: That's not good. If you're carrying that much weight around all day, you're bound to have some problems.

　　　W: 背中がとても痛いわ。バックパックの中にこれらの本を全部入れているから，とても重いのよ。

　　　M: それはよくないな。一日中そのすごい重さを抱えていたら，問題が起きるはずだよ。

What does the man suggest to the woman?	男性は女性に何を提案していますか。
(A) She should not read so many books.	(A) そんなに多くの本を読むべきではない。
(B) She should weigh her backpack.	(B) バックパックの重さを測るべきだ。
(C) She ought to carry a lighter backpack.	(C) 軽くしたバックパックを持ち運ぶべきだ。
(D) She ought to exercise to strengthen her back.	(D) 背中を鍛える運動をするべきだ。

解法 設問を先読みしてから会話を聞き，会話内で男性が提案していることを聞き取る。問題の解決策を問う問題。女性のバックパックが重くて背中が痛いという問題点について，男性は If you're carrying that much weight around all day, you're bound to have some problems. と述べている。男性は解決方法として，重いバックパックをどうにかしなければならないと思っているので，正解は (C)。

重要語
- ☐ **bother**「～を悩ませる」
- ☐ **weigh a ton**「とても重い」
- ☐ **be bound to** *do*「～するはずだ」

12.

解答：D

◀))) 054

W: Excuse me. Is this where the lost-and-found is located? I left my glasses in the humanities building yesterday after class.

M: You need to go over to the campus security office on the first floor of the administration building. I'm sure you know where that is, don't you?

　W: すみません。こちらに遺失物預かり所はありますか？　昨日人文科学棟で，授業の後メガネを置き忘れてしまったのですが。

　M: 事務棟の1階の構内保安課に行ってください。どこにあるかおわかりになりますよね。

What is the woman's problem?　　　　　　　女性の問題は何ですか。

(A) She does not know where the security office is.　(A) 保安課の場所がわからない。

(B) She missed her humanities class.　　　(B) 人文科学の授業を欠席した。

(C) She got lost walking around campus.　(C) キャンパスを歩いていて迷った。

(D) She left her glasses in a classroom.　(D) 教室にメガネを忘れた。

解法 設問を先読みしてから会話を聞き，会話内で女性の問題点を聞き取る。女性の問題点は，授業の後メガネを置き忘れたこととなので，正解は (D)。

重要語

□ **lost-and-found**
「遺失物取扱所」

□ **humanities**「人文科学」

□ **security office**「保安課」

13.-16.

Long Conversation

◀))) 055

Listen to the following conversation between two students at school.

W: Dominic, you look so tired.

M: Yes, I've been up studying late three nights in a row. I've got mid-term exams in all four of my classes. They're really killing me.

W: No kidding. I lucked out this semester. I've only got a couple. So how many do you have out of the way?

M: That's the bad part. Only one. I've got two tomorrow and one the day after. The thing is, I'm planning to go to grad school, so I really need to get my GPA up. The first two years I was here, I wasn't a very serious student, to say the least. So now, if I want to raise my grades, my work is really cut out for me.

W: What are you thinking of going on and studying in?

M: I'm a math major with a business minor, and I'm becoming more and more interested in statistics. I figure that with my math degree, and maybe a master's in either business or accounting, I could get a really good job in an insurance company. Basically, I'd like a job that's pretty secure and pays a good income.

W: Wouldn't we all!

学校で2人の学生が交わす次の会話を聞きなさい。

W: ドミニク，ずいぶん疲れているようね。

M: ああ，3日間連続で遅くまで勉強していてね。僕のとっている授業は4つとも中間試験があって，ほんとうに死にそうだよ。

W: ほんとう？　私は今学期運がよかったわ。2つしかなかったもの。それでいくつ終わったの？

M: それがまずいことにひとつだけだよ。明日2つ，あさってひとつある。実は大学院に行くことを考えているから，どうしても学業平均値（GPA）を上げる必要があるんだ。ここでの最初の2年間，僕は控えめに言ってもあまりまじめな学生じゃなかった。だから今評価を上げようとするなら，本当に身を削って勉強しなきゃ。

W: 何を引き続き勉強しようと考えているの？

M: 僕は専攻が数学，副専攻がビジネスで，だんだん統計学に興味が出てきた。僕の数学の学位に，ビジネスか会計学の修士号があれば，保険会社で本当にいい仕事につけると思う。基本的に，かなり安定して収入のいい仕事につきたいと思っているんだよ。

W: 皆そうよ！

◈ 設問を素早く先読みしてから会話を聞き，次の点を聞き取る。

13. 男性が疲れている理由，　　**15.** 男性が後悔していること，
14. 男性の試験数，　　　　　　**16.** 男性の専攻

13.

解答：C

◀)) 056　Why is the man tired?　　　　　　　　男性はなぜ疲れているのですか。

(A) He just finished taking a test.　　　　(A) 彼はちょうど試験を受けてきた。
(B) He has a part-time job at night.　　　(B) 彼は夜アルバイトをしている。
(C) He has been studying a lot.　　　　　(C) 彼はずっとかなり勉強している。
(D) He is preparing grad school applications.　(D) 彼は大学院出願の準備をしている。

> **解法**　会話内の情報に関する問題。男性が疲れているのは，I've been up studying late three nights in a row.「3日間連続で遅くまで勉強していた」ためである。正解は (C)。

14.

解答：C

◀)) 056　How many mid-term exams does the man have?　男性の中間試験はいくつありますか。

(A) Two　　　　　　　　　　　　　　　(A) 2
(B) Three　　　　　　　　　　　　　　(B) 3
(C) Four　　　　　　　　　　　　　　 (C) 4
(D) Five　　　　　　　　　　　　　　 (D) 5

> **解法**　会話内の情報に関する問題。男性は I've got mid-term exams in all four of my classes. と言っているので，正解は (C)。数字などの情報は設問ポイントになることがあるため，会話内に出てきたときには注意するべきである。

15.　　　　　　　　　　　　　　　　　　　　　　　　解答：A

◀)) 056　What does the man regret about his first few
　　　years at the university?

(A) He received rather low grades.

(B) He chose the wrong major.

(C) He spent too much time working.

(D) He did not know what he wanted to study.

男性は大学での最初の数年間について何を後悔し
ていますか。

(A) やや低い成績だった。

(B) 専攻の選択を間違った。

(C) 働くことに時間を費やしすぎた。

(D) 自分の勉強したいことがわからなかった。

> **解法**　推測に関する問題。男性は I really need to get my GPA up. I wasn't a very serious student.
> と述べている。成績が低かったことが推測できるので，正解は (A)。

16.　　　　　　　　　　　　　　　　　　　　　　　　解答：A

◀)) 056　What field is the man majoring in?

(A) Math

(B) Business

(C) Accounting

(D) Computer science

男性はどの分野を専攻していますか。

(A) 数学

(B) ビジネス

(C) 会計学

(D) コンピュータサイエンス

> **解法**　会話内の情報に関する問題。男性は I'm a math major や with my math degree と述べている
> ので，正解は (A)。

> **重要語**　□ **in a row**「連続で」　　　　　　　　□ **GPA**「学業平均値」(< grade point average)
> 　　　　　　□ **luck out**「運がよい，うまくいく」　　□ **statistics**「統計学」

Section 1　Part C（トーク問題）の概要

　Listening Comprehension セクションは以下の構成になっている。本節では Talks を攻略する（赤色の部分）。

Listening Comprehension（50問：約35分）

Part A（30問）	Part B（8または9問）	Part C（12または11問）
Short Conversations	Long Conversations	Talks

> **主な特徴**
>
> ◈ 全問とも四肢択一形式。
> ◈ 3つのトークが出題され，それぞれに 3-5 つの設問がある。
> ◈ 音声に合わせて試験が進行するため，解答時間を自分で配分することができない。
> ◈ 問題用紙に設問と選択肢が印刷されている。

Talks

　大学の教官1名によって行われる講義などのトークを聞き取り，その内容についての質問に答える出題形式。

Listening Comprehension Part C のストラテジー

　本節も前節と同様に，全問題共通の［総合的なストラテジー］と，頻出の設問形式・設問ポイントを元に分類した［特有のストラテジー］の2種類に分けて学習を進める。

総合的なストラテジー

1. Part C 総合的なストラテジー

　　　　「キーワード」を聞き取る

　　　　「設問を先読み」して答えに関する情報を聞き取る

　　　　「繰り返される情報」に注意する

特有のストラテジー

2. Part C 特有のストラテジー1　話者の主張や話の流れをつかむ問題

　　　　講義の主題やトピックを問う設問

　　　　前後の講義を推測する設問

　　　　話者のトーンを問う設問

3. Part C 特有のストラテジー2　細部の詳細情報を聞き取る問題

　　　　名前，数字，年号，統計など，具体的な詳細情報を問う設問

　　　　講義で述べる定義や理論を問う設問

　　　　時系列に列挙する設問

1．Part C 総合的なストラテジー

最重要ストラテジー ▶▶▶

◆「キーワード」を聞き取る

◆「設問を先読み」して答えに関する情報を聞き取る

◆「繰り返される情報」に注意する

　各トークは1分半〜2分程度のものが多く，会話問題に比べ格段に英文が長くなる。そのため，いっそう焦点を絞ったリスニングが求められる。ただし，基本ストラテジーは会話問題で学んだ方略と同様である。

「キーワード」を聞き取る

　英文の中で強調され，はっきりと発音される「キーワード」をしっかり聞き取ることで，会話のトピックや主要な情報をつかむ。聞き取ったキーワードを断片的にとらえるだけでなく，5W1H（=who, what, when, where, why, how）を意識して話の流れを整理するように心がけよう。

「設問を先読み」して答えに関する情報を聞き取る

　トークを漫然と聞かず，常に設問で問われていることを意識して，答えに結びつく情報にフォーカスしてリスニングを行う。Part C でよく問われる設問ポイントについては，次項からの「Part C 特有のストラテジー」で学習する。

「繰り返される情報」に注意する

　設問に対する答えは，トークのポイントとなる重要な情報として，表現を変えて何度も繰り返されることが多い。

Section 1　Part C　特有のストラテジー

2.　Part C 特有のストラテジー 1

最重要ストラテジー ▶▶▶

◆ 講義の主題やトピックを問う設問「講義の主題は何ですか」「講義によれば〜は何ですか」

◆ 前後の講義を推測する設問「前回の講義では何を学習していましたか」

◆ 話者のトーンを問う設問「話者の口調はどうですか」

　トーク問題の設問のポイントは，大きく分けて話者の主張や話の流れをつかむ Idea Questions と，数字や定義など細部の情報をつかむ Factual Questions になる。本項では Idea Questions を主に扱う。

　この種の問題には，「講義のトピックは何ですか」「この前の［後の］講義では何を学習していた［する］と思われますか」「話者の論調はどうですか」「講義によれば〜は何ですか」「教授によれば〜は何ですか」などがある。解答のためには，まず講義の流れをつかみ，主題が何かを把握する必要がある。

トークの流れ

トークの流れは大まかに以下のようになっている。

序論　導入

◈ 前回の講義で何を学んだのか，今日の講義で何を採り上げるのかをまず述べる。

> Today, we're going to discuss …
> Let's focus on …
> I'd like to talk about …

◈ 主張や主題をここで明確に述べることが多い。

展開　論の展開

◈ トピックに従って，具体的な事例を採り上げて論を展開。採り上げる事例は 2〜3 にまたがる。

結論　まとめ

◈ 冒頭で述べた主張を再び強調。次の話題の導入もここで述べられる。

◈ ただし，結論部は省略され，展開部でトークが終わることも多い。

Section Ⅰ Part A/B

Section Ⅰ Part C

Section 2

Section 3

総合模試

総合模試 解答・解説

89

話の流れをつかむためには，つなぎことば（discourse markers）がヒントになる。

話の転換を表すつなぎことば

- but, however, nevertheless, conversely, on the contrary, on the other hand

序列，列挙などを表すつなぎことば

- first, second, next, finally, in conclusion, to begin with
- one … , another …

結論を表すつなぎことば

- as a result, in a nutshell, after all

その他

- basically, at any rate, in other words, as a matter of fact, furthermore

設問例

講義の主題やトピックを問う設問

講義冒頭にヒントが述べられる

- ☐ What is the speaker's main point?
- ☐ What is the speaker discussing?
- ☐ What is the lecture mainly about?
- ☐ What is the main purpose [topic] of the lecture?

前後の講義を推測する設問

講義冒頭もしくは最後にヒントが述べられる

☐ What was probably discussed in the previous class?

☐ Which of the following was the professor probably talking about in the previous class?

☐ What will the class probably do next?

☐ What topic will be discussed next?

話者のトーンを問う設問

講義全体のトーンや話者の語調をつかむためには，口調やイントネーションもヒントとなる

☐ Which of the following best represents the speaker's attitude toward ...?

Section 1 Part A/B　Section 1 Part C　Section 2　Section 3　総合模試　総合模試 解答・解説

1. What is the main purpose of this talk?

   (A) To clarify the concept of propaganda

   (B) To understand how harmful propaganda can be

   (C) To identify where propaganda comes from

   (D) To find ways to resist the effects of propaganda   Ⓐ Ⓑ Ⓒ Ⓓ

2. Why does the professor feel that brainwashing is not a good definition of propaganda?

   (A) Propaganda is not as effective as brainwashing.

   (B) Propaganda is not as dangerous as brainwashing.

   (C) Brainwashing mainly involves political beliefs.

   (D) Brainwashing is too narrow of a definition.   Ⓐ Ⓑ Ⓒ Ⓓ

3. According to the professor, what is the most important characteristic of propaganda?

   (A) It must be associated with a cause.

   (B) It must be identified with a group.

   (C) It must be selectively distributed.

   (D) It must be damaging to the receiver.   Ⓐ Ⓑ Ⓒ Ⓓ

4. Which of the following does the professor regard as propaganda?

   (A) Pop music

   (B) Television news

   (C) Government press releases

   (D) Advertising   Ⓐ Ⓑ Ⓒ Ⓓ

練習問題　解答・解説　▶▶▶

1.-4.　　　　　　　　　　　　　　　　　Sociology: Mass Communication

◆) 057　Listen to the following talk in a mass communications class.

1　　Today, let's shift our focus on mass media and discuss the questions, "What is propaganda?" and "What distinguishes it from other forms of communication?"

2　　Many people associate propaganda with brainwashing. You know, people want you to believe something without your knowing it. Like a religious cult. Some sociologists and communication specialists have defined propaganda that narrowly, but I have to agree with most scholars who have a broader conception of propaganda. This is because there are many messages and images which attempt to persuade us but don't necessarily try to completely change our belief systems. Let me offer you a definition from one of my dictionaries: "Propaganda refers to ideas, facts, images, and claims deliberately spread in order to further a particular cause." So, what are the important characteristics in this definition? "Cause" is probably foremost. There needs to be a strong cause or purpose, which could be religious, political, or economic. I personally regard advertising as a form of propaganda, for instance, because the purpose of advertising is unmistakably to promote the consumption of a product.

マスコミュニケーションのクラスでの次の話を聞きなさい。

1　　今日は焦点をマスメディアに移して，「プロパガンダとは何か」「プロパガンダと他のコミュニケーション形式では何が異なるのか」という問題を議論しましょう。

2　　多くの人々はプロパガンダを洗脳と結びつけて考えます。人は他人がそうと気づかないうちに何かを信じさせようとします。カルト集団のように。社会学者やコミュニケーション専門家の一部はそのように狭義でプロパガンダを定義してきましたが，もっと広いプロパガンダの概念を持つ多くの学者に私は同意せざるを得ません。なぜなら，メッセージやイメージの多くは，私たちを説得しようと試みますが，必ずしも私たちの思考体系を完全に変えようとまではしないからです。私が持っている辞書の中からひとつの定義を披露しましょう。「プロパガンダとは，特定の主張を推進するために意図的に広められる考え，事実，イメージ，見解を指す。」では，この定義の中で重要な特徴は何でしょうか。「主張」がおそらく一番に来ますね。強い主張や目的が必要であり，それは宗教的，政治的，経済的なものだったりしますが，私自身はたとえば広告も一種のプロパガンダであると考えています。広告の目的は，明らかに製品の消費を促進することだからです。

93

◆ 設問を素早く先読みしてからトークを聞き，次の点を聞き取る。

1. 話の目的，　　　　　　　**3.** プロパガンダの特徴，

2. プロパガンダの定義，　　**4.** プロパガンダとみなされるもの

1.

🔊 058 **設問訳** この話の一番の目的は何ですか。

(A) プロパガンダの概念を明確にすること

(B) プロパガンダがどれほど有害になりうるかを理解すること

(C) プロパガンダがどこから生まれるかを明らかにすること

(D) プロパガンダの影響に抵抗する方法を見つけること

> **解法** この話の目的，主題を問う問題。トークの目的や主題は導入部分で明確に述べることが多い。導入における次の文に注目しよう。目的は (A)「プロパガンダの概念を明確にすること」だとわかる。
>
> 》Today, let's shift our focus on mass media and discuss the questions, "What is propaganda?" and "What distinguishes it from other forms of communication?" **❶**

2.

🔊 058 **設問訳** 教授はなぜ洗脳がプロパガンダの定義としてふさわしくないと感じているのですか。

(A) プロパガンダは洗脳ほど影響力が強くないから。

(B) プロパガンダは洗脳ほど危険ではないから。

(C) 洗脳は主に政治的信条に関わっているから。

(D) 洗脳は定義として狭すぎるから。

> **解法** 定義づけと，それに対する話者の考えを問う問題。次の文中に定義づけと話者の考えが示されている。話者は洗脳よりもっと広いプロパガンダの概念を持つ多くの学者に賛成していることが agree, a broader conception からわかる。正解は (D)。
>
> 》but I have to agree with most scholars who have a broader conception of propaganda. **❷**

3.　　　　　　　　　　　　　　　　　　　　　　　　　　　　　　　　　　　　　解答：A

◀)) 058　**設問訳**　教授によれば，プロパガンダの最も重要な特徴は何ですか。

(A) 主張と結びついていなくてはならない。

(B) 集団と一体感がなければならない。

(C) 選別された相手に届けられなければならない。

(D) 受け手にダメージを与えなければならない。

> **解法**　定義づけに関する問題。話者が重要な点を強調したいときに，質問をして，自らそれに答えることがよくある。ここでは，「プロパガンダの最も重要な特徴は何か」と質問し，その答えの中の cause がキーワードとなる。正解は (A)。
>
> 》So, what are the important characteristics in this definition?｀Cause"is probably foremost. There needs to be a strong cause or purpose, which could be religious, political, or economic.　**❷**

4.　　　　　　　　　　　　　　　　　　　　　　　　　　　　　　　　　　　　　解答：D

◀)) 058　**設問訳**　次のうち，教授がプロパガンダだと考えているものはどれですか。

(A) ポップス

(B) テレビのニュース

(C) 政府公報

(D) 広告

> **解法**　話者の考えに関する問題。広告がプロパガンダに含まれることについては次のように述べている。正解は (D)。このように繰り返される情報はよく設問として採り上げられるので注意。
>
> 》I personally regard advertising as a form of propaganda, for instance, because the purpose of advertising is unmistakably to promote the consumption of a product.　**❷**

重要語　□ **sociologist**「社会学者」　　　　　□ **deliberately**「故意に」
　　　　　□ **belief system**「思想体系」　　　□ **cause**「主張，理由，運動」

3.　Part C 特有のストラテジー2

最重要ストラテジー ▶▶▶

◆ 名前，数字，年号，統計など，具体的な詳細情報を問う設問

◆ 講義で述べる定義や理論を問う設問

◆ 時系列に列挙する設問

　前項で学んだ，大きな話の流れや主張を聞き取る設問に対し，本項では数字など細部の詳細情報を聞き取る設問を扱う。設問の形式とポイントには次のようなものがある。

設問例

🐾 名前，数字，年号，統計など，具体的な詳細情報を問う設問

☐ What percentage of the mouse genome is common to humans?

☐ According to the speaker [lecture], how long does it take to ...?

☐ What specialized word does the professor use to refer to ...?

　講義の主題に密接に関わる詳細情報が問われやすい。名前，数字など，重要と思われる具体情報には特に気をつけて把握し，覚えておくように努めよう。

🐾 講義で述べる定義や理論を問う設問

☐ According to the lecture, what does the "intrinsic value" of a stock refer to?

☐ Which of the following is true about the definition of ...?

　講義の中で，話者により用語，理論などが「定義」されることがある。この定義は設問のポイントとなる。定義されるものは強調して発音され，認識しやすいので，その前後に述べる内容に注意しよう。英文中の define/definition，theory，term，word といった語もヒントとなる。

🐾 時系列に列挙する設問

　ある事柄の経過や過程に関する言及は，時系列に列挙する設問と結びつく可能性がある。つなぎことばを意識して聞き，また年号や月日などの時を表す語句に注意しよう。

練習問題 ▶▶▶　☞ 講義の中で述べられる数字，定義，理論など細かな情報に注意して聞き，解答しなさい。

🔊 059
060

5. What are the students studying in this chemistry course?

(A)　The analyzing of chemical elements

(B)　The synthesizing of compounds

(C)　The general concepts of chemistry

(D)　The process of laboratory research　　Ⓐ Ⓑ Ⓒ Ⓓ

6. Which theory does the professor refer to in explaining states of matter?

(A)　Particles in motion

(B)　Electromagnetic waves

(C)　Nuclear element decay

(D)　Solid state　　Ⓐ Ⓑ Ⓒ Ⓓ

7. What fact about chemistry appears to most impress the professor?

(A)　All things can be viewed as matter or energy.

(B)　The whole universe is composed of about 100 elements.

(C)　The universe constantly changes physical states.

(D)　Nuclear changes produce enormous amounts of energy.

Ⓐ Ⓑ Ⓒ Ⓓ

8. According to the lecture, how many compounds exist in the universe?

(A)　1 million

(B)　5 million

(C)　7 million

(D)　11 million　　Ⓐ Ⓑ Ⓒ Ⓓ

5.-8.

◀)) 059　　Listen to the following lecture given in a chemistry class.

1　　Since we're focusing on "concepts of chemistry" in this course, rather than, say, actually analyzing or synthesizing compounds in the laboratory, I want to do my best to keep in mind the broad view.

2　　Basically, a chemist wants to understand how the universe is put together. Along with physicists, chemists have discovered that all things in the universe can be classified as matter or energy, and each of these can be converted to the other. Matter itself can be further classified into three physical states: solid, liquid, or gas. These are the three forms of matter that chemists routinely work with.

3　　Furthermore, study of matter in these three states has led to the conclusion that the behavior of matter can be explained by the assumption that matter is made up of particles in motion. The particles-in-motion theory—sometimes called the kinetic-molecular theory of matter—explains many common phenomena such as the evaporation of liquids and the diffusion of gases. It also explains the systematic kinds of changes that matter goes through as it changes from one state to another, such as when water changes from solid to liquid to gas, for instance.

4　　An important general point to remember: The careful study of matter over the past 150 years has helped chemists to discover that the whole universe is composed of around 100 elements—"elements" meaning substances that cannot be further decomposed into simpler substances. To be exact, about 92 elements can be found in nature, and around 20 can be produced artificially. Just think—everything from the most distant star to your fingernail is made up of around 100 elements. This is an astonishing discovery. Of course, the incredible multiplicity of matter that one actually observes in the universe is a result of the extraordinary number of ways these elements can be combined. Currently, the number of known compounds, both naturally occurring and artificially produced in the lab., stands at about 7 million.

化学のクラスでの次の講義を聞きなさい。

1　このクラスでは実験室で実際に化合物を分析したり合成したりするのではなく，「化学の概念」に焦点を当てますので，広い視野を心に留めておきたいと思います。

2　基本的に，化学者というものは万物がどのようにして成り立っているかを理解したいものです。物理学者とともに，化学者はこの世のあらゆる事物は物質，もしくはエネルギーに分類することができ，なおかつ両者は互いに変換できるということを発見しました。物質はそれ自体 3 つの物理的な状態，すなわち固体，液体，気体に分類できます。これらは化学者が日常的に研究対象とする物質の 3 形態です。

3　さらに，これら 3 つの状態にある物質を研究するうちに，物質は運動している粒子から成るという仮説を用いることで，物質の挙動を説明できるという結論になりました。粒子運動論（particles-in-motion theory），時には物質の分子運動論（kinetic-molecular theory of matter）と呼ばれる理論により，液体の蒸発や気体の拡散といった多くの一般的な現象は説明されます。また，物質がある状態から別の状態へ変わるときの規則的な変化，たとえば水が固体から液体になり，気体になるといったこともこれで説明されるのです。

4　ひとつ覚えておいてもらいたい重要なポイントがあります。過去 150 年に及ぶ物質に関する注意深い研究により，化学者は全宇宙が 100 ほどの元素から成り立っていることを発見しました。「元素」とは，それ以上単純な形に分割することのできない物質のことです。正確に言えば，約 92 の元素が自然界に存在し，約 20 の元素が人工的に作ることができます。考えてみてください。はるか彼方の星からあなたたちの指の爪まで，何もかもが 100 種ほどの元素でできているのです。これは驚くべき発見です。もちろん，宇宙において実際に目にする物質は途方もなく多様な形をとりますが，それはこれらの元素の結合の仕方がきわめて多様である結果なのです。現在判明している化合物の数は，自然界に存在するものと実験室で人工的に作られるものを合わせて 700 万ほどにのぼります。

◈ 設問を素早く先読みしてからトークを聞き，次の点を聞き取る。

5. 講義のトピック，　　　　　　　**7.** 教授が感銘を受けた事実，

6. 物質の状態を説明する理論，　**8.** 宇宙の化合物の数

5.
解答：C

◀))〔060〕 **設問訳** この化学のクラスで学生は何の勉強をしていますか。

(A) 化学元素の分析

(B) 化合物の合成

(C) 化学の一般概念

(D) 実験研究の手順

解法 講義のトピックを問う問題。主要なトピックは，講義の冒頭の部分で次のように説明されている。正解は (C)。このように，クラスの目的や主な内容は最初に説明されることが多い。

》Since we're focusing on "concepts of chemistry" in this course, rather than, say, actually analyzing or synthesizing compounds in the laboratory, I want to do my best to keep in mind the broad view. (**1**)

6.
解答：A

◀))〔060〕 **設問訳** 教授は物質の状態を説明するときにどの理論について述べましたか。

(A) 粒子運動

(B) 電磁波

(C) 元素核崩壊

(D) 固体物理

解法 定義・理論に関する問題。物質の状態を説明するのに使われる理論は分子運動論（particles in motion）で，次のように 2 度続けて言及されている。正解は (A)。トーク問題では用語や概念が定義されることがしばしばあり，設問のポイントにもなる。theory, term, define/definition などの単語が聞こえたら，設問のポイントとなることが考えられる。

》Furthermore, study of matter in these three states has led to the conclusion that the behavior of matter can be explained by the assumption that matter is made up of particles in motion. The particles-in-motion theory—sometimes called the kinetic-molecular theory of matter—explains many common phenomena such as the evaporation of liquids and the diffusion of gases. (**3**)

Section 1　Part A/B

Section 1　Part C

Section 2

Section 3

総合模試

総合模試　解答・解説

7.　　　　　　　　　　　　　　　　　　　　　　　　　　　　解答：B

◀)) 060　**設問訳**　教授が最も感銘を受けた化学に関する事実は何だと思われますか。

(A) 万物は物質もしくはエネルギーと見なすことができる。

(B) 全宇宙は 100 ほどの元素でできている。

(C) 宇宙は常に物理状態を変化させている。

(D) 核変化は巨大なエネルギーを生み出す。

解法　話者の考えを推測する問題。繰り返される情報やイントネーションから解答を見つけ出す。次の部分から，正解は (B) であることがわかる。An important general point to remember と教授が強調して話しており，次に重要なことを述べようとしていることに注目しよう。This is an astonishing discovery. と述べていることからもわかる。

》 An important general point to remember: The careful study of matter over the past 150 years has helped chemists to discover that the whole universe is composed of around 100 elements—"elements" meaning substances that cannot be further decomposed into simpler substances. To be exact, about 92 elements can be found in nature, and around 20 can be produced artificially. Just think—everything from the most distant star to your fingernail is made up of around 100 elements. This is an astonishing discovery. (**4**)

8.　　　　　　　　　　　　　　　　　　　　　　　　　　　　解答：C

◀)) 060　**設問訳**　講義によれば，宇宙にはいくつの化合物が存在しますか。

(A) 100 万

(B) 500 万

(C) 700 万

(D) 1,100 万

解法　数の問題。数字などの具体的な情報は設問ポイントとなることを認識しておこう。次の文にあるように正解は (C)。トークには他の数字も登場するため，情報を整理しながら聞かなくてはならない。

》 Currently, the number of known compounds, both naturally occurring and artificially produced in the lab., stands at about 7 million. (**4**)

重要語　□ **synthesize**「～を合成する」　　　□ **gas**「気体」

□ **compound**「化合物」　　　　　　□ **particle**「粒子」

□ **chemist**「化学者」　　　　　　　□ **molecular**「分子の」

□ **physicist**「物理学者」　　　　　　□ **evaporation**「蒸発」

□ **matter**「物質」　　　　　　　　　□ **diffusion**「拡散」

□ **solid**「固体」　　　　　　　　　　□ **element**「元素」

□ **liquid**「液体」

101

061
062

9. Which of the following is the main target of the gypsy moth?

(A) Small bushes

(B) Garden vegetables

(C) Grain crops

(D) Leafy trees   Ⓐ Ⓑ Ⓒ Ⓓ

10. When does the adult moth usually lay eggs?

(A) During the winter

(B) In early spring

(C) In the middle of the summer

(D) Near the beginning of fall   Ⓐ Ⓑ Ⓒ Ⓓ

11. How are the eggs protected?

(A) They are laid inside tree trunks.

(B) The male shields them with his body.

(C) The female covers them with hair.

(D) They have a tough outer skin.   Ⓐ Ⓑ Ⓒ Ⓓ

12. Which of the following characteristics differentiate the male and female gypsy moth?

(A) Capability of sustained flight

(B) Darkness of coloration

(C) Amount of food consumed

(D) Length of maturation period   Ⓐ Ⓑ Ⓒ Ⓓ

練習問題　解答・解説　▶▶▶

9.-12. .... Zoology: Gypsy Moth

🔊 061　Listen to part of a talk given in a zoology class.

1　We continue our study of agricultural pests by looking at the gypsy moth, whose destructive larva defoliates and subsequently kills all kinds of shade trees, fruit trees, and woodland trees. More than 500 species of deciduous trees are attacked by the gypsy moth, not to mention the occasional shrub or garden plant, and millions of dollars are spent each year trying to combat it.

2　The gypsy moth passes through the winter in the egg stage. The female moth lays eggs in mid-summer, soon after emerging from the cocoon herself in mid-to-late July. The eggs are deposited in yellowish masses on the trunks of trees or the sides of buildings. Each mass, which contains anywhere from 200 to 1,000 eggs, is then covered with hair from the female's body for protection. The eggs usually hatch in spring after the weather warms up. The young larvae are pale brown caterpillars with long tufts of hair projecting from their bodies. They are voracious eaters and will consume many times their own body weight in leaves every day.

3　Males and females vary greatly in appearance. The female is much larger and incapable of flying for any continuous period of time—the best she can do is to flutter short distances.

動物学のクラスでの話の一部を聞きなさい。

1　農害虫の学習として，次にマイマイガについて見ていきます。破壊力のあるマイマイガの幼虫は木の葉を落とし，その結果あらゆる種類の日陰を作る樹木，果樹，森林樹を枯らしてしまいます。500 種以上の落葉樹がマイマイガによる被害を受け，もちろん時には低木や園芸植物も被害にあい，その駆除のために毎年数百万ドルが費やされています。

2　マイマイガは卵の状態で冬を越します。メスのマイマイガは盛夏のころ卵を産みます。それは 7 月中旬から下旬にマユから出てまもなくのことです。卵は木の幹や建物の側壁などに黄色い塊の状態で産みつけられます。ひとつの卵塊の中にはおおよそ 200 から 1,000 の卵が含まれており，保護のためメスの体毛で覆われます。卵は通常春に暖かくなってから孵化します。幼虫はうす茶色の毛虫で，体から長いふさ状の体毛が出ています。貪欲に食べ，毎日自分の体重の何倍もの葉を食べます。

3　オスとメスで見た目は大きく異なります。メスのほうがずっと大きく，まとまった時間継続して飛ぶことはできず，せいぜい短い距離をひらひら飛ぶ程度です。

◈ 設問を素早く先読みしてからトークを聞き，次の点を聞き取る。
　　9. マイマイガの標的，　**10.** 産卵時期，　**11.** 卵の保護方法，　**12.** オスとメスの異なる特徴

9. 　　　　　　　　　　　　　　　　　　　　　　　　　　　　　　解答：D

◀) 062　**設問訳** 　次のうち，マイマイガの主な標的はどれですか。

　　(A) 小さな低木
　　(B) 園芸野菜
　　(C) 穀物
　　(D) 葉の多い樹木

　解法 　講義で述べられた情報を把握する問題。主な標的は，次の部分から考えて (D)「葉の多い樹木」
　であることがわかる。

　　》 ... whose destructive larva defoliates and subsequently kills all kinds of shade trees,
　　fruit trees, and woodland trees. (**1**)
　　》 More than 500 species of deciduous trees are attacked by the gypsy moth, ... (**1**)

10. 　　　　　　　　　　　　　　　　　　　　　　　　　　　　　解答：C

◀) 062　**設問訳** 　成虫のマイマイガは通常いつ卵を産みますか。

　　(A) 冬の間
　　(B) 早春
　　(C) 真夏
　　(D) 秋の初めごろ

　解法 　講義で述べられた情報を把握する問題。次の部分からマイマイガは真夏に卵を産むので，正解
　は (C) であることがわかる。

　　》 The female moth lays eggs in mid-summer, ... (**2**)

11. 　　　　　　　　　　　　　　　　　　　　　　　　　　　　　解答：C

◀) 062　**設問訳** 　卵はどのように保護されますか。

　　(A) 木の幹の中に産みつけられる。
　　(B) オスが自らの体で卵をかくまう。
　　(C) メスが体毛で卵を覆う。
　　(D) 卵は堅い外皮を持っている。

　解法 　講義で述べられた産卵時の特徴に関する問題。産卵時の特徴については次のように述べている。
　メスが体毛で卵を覆うので，正解は (C)。

　　》 Each mass, which contains anywhere from 200 to 1,000 eggs, is then covered with
　　hair from the female's body for protection. (**2**)

12.　　　　　　　　　　　　　　　　　　　　　　　　　　　　解答：A

◀) 062　**設問訳**　次のうち，オスとメスのマイマイガで異なる特徴はどれですか。

(A) 継続飛行の能力

(B) 色の濃さ

(C) 食べものの消費量

(D) 成虫になる時期の長さ

解法　講義で対比された事実を問う問題。教授はオスとメスのマイマイガを対比させている。列挙や
対比，分類は設問ポイントになりやすい。次の英文から，オスとメスは継続飛行の能力に違い
があることがわかる。正解は (A)。

》The female is much larger and incapable of flying for any continuous period of time（**3**）

重要語　□ **zoology**「動物学」　　　　　　　　　□ **mass**「かたまり」

□ **agricultural pest**「農害虫」　　　　　□ **trunk**「(木の) 幹」

□ **gypsy moth**「マイマイガ」　　　　　　□ **hatch**「孵化する」

□ **larva**「幼虫」(複数形：larvae)　　　　□ **tuft**「ふさ」

□ **defoliate**「〜を落葉させる」　　　　　□ **voracious**「貪欲な」

□ **deciduous tree**「落葉樹」　　　　　　□ **flutter**「はためく，ひらひらする」

□ **shrub**「低木」

Section 1 Part A/B

Section 1 Part C

Section 2

Section 3

総合模試

総合模試 解答・解説

105

集中練習問題 ❶ 1 題 4 問

BURST ONE

1. What distinction did Sinclair Lewis achieve as a writer?

   (A) He was the first American writer widely read in Europe.

   (B) He was given special recognition by the American government.

   (C) He was regarded by American critics as the finest writer of his time.

   (D) He was the first American to win the Nobel Prize for literature.

             Ⓐ Ⓑ Ⓒ Ⓓ

2. According to the professor, what type of writer was Sinclair Lewis?

   (A) A social critic

   (B) A realist

   (C) A romantic

   (D) An idealist

             Ⓐ Ⓑ Ⓒ Ⓓ

3. According to the professor, who should especially read Lewis' books?

   (A) Political science majors

   (B) History students

   (C) Art historians

   (D) Cultural critics

             Ⓐ Ⓑ Ⓒ Ⓓ

4. What was Lewis' job before he achieved success as a novelist?

   (A) Reporter

   (B) Photographer

   (C) Publisher

   (D) Editor

             Ⓐ Ⓑ Ⓒ Ⓓ

集中練習問題 ❶　解答・解説

1.-4.　　　　　　　　　　　　　　　　　　　　　**American Literature: Sinclair Lewis**

🔊 063　Listen to the following talk in an American literature class.

1　Sinclair Lewis, American novelist, 1885 to 1951. How many of you have read him? That's what I thought, hardly anyone. In fact, Sinclair Lewis was the first American writer to win the Nobel—quite a distinction, I think. So, why is it that this Nobel prize-winner is so seldom read these days?

2　I suppose part of it is that Lewis was above all a social critic. His novels are brilliant exposés of the shallowness and hypocrisy of early 20th-century American culture. In fact, and I mean this in all seriousness, Lewis may be the finest social critic—in the form of a novelist—that American culture has ever produced. The problem is that when the period that a writer like Lewis criticizes passes, the writing itself seems outdated. That is, since the writer's work has focused on the lives of people and society rather than on art and beauty, the following generations are not that interested in the topic. Indeed, the most important place where Lewis' books should be studied today is in history classes. As you know, I strongly maintain that novelists' depictions of history are far fuller and truer-to-life than the versions created by historians, using facts of political history and economics.

3　Harry Sinclair Lewis was born on February 7, 1885, in Sauk Centre, Minnesota. As a boy, he read everything he could get his hands on, and for college, he went east and graduated from Yale University in 1907. For a time, like Hemingway after him, he worked as a reporter, but even during his work as a newspaperman he never lost sight of his ambition to become a serious novelist. His first novel, *Our Mr. Wrenn*, in 1914, was favorably received by critics but had few readers. It was the publication of *Main Street* in 1920 that made his literary reputation. The power of *Main Street* stems from Lewis' careful rendering of local speech, customs, social conventions, and his satire. *Main Street* became not just a novel but the textbook on provincial America of that time.

アメリカ文学のクラスでの次の話を聞きなさい。

1 シンクレア・ルイスはアメリカの小説家で，1885 年に生まれ 1951 年に没しました。みなさんの中で何人が彼の作品を読んだことがありますか。思ったとおり，ほとんどだれも読んでいませんね。実のところ，シンクレア・ルイスはノーベル賞を受賞した最初のアメリカ人作家なのです。大きな功績だと思います。では，なぜ今ではこのノーベル賞作家の作品はめったに読まれていないのでしょうか。

2 私はこの理由の一部には，ルイスが何より社会批評家であったことがあると思います。彼の小説では 20 世紀初頭のアメリカ文化の浅はかさと偽善が見事に暴かれていました。実際，まじめな話，ルイスはアメリカ文化が作り上げた，小説家の姿をした最高の社会批評家かもしれません。問題は，ルイスのような作家が批判する時期が過ぎ去ってしまえば，作品そのものも時代遅れに感じられてしまうということです。つまり，そうした作家の作品は芸術や美の追究ではなく，人々の生活や社会に焦点を合わせているため，次の世代の人々はその話題にそれほど興味を抱かないのです。確かに今日ルイスの本が研究されるべき最も重要な場所は歴史学のクラスです。ご承知のように，歴史学者が政治の経緯や経済に関する事実を並べて書いたものよりも，小説家の歴史描写ははるかに充実して事実に近いものであることを強く主張しておきたいと思います。

3 ハリー・シンクレア・ルイスは，1885 年 2 月 7 日ミネソタ州ソークセンターで生まれました。少年時代の彼は手に入るものは何でも読み，大学進学のために東部に移り，1907 年イェール大学を卒業しました。しばらくの間，後日ヘミングウェイもそうしたように，彼は記者として働きましたが，新聞社に勤める間も純文学作家になりたいという夢を忘れることはありませんでした。1914 年の最初の小説，『わが社のレン氏』は批評家には好意的に受け入れられましたが，読者は多くありませんでした。彼が文学的名声を得たのは，1920 年の『本町通り』の刊行によるものでした。『本町通り』の魅力は，方言，地方習慣，社会的因習の細かい描写と，彼の風刺によるものです。『本町通り』は単なる小説ではなく，当時のアメリカの地方社会に関する教科書にもなりました。

◆ 設問を素早く先読みしてからトークを聞き，次の点を聞き取る。

1. ルイスが得た栄誉，　**2.** 彼の作家としてのタイプ，　**3.** 彼の本を読むべき人，　**4.** 彼が経験した職業

1.

解答：D

🔊 064 What distinction did Sinclair Lewis achieve as a writer?

(A) He was the first American writer widely read in Europe.
(B) He was given special recognition by the American government.
(C) He was regarded by American critics as the finest writer of his time.
(D) He was the first American to win the Nobel Prize for literature.

シンクレア・ルイスは作家としてどのような栄誉を得ましたか。

(A) ヨーロッパで広く読まれた最初のアメリカ人作家だった。
(B) アメリカ政府により特別に表彰された。
(C) アメリカ人批評家に，その時代の最もすばらしい作家と認められた。
(D) ノーベル文学賞を受賞した最初のアメリカ人だった。

解法 繰り返される情報がポイントとなる。この講義は Sinclair Lewis の生涯と業績を述べている。ルイスはノーベル文学賞を受賞した最初のアメリカ人だったので，正解は (D)。ノーベル賞については次のように2度続けて述べている。

》 In fact, Sinclair Lewis was the first American writer to win the Nobel—quite a distinction, I think. (**1**)
》 So, why is it that this Nobel prize-winner is so seldom read these days? (**1**)

2.

解答：A

🔊 064 According to the professor, what type of writer was Sinclair Lewis?

(A) A social critic
(B) A realist
(C) A romantic
(D) An idealist

教授によれば，シンクレア・ルイスはどのようなタイプの作家でしたか。

(A) 社会批評家
(B) 現実主義者
(C) ロマン派の作家
(D) 理想主義者

解法 繰り返される情報がポイントとなる。above all「何より」の後に続く語句 a social critic に注意。critic に関する表現は次のように繰り返し用いられている。正解は (A)。

》 Lewis was above all a social critic. (**2**)
》 Lewis may be the finest social critic (**2**)
》 the period that a writer like Lewis criticizes passes (**2**)

3. 解答：B

🔊 064 According to the professor, who should especially read Lewis' books?

教授によれば，特にルイスの本を読むべきなのはだれですか。

(A) Political science majors

(B) History students

(C) Art historians

(D) Cultural critics

(A) 政治学専攻の学生

(B) 歴史学の学生

(C) 美術史研究家

(D) 文化批評家

解法 the most important place は次に重要な情報がくるシグナルと考えられるので，注意する。歴史学のクラスと言っているので正解は (B)。歴史に関する話は次のように，その後にも続いている。

》 Indeed, the most important place where Lewis' books should be studied today is in history classes. (**2**)

》 As you know, I strongly maintain that novelists' depictions of history are far fuller and truer-to-life than the versions created by historians, using facts of political history and economics. (**2**)

---

4. 解答：A

🔊 064 What was Lewis' job before he achieved success as a novelist?

小説家として成功する前のルイスの職業は何でしたか。

(A) Reporter

(B) Photographer

(C) Publisher

(D) Editor

(A) 記者

(B) 写真家

(C) 出版業者

(D) 編集者

解法 ルイスは小説家になる前は記者をしていたことが次の英文からわかる。正解は (A)。

》 he worked as a reporter, but even during his work as a newspaperman he never lost sight of his ambition to become a serious novelist. (**3**)

重要語 □ **hypocrisy**「偽善」　　　　　　□ **render**「〜を描写する」

□ **outdated**「時代遅れの」　　　　□ **satire**「風刺，皮肉」(形容詞：satirical)

□ **stem from ...**「〜に由来する」

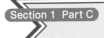

集中練習問題 ❷　1題4問

BURST TWO

1. What does the professor say about Halley's Comet?

   (A)　Most people have never heard of it.

   (B)　It will likely appear twice during the 21st century.

   (C)　Most people do not pronounce its name correctly.

   (D)　It sometimes comes dangerously close to the Earth.　

2. What most influences the amount of time it takes Halley's Comet to revolve around the Sun?

   (A)　The gravity of the planets it encounters

   (B)　The angle of its approach to the Sun

   (C)　The quantity of mass it loses along the way

   (D)　The amount of time it spends at perihelion　

3. What does the professor say makes Halley's Comet unique among comets?

   (A)　The absolute regularity of its orbit

   (B)　The speed at which it travels

   (C)　The brightness it exhibits

   (D)　The direction of its revolution　

4. When is Halley's Comet at its brightest when seen from Earth?

   (A)　Immediately after it crosses the Earth's orbital path

   (B)　Just before it reaches the point of perihelion

   (C)　Shortly after it first begins to move away from the Sun

   (D)　During the last few weeks of its approach to the Sun

1.-4.
Astronomy: Halley's Comet

🔊 065 Listen to the following talk given in an astronomy class.

1   Good morning. Today we're going to talk about the most famous of all comets: Halley's Comet. Note the pronunciation. Most people mistakenly pronounce it as "Haley's" Comet.

2   Anyway, Halley's Comet is unique for several reasons. To begin with, it was the very first comet to be recognized as being periodic. That means it reappears on a relatively regular basis. So how long is that period? Well, every 76 to 79 years, depending on disturbances caused by the gravitational fields of the planets the comet encounters during its revolution.

3   Another reason Halley's Comet is unusual is that it is the only comet that predictably becomes bright enough to be seen by the naked eye. During its peak viewing period, the three to four weeks after perihelion—that's the point when the comet begins its outward journey away from the Sun—Halley's Comet rivals even the brightest stars.

天文学のクラスでの次の話を聞きなさい。

1   おはよう。今日は彗星の中で最も有名なハレー彗星の話をしましょう。発音に気をつけてください。ほとんどの人は「ヘイリー」彗星と間違って発音しますから。

2   それはさておき，ハレー彗星はいくつかの理由からユニークな彗星です。まず，周期的であると認識されたまさに最初の彗星であること。つまり，比較的規則正しく出現するということです。その周期はどれくらいでしょうか。周回中に接近する惑星の重力場に起因する妨害によって異なりますが，76 年から 79 年周期になります。

3   ハレー彗星が特別だというもうひとつの理由は，予想どおり裸眼で見えるほど明るくなる唯一の彗星だということです。最もはっきり見える時期は，ちょうど彗星が太陽から遠ざかり始めるときである近日点を過ぎて 3，4 週間経ったころで，ハレー彗星は他の最も明るい星に匹敵するほど明るくなります。

◈ 設問を素早く先読みしてからトークを聞き，次の点を聞き取る。

1. ハレー彗星に関する教授の言及，　　**3.** ハレー彗星のユニークな点，

2. 周回する時間に影響するもの，　　　**4.** 最も明るい時期

1.
解答：C

🔊 066 | What does the professor say about Halley's Comet? | 教授はハレー彗星について何と言っていますか。

(A) Most people have never heard of it.

(B) It will likely appear twice during the 21st century.

(C) Most people do not pronounce its name correctly.

(D) It sometimes comes dangerously close to the Earth.

(A) ほとんどの人が聞いたことがない。

(B) 21 世紀には 2 回出現するだろう。

(C) ほとんどの人は正しくその名前を発音していない。

(D) ときには危険なほど地球に接近する。

> **解法** この講義は Halley's Comet に関するものである。最初の部分で，ハレー彗星をほとんどの人が間違って発音すると述べている。正解は (C)。
>
> 》 Note the pronunciation. Most people mistakenly pronounce it as "Haley's" Comet. (**1**)

2.
解答：A

🔊 066 | What most influences the amount of time it takes Halley's Comet to revolve around the Sun? | ハレー彗星が太陽の周りを回る時間の長さに最も影響するのは何ですか。

(A) The gravity of the planets it encounters

(B) The angle of its approach to the Sun

(C) The quantity of mass it loses along the way

(D) The amount of time it spends at perihelion

(A) 接近する惑星の重力

(B) 太陽への接近角度

(C) 周回中に失う質量

(D) 近日点で費やす時間の長さ

> **解法** ハレー彗星の周期は，周回中に接近する惑星の重力場に起因する妨害によって異なり，76 年から 79 年周期になるので，ハレー彗星が太陽の周りを回る時間の長さに最も影響するのは，(A)「接近する惑星の重力」である。
>
> 》 Well, every 76 to 79 years, depending on disturbances caused by the gravitational fields of the planets the comet encounters during its revolution. (**2**)

3.

解答：C

066 What does the professor say makes Halley's Comet unique among comets?

(A) The absolute regularity of its orbit

(B) The speed at which it travels

(C) The brightness it exhibits

(D) The direction of its revolution

ハレー彗星は彗星の中でどんな点がユニークだと教授は述べていますか。

(A) 軌道の絶対的な規則性

(B) 移動のスピード

(C) 示す明るさ

(D) 周回の方向

解法 ハレー彗星がユニークなのは，次の英文のとおり裸眼で見えるくらいに明るいことなので，正解は (C)。教授が彗星の特徴を列挙する際に使っている To begin with，Another reason などの語句は，重要なポイントを整理しながら聞くヒントになる。

》 Another reason Halley's Comet is unusual is that it is the only comet that predictably becomes bright enough to be seen by the naked eye. (**3**)

4.

解答：C

066 When is Halley's Comet at its brightest when seen from Earth?

(A) Immediately after it crosses the Earth's orbital path

(B) Just before it reaches the point of perihelion

(C) Shortly after it first begins to move away from the Sun

(D) During the last few weeks of its approach to the Sun

地球から見てハレー彗星の最も明るい時期はいつですか。

(A) 地球の公転軌道と交わった直後

(B) 近日点に着く直前

(C) 最初に太陽から遠ざかり始めてまもなく

(D) 太陽に接近しているときの最後の数週間

解法 地球から見てハレー彗星の最も明るい時期は，近日点（彗星が太陽から遠ざかり始めるとき）の 3，4 週間後である。正解は (C)。

》 During its peak viewing period, the three to four weeks after perihelion—that's the point when the comet begins its outward journey away from the Sun—Halley's Comet rivals even the brightest stars. (**3**)

重要語
- **comet** 「彗星」
- **periodic** 「周期的な」
- **on a regular basis** 「定期的に」(= regularly)
- **disturbance** 「妨害，障害」
- **gravitational** 「重力の」
- **revolution** 「回転，公転」(動詞：revolve)
- **predictably** 「予想されたとおり」
- **perihelion** 「近日点」(遠日点は aphelion)
- **rival** 「〜に匹敵する」

Section 1 Part C

集中練習問題 ❸　1題4問

Section I Part A/B

Section I Part C

Section I Part C

Section 2

Section 3

総合模試

総合模試 解答・解説

BURST THREE

1. According to the professor, where did the Pueblo peoples come from?

   (A)　They were descendants of two different native groups.

   (B)　They immigrated from northern California.

   (C)　They moved from Central America.

   (D)　They evolved from a warlike desert tribe.　　

2. What point does the professor make about the phrase "Native American"?

   (A)　It refers equally to western and eastern early American peoples.

   (B)　It is a more precise term than the phrase "indigenous peoples."

   (C)　It is inaccurate because no peoples were native to the Americas.

   (D)　It was introduced as a neutral term to replace the word "Indian."

3. What are the Pueblos most known for?

   (A)　Their dwellings

   (B)　Their art

   (C)　Their hunting

   (D)　Their farming　　

4. According to the lecture, which of the following words could be used to describe Pueblo culture?

   (A)　Tranquil

   (B)　Primitive

   (C)　Conservative

   (D)　Militant

集中練習問題 ❸ 解答・解説

1.-4.　　　　　　　　　　　　　　　　　　　American History: Native Americans

🔊 067　　Listen to the following lecture in an American history class.

1　　Let's turn our attention now from indigenous cultures of the Eastern seaboard to the American West. The group of Native Americans called Pueblos—known for their art and farming and above all their architecture—were perhaps the most famous residents of the American Southwest. Interestingly, the Pueblos and their culture emerged from the mingling of two different groups: the Basket Makers who inhabited the Southwest before them, and a new group of peoples who migrated in from the Colorado and Utah regions. However, when one talks about "origins" of Native American groups we should remember that even the word "Native American" is problematic, because archaeologically there were no peoples "native" to the New World—everyone's ancestors came at one time over the land bridge from Siberia through what is now Alaska.

2　　The Pueblos are best known for their houses. Most hills in the Southwest are mesas; that is, they have flat tops and very steep, rocky sides. The Pueblos built their dwellings—whole towns and cities, in fact—just below the tops of these mesas. These high cliff-dwellings are some of the most beautiful residences that humans have ever constructed—the ultimate "rooms with a view."

3　　As far as we can judge, Pueblo culture was peaceful. Few indications of fighting have been found, and it appears that when Pueblo people had differences they settled them without resorting to clubs and spears. Village life seems to have been built around consensus and equality, and there are few signs of special treatment for important individuals such as elaborate burials or palaces for the elite.

　　アメリカ史のクラスでの次の講義を聞きなさい。

1　　ここで東海岸の土着文化からアメリカ西部へ目を向けてみましょう。プエブロ族と呼ばれるアメリカ先住民族は，その芸術と農業，そしてとりわけ建築で知られていますが，アメリカ南西部のおそらく最も有名な居住者でした。おもしろいことにプエブロ族とその文化は，彼らの前から南西部に住んでいたバスケットメーカー文化に属する先住民と，コロラドやユタ地域から移り住んできた新しい集団という2つの異なる集団の混成から生まれたものでした。しかし，ネイティブ・アメリカンの集団の「源」について話すとき，「ネイティブ・アメリカン」ということばさえも問題があることを覚えておかなければなりません。なぜなら考古学的には新大陸「生まれ」の民族というものはいなかったのです。どんな人の祖先も，ある時期に現在のアラスカを通ってシベリアから陸橋を渡ってきたのです。

2　　プエブロ族はその住居で最もよく知られています。南西部のほとんどの小山はメサ，つまり上が

Section 1 Part A/B
Section 1 Part C
Section 2
Section 3
総合模試
総合模試 解答・解説

平らで，周囲は岩で切り立っています。プエブロ族は自分たちの住居，実際には町や村すべてを，これらメサの頂上のすぐ下に造りました。こうした高い断崖の住居は人類が建設した最も美しい住宅のひとつで，究極の「眺めのよい部屋」です。

3　私たちが判断できる範囲では，プエブロ文化は平和的でした。戦闘を示す痕跡はほとんど見つかっておらず，意見の相違があったときもこん棒や槍に頼ることなく解決していたようです。集落生活は合意と平等のもとに成り立っていたと思われ，念入りな埋葬やエリートのための豪邸のような重要人物に対する特別扱いの痕跡もほとんどありません。

◆ 設問を素早く先読みしてからトークを聞き，次の点を聞き取る。

1. プエブロ族の由来，

2. ネイティブ・アメリカンという用語に関する言及，

3. プエブロ族の有名な点，

4. プエブロ文化を描写する語

1.
解答：A

🔊 **068**

According to the professor, where did the Pueblo peoples come from?

(A) They were descendants of two different native groups.

(B) They immigrated from northern California.

(C) They moved from Central America.

(D) They evolved from a warlike desert tribe.

教授によれば，プエブロ族はどこからやってきましたか。

(A) 2つの異なる土着集団の子孫であった。

(B) 北カリフォルニアから移住してきた。

(C) 中央アメリカから移ってきた。

(D) 好戦的な砂漠民族から転化した。

> **解法** プエブロ族は，バスケットメーカー文化に属する先住民と，コロラドやユタ地域からの新しい集団の混成から生まれたので，正解は (A)。
>
> 》 Interestingly, the Pueblos and their culture emerged from the mingling of two different groups: the Basket Makers who inhabited the Southwest before them, and a new group of peoples who migrated in from the Colorado and Utah regions. **1**

2.
解答：C

🔊 **068**

What point does the professor make about the phrase "Native American"?

(A) It refers equally to western and eastern early American peoples.

(B) It is a more precise term than the phrase "indigenous peoples."

(C) It is inaccurate because no peoples were native to the Americas.

(D) It was introduced as a neutral term to replace the word "Indian."

教授は「ネイティブ・アメリカン」という用語について何を述べていますか。

(A) それは西部と東部にいた初期のアメリカ民族を同等に表している。

(B) それは「原住民」よりも正確な用語である。

(C) アメリカで生まれた民族はないため，その用語は不正確である。

(D)「インディアン」ということばに代わる中立的な語として導入された。

解法 考古学的にはアメリカで生まれた民族というものはいないため,「ネイティブ・アメリカン」ということばは不正確である。話者は何を問題視しているかを聞き取ろう。次の部分に注意。正解は (C)。

》 However, when one talks about "origins" of Native American groups we should remember that even the word "Native American" is problematic, because archaeologically there were no peoples "native" to the New World ... (**1**)

3.

解答：A

🔊 068 What are the Pueblos most known for? | プエブロ族は何が一番有名ですか。

(A) Their dwellings
(B) Their art
(C) Their hunting
(D) Their farming

(A) 住居
(B) 芸術
(C) 狩猟
(D) 農業

解法 プエブロ族については,その住居が最もよく知られているので,正解は (A)。

》 The Pueblos are best known for their houses. (**2**)

4.

解答：A

🔊 068 According to the lecture, which of the following words could be used to describe Pueblo culture? | 講義によれば,プエブロ文化を描写するのによいことばは次のどれですか。

(A) Tranquil
(B) Primitive
(C) Conservative
(D) Militant

(A) 平穏な
(B) 原始的な
(C) 保守的な
(D) 好戦的な

解法 「プエブロ文化は平和的であった」と述べているので,正解は (A)。peaceful と述べてから,その説明のために,戦闘を示す痕跡はほとんど見つかっていないことや,意見の相違があったときにもこん棒や槍に頼ることなく解決していたようであることを挙げている。

》 Pueblo culture was peaceful. (**3**)

重要語
- **indigenous**「土着の,土地固有の」
- **mingle**「混ざる」
- **migrate**「移住する」
- **archaeologically**「考古学的に」
- **dwelling**「住居」
- **resort to ...**「(手段) に訴える,頼る」
- **consensus**「合意」
- **elaborate**「入念な,精巧な」
- **burial**「埋葬,葬式,墓」

II

Section 2
Structure and Written Expression
攻略ストラテジー＋練習問題

Section 2 の概要

Structure and Written Expression セクションは以下の構成になっている。

Structure and Written Expression（40問：25分）	
Structure（15問）	空所補充問題
Written Expression（25問）	誤文訂正問題

主な特徴

◆ 全問とも四肢択一形式。

◆ 空所補充問題と誤文訂正問題は，それぞれまとまって出題される。

Structure

一部が欠けた不完全な英文の空所に最も適する語またはフレーズを4つの選択肢の中から選ぶ。

Written Expression

問題文の4か所に下線が引かれている。その中から文法的に誤っているものをひとつ選び出して解答する。

Structure and Written Expression のストラテジー

　本章では出題されるポイントを文法項目から 13 に分け，それぞれを ［「文レベル」のストラテジー］ ［「単語レベル」のストラテジー］ ［「チャンクレベル」のストラテジー］ の 3 項目に分類した。以下の順に学習する。

「文レベル」のストラテジー

1. 主語と動詞
2. 一致
3. 並列

「単語レベル」のストラテジー

4. 名詞
5. 代名詞
6. 動詞
7. 形容詞・副詞
8. 接続詞・前置詞
9. 冠詞
10. 品詞

「チャンクレベル」のストラテジー

11. 語順
12. 脱落
13. 重複

1. 主語と動詞

最重要ストラテジー ▶▶▶

正しい文構造となる選択肢を選ぶ，または正しい文構造になるように下線部を訂正する問題。主語と述語動詞は，原則として文あるいは節にひとつずつ含まれる。まずは主語と述語動詞を正確に把握することが，文の構成を理解し，正解を見つけるのに必要な基本ステップである。

練習問題 ▶▶▶

1. <u>Atoms they</u> combine <u>in</u> a great variety of <u>ways</u> <u>to form</u> compounds.
     A   B   C   D

Ⓐ Ⓑ Ⓒ Ⓓ

2. ------- study of the behavior of basic economic units, such as companies, industries, or households.

(A) It is microeconomics that

(B) Microeconomics

(C) Microeconomics is the

(D) That microeconomics

Ⓐ Ⓑ Ⓒ Ⓓ

3. A miniature is a small painting, -------, executed in watercolor.

(A) typically a portrait

(B) is a typical portrait

(C) it is a typical portrait

(D) a portrait is typical

Ⓐ Ⓑ Ⓒ Ⓓ

練習問題　解答・解説　▶▶▶

1.

解答：A　they を削除して Atoms とする

Atoms combine in a great variety of ways to form compounds.

訳 原子はさまざまな形で結合し、化合物を形成する。

解法 ひとつの文で atoms と they の両方が主語になるのは誤り。atoms が主語になる場合 they は不要なので、これを削除する。

重要語
- □ **atom**「原子」
- □ **combine**「結合する」
- □ **a variety of ...**「多様な〜」
- □ **compound**「化合物」

2.

解答：C

Microeconomics is the study of the behavior of basic economic units, such as companies, industries, or households.

訳 ミクロ経済学は、企業、産業、世帯など、基本的な経済単位の行動に関する学問である。

解法 問題文には空所の後に主語と動詞がないので、主語と動詞が含まれている選択肢を選ぶ。主語は microeconomics、動詞は is である。(A) は that に続いて動詞が必要。

重要語
- □ **behavior**「行動」
- □ **unit**「単位」
- □ **industry**「事業、産業」
- □ **household**「世帯、家庭」

3.

解答：A

A miniature is a small painting, **typically a portrait,** executed in watercolor.

訳 細密画は小さな絵画で、概して肖像画であり、水彩絵の具によって描かれている。

解法 問題文は主語 miniature、動詞 is、補語 a small printing がそろっており、空所がなくても文として成立している。カンマではさまれた部分は a small painting を説明する同格部分であり、ここに主語や動詞は不要。executed は過去分詞で painting を修飾する。

重要語
- □ **typically**「概して、典型的には」
- □ **execute**「〜を製作する」
- □ **portrait**「肖像画」

⚠ チェックポイント

□ 文の構成が単文、重文、複文のいずれかを見極める。

- **単文** 主部と述部が1つずつの文
- **重文** 主部と述部が2つ以上あり、等位接続詞によって結ばれている文
- **複文** 主節と従属節を含む文で、それぞれの節には原則的に主語と述語動詞が含まれる

□ **空所補充問題の場合** 空所以外の部分に主語と述語動詞があるかどうかを確認する。ないときは、適切な主語と述語動詞の両方またはいずれかを含む選択肢を選ぶ。

□ **誤文訂正問題の場合** 主語や述語動詞が重複していないか、または欠けていないかどうかを確認する。

※ 節は主語と述語動詞を含み、句はそれらを含まない語の集まりである。
※ 名詞の後に置かれ、カンマではさまれた同格部分に述語動詞は不要である。

2. 一致

最重要ストラテジー ▶▶▶

　一致とは，数・格・人称・性などの呼応を指す。特に TOEFL ITP では，主語と述語動詞の数の呼応，代名詞とそれの指す名詞の数や人称の一致を確認する必要がある。下線部または選択肢に動詞や代名詞がある場合には，対応する部分を文中から探し出し，一致しているかどうかを確認する必要がある。

練習問題 ▶▶▶

4. <u>Technically</u>, two systems are at <u>the same</u> temperature if no heat
　　　A 　　　　　　　　　　　　　　　　B

　　 <u>flow</u> from one to <u>the other</u>.
　　　C 　　　　　　D

　　　　　　　　　　　　　　　　　　　　　　　　　Ⓐ Ⓑ Ⓒ Ⓓ

5. Vignettes <u>are</u> sketches or short works <u>of</u> literature <u>noted</u> for <u>its</u> precise detail.
　　　　　　　A 　　　　　　　　　　　B 　　　　　C 　　　D

　　　　　　　　　　　　　　　　　　　　　　　　　Ⓐ Ⓑ Ⓒ Ⓓ

6. The life cycle of <u>an</u> annual plant, <u>such as</u> corn or beans, <u>are</u>
　　　　　　　　　　　A 　　　　　　　B 　　　　　　　　C

　　 completed in a single year <u>or</u> growing season.
　　　　　　　　　　　　　　　D

　　　　　　　　　　　　　　　　　　　　　　　　　Ⓐ Ⓑ Ⓒ Ⓓ

練習問題　解答・解説 ▶▶▶

4.
解答：C　flow を flows にする

Technically, two systems are at the same temperature if no heat **flows** from one to the other.

訳　熱が一方から他方へ流れなければ，厳密には 2 つのシステムは同じ温度である。

解法　if 節の主語 heat は，「熱」を意味するときは不可算名詞扱いである。したがって，動詞はこの主語に合わせて，flow ではなく flows にする必要がある。

重要語
- □ **technically**「厳密に言えば，技術的に」
- □ **temperature**「温度」
- □ **flow**「流れる，通る」

5.
解答：D　its を their にする

Vignettes are sketches or short works of literature noted for **their** precise detail.

訳　ビネットとは，細部を描き込むことで知られる文芸小品や短編のことである。

解法　主語 vignettes は複数形であり，それに対応する所有格の代名詞は単数形の its ではなく，複数形の their を用いる。

重要語
- □ **literature**「文学，文芸」
- □ **precise**「正確な」
- □ **detail**「詳細」

6.
解答：C　are を is にする

The life cycle of an annual plant, such as corn or beans, **is** completed in a single year or growing season.

訳　とうもろこしや豆のような 1 年生植物の寿命は，1 年または成育期間の終了とともに終わる。

解法　主語 life cycle は単数形であるから，動詞もそれに合わせて are ではなく is を用いる。挿入句などによって主語と動詞が離れている場合は，特に注意が必要である。

重要語
- □ **annual**「1 年の」
- □ **complete**「〜を完了させる」

⚠ チェックポイント

□ 述語動詞に下線が引かれている場合

述語動詞が，主語の人称や数（単数形・複数形）に正しく呼応しているかどうかを確認する。特に，主語の後に同格を表す句などが挿入されて主語と動詞が離れているときには，対応する主語がどれかということに注意して確認する。

□ 代名詞に下線が引かれている場合

まず代名詞が文中のどの名詞を指しているかを把握する。その名詞と代名詞の人称や数が正しく呼応しているかどうかを確認する。

125

3. 並列

並列とは，重要度の等しい複数の情報を列挙するとき，同じ品詞や文法的に同じ形の語句を並べることである。例えば A, B, and C の形で情報が列挙される場合，A，B，C の 3 要素は形容詞なら形容詞，動名詞なら動名詞で形を統一しなければならない。並列語句を見つけるには，語句をつなぐカンマや and，or がヒントになる。これらに注意したうえで，文の意味と構成をよく理解し，正しく並列されているかどうかを判断することが重要である。

練習問題 ▶▶▶

7. The retina of the eye is <u>most</u> sensitive to the primary <u>colors</u> of red,
    <u>   </u>
A   B   C

<u>greenish</u>, and blue.
   D

Ⓐ Ⓑ Ⓒ Ⓓ

8. Deforestation causes fertile soil to be blown away or washed into rivers, leading to soil erosion, droughts, and -------.

(A) floods

(B) there is flooding

(C) the floods

(D) a flooding

Ⓐ Ⓑ Ⓒ Ⓓ

9. Price controls <u>are</u> government regulations freezing or <u>to limit</u> prices <u>during</u>
                  A   B   C

times of <u>emergency</u>.
      D

Ⓐ Ⓑ Ⓒ Ⓓ

練習問題　解答・解説　▶▶▶

7.　　　　　　　　　　　　　　　　　　　　解答：D　　greenish を green にする

The retina of the eye is most sensitive to the primary colors of red, **green**, and blue.

訳　目の網膜は赤，緑，青の三原色に最も敏感である。

解法　並列されている三色のうち，red と blue は前置詞 of の後にきているので名詞である。red およびblue という名詞と並列するために，形容詞 greenish（緑がかった）は，名詞 green にする必要がある。

> **重要語**　□ **retina**「網膜」　　　　　　□ **primary**「主要な」
> 　　　　　□ **sensitive**「敏感な」

8.　　　　　　　　　　　　　　　　　　　　　　　　　　　解答：A

Deforestation causes fertile soil to be blown away or washed into rivers, leading to soil erosion, droughts, and **floods**.

訳　森林伐採は，肥よくな土壌が風で飛ばされたり雨で川に流されたりする原因となり，土壌浸食，干ばつ，洪水を引き起こす。

解法　soil erosion および droughts と並列するために，空所には無冠詞の名詞を入れる必要がある。(A) floods が正解。

> **重要語**　□ **deforestation**「森林伐採」　　□ **drought**「干ばつ」
> 　　　　　□ **fertile**「肥よくな」　　　　□ **flood**「洪水」
> 　　　　　□ **erosion**「浸食」

9.　　　　　　　　　　　　　　　　　　　解答：B　　to limit を limiting にする

Price controls are government regulations freezing or **limiting** prices during times of emergency.

訳　物価統制とは，非常時に物価を凍結したり制限したりする政府の規制のことである。

解法　government regulations を修飾する現在分詞 freezing に合わせて並べるために，(B) の不定詞 to limit は limiting にしなければならない。

> **重要語**　□ **regulation**「規制，調整」　　□ **emergency**「非常時」
> 　　　　　□ **freeze**「〜を凍結する」

⚠ チェックポイント

□ カンマや and，or などでつながれた並列語句があることを確認する。

□ 並列される語句の品詞や形がそろっているかどうかを確認する。そろっていない場合，正しい品詞や形は何であるかを前後の要素から判断する。

4. 名詞

最重要ストラテジー ▶▶▶

名詞の出題ポイントは数の扱いに関するものが多い。下線の引かれている語が可算名詞の場合には，単数形あるいは複数形のどちらが正しいか，不可算名詞の場合には複数形の-s が付いていないかどうか，また much や few など名詞を修飾する数量形容詞の使い分けが適切かどうかといったことがポイントとなる。

練習問題 ▶▶▶

10. <u>Most people</u> are <u>unaware</u> that San Jose, California, <u>is one of</u> the ten largest
     A   B   C

<u>city</u> in the United States.
D

Ⓐ Ⓑ Ⓒ Ⓓ

11. <u>Much</u> earthquakes occur at <u>the</u> boundaries <u>between</u> tectonic plates,
    A   B   C

<u>especially</u> in the Pacific Ocean and mid-Atlantic zones.
D

Ⓐ Ⓑ Ⓒ Ⓓ

12. In heavy <u>manufacturing</u>, the <u>greatest</u> capital expense <u>is</u> the purchase of
          A   B   C

manufacturing <u>equipments</u>.
D

Ⓐ Ⓑ Ⓒ Ⓓ

練習問題　解答・解説　▶▶▶

10.

解答：D　city を cities にする

Most people are unaware that San Jose, California, is one of the ten largest **cities** in the United States.

訳　ほとんどの人は，カリフォルニア州サンノゼが全米 10 大都市に含まれていることを知らない。

解法　one of の後は可算名詞の複数形がくる。(D) の city を cities にする必要がある。

重要語　□ **unaware**「知らない，気づかない」

11.

解答：A　Much を Many にする

Many earthquakes occur at the boundaries between tectonic plates, especially in the Pacific Ocean and mid-Atlantic zones.

訳　地震の多くは地殻プレート同士の境目，とくに太平洋と大西洋中部で起こっている。

解法　earthquake のように数えられる名詞に用いる数量形容詞は，much ではなく many である。much は不可算名詞とともに用いる。

重要語　□ **boundary**「境界」　　　□ **the Pacific Ocean**
　　　　　□ **tectonic plate**　　　　　　「太平洋」
　　　　　　「地殻構造プレート」　　　□ **Atlantic**「大西洋の」

12.

解答：D　equipments を equipment にする

In heavy manufacturing, the greatest capital expense is the purchase of manufacturing **equipment**.

訳　重工業で最大の資本支出となるのは製造設備の購入費である。

解法　equipment は不可算名詞なので複数形はない。equipments ではなく，equipment としなければならない。

重要語　□ **manufacture**　　　　　□ **purchase**「購入」
　　　　　　「〜を製造する，生産する」　□ **equipment**「設備，装置」
　　　　　□ **capital**「資本」

⚠ チェックポイント

□ 下線部の名詞は可算名詞か不可算名詞かを確認する。

可算名詞　単数形あるいは複数形でよいのかどうかを確認する
不可算名詞　複数形の -s が付いていないかどうかを確認する

□ 名詞を修飾する数量形容詞が適切かどうかを確認する。

◆ many, few, several ＋可算名詞
◆ much, little ＋不可算名詞
◆ each/every ＋単数可算名詞
◆ a group [bunch/series/number] of ＋複数可算名詞

5. 代名詞

TOEFL ITP に出題される代名詞問題は人称代名詞，関係代名詞の用法である。代名詞に下線が引かれている場合には，その代名詞の格・人称・数が正しく使われているかを確認しよう。代名詞の指す名詞との数の一致，動詞との呼応，先行詞との関係，関係詞節中での働きなどが解答のヒントとなる。

練習問題 ▶▶▶

13. Hannibal Hamlin <u>served</u> as vice president under Abraham Lincoln but
                 A

was not <u>nearly</u> as well-known as the man <u>who</u> was <u>its</u> boss.
       B   C   D   ⒶⒷⒸⒹ

14. Hay fever is <u>an</u> allergy, <u>which</u> symptoms include sneezing, runny nose,
              A   B

and watery eyes, <u>that occurs</u> seasonally on exposure <u>to</u> pollen.
               C   D   ⒶⒷⒸⒹ

15. The poet William Carlos Williams supported <u>him</u> as <u>a</u> physician <u>during</u>
                                   A   B   C

the four decades before his poems made him <u>famous</u>.
                                     D   ⒶⒷⒸⒹ

練習問題　解答・解説　▶▶▶

13.　　　　　　　　　　　　　　　　　　　　解答：D　　its を his にする

Hannibal Hamlin served as vice president under Abraham Lincoln but was not nearly as well-known as the man who was **his** boss.

> **訳**　ハンニバル・ハムリンはエイブラハム・リンカーンのもとで副大統領を務めたが，知名度の点では自分の上司にとても及ばなかった。

> **解法**　Hannibal Hamlin は人名なので，人称代名詞は its ではなく his でなければならない。

> | **重要語**　□ **vice president**「副大統領」 | □ **well-known**「有名な」 |
> |---|---|
> | □ **not nearly**「とうてい～でない」 | |

14.　　　　　　　　　　　　　　　　　　　解答：B　　which を whose にする

Hay fever is an allergy, **whose** symptoms include sneezing, runny nose, and watery eyes, that occurs seasonally on exposure to pollen.

> **訳**　花粉症はアレルギーの一種で，くしゃみ，鼻水，涙目などの症状があり，ある季節になると花粉に接触することで起きる。

> **解法**　関係詞節には主語 symptoms，動詞 include，目的語 sneezing ... watery eyes がそろっているので，主格，目的格で用いる関係代名詞 which は誤り。allergy を先行詞として symptoms を修飾する所有格 whose を用いる。

> | **重要語**　□ **hay fever**「花粉症」 | □ **pollen**「花粉」 |
> |---|---|
> | □ **sneezing**「くしゃみ」 | |

15.　　　　　　　　　　　　　　　　　　　　解答：A　　him を himself にする

The poet William Carlos Williams supported **himself** as a physician during the four decades before his poems made him famous.

> **訳**　詩人ウィリアム・カーロス・ウィリアムズは詩で有名になる前の 40 年間，医者として生計を立てた。

> **解法**　他動詞の目的語となる代名詞が主語自身を指す場合は，再帰代名詞を用いる。

> | **重要語**　□ **support** *oneself*「自活する」 | □ **physician**「医者」 |
> |---|---|

⚠ チェックポイント

□ 下線部の代名詞がどの名詞を指しているのかを見きわめ，次の点を確認する。

> **人称代名詞**　人称（1 人称，2 人称，3 人称）・格（主格，所有格，目的格）・数（単数，複数）が正しいかどうかを確認する。

> **関係代名詞**　先行詞の有無と種類（人，人以外のもの）・格（主格，所有格，目的格）が正しいかどうかを確認する。

6. 動詞

TOEFL ITP で特に注意が必要なのは，動詞の時制と動名詞・不定詞・分詞の用法である。次の点を確認しておこう。

動名詞 動詞的機能と名詞的機能を併せ持つ語で -ing の形をとる。

不定詞 to 不定詞と原形不定詞があり，to 不定詞には名詞，形容詞，副詞の用法がある。原形不定詞は，知覚動詞や使役動詞などとともに用いられる。

分詞 動詞的機能と形容詞的機能を持つが，ほかに動詞と接続詞の機能を持った分詞構文もある。分詞には現在分詞と過去分詞がある。現在分詞は進行形などを作り，形容詞的には能動的な意味を持つ。過去分詞は完了形や受動態などを作り，形容詞的には受動的な意味を持つ。

練習問題 ▶▶▶

16. In the United States, the industrial revolution is generally agreed to -------
at the time of the Civil War.

(A) begin

(B) beginning

(C) be beginning

(D) have begun Ⓐ Ⓑ Ⓒ Ⓓ

17. The run of a local school district is usually the responsibility of the
     A   B   C   D
superintendent of schools. Ⓐ Ⓑ Ⓒ Ⓓ

18. Silicon is the second most abundant element in the Earth's crust,
                 A   B
make up nearly 28 percent of its total mass.
  C   D Ⓐ Ⓑ Ⓒ Ⓓ

練習問題　解答・解説　▶▶▶

16.　　　　　　　　　　　　　　　　　　　　　　　　　　　　解答：D

In the United States, the industrial revolution is generally agreed to **have begun** at the time of the Civil War.

訳　米国では，産業革命は南北戦争時に始まったと一般的に認識されている。

解法　「始まった」という過去の事柄を不定詞で表すとき，to の後は《have＋過去分詞》になるので，ここでは (D) の have begun が正しい。

重要語　□ **industrial revolution**　　　　□ **the Civil War**「南北戦争」
　　　　　「産業革命」

17.　　　　　　　　　　　　　　　　　　解答：A　　run を running にする

The **running** of a local school district is usually the responsibility of the superintendent of schools.

訳　地元の学区運営は一般に教育長の責務である。

解法　run の名詞としての意味は，「走ること，競走，流れ」などであり，この文に適した「運営」を意味する語は動名詞 running である。似た語の意味の違いに注意。

重要語　□ **responsibility**「責任，責務」　　□ **superintendent**「教育長」

18.　　　　　　　　　　　　　　　　解答：C　　make up を making up にする

Silicon is the second most abundant element in the Earth's crust, **making up** nearly 28 percent of its total mass.

訳　ケイ素は地殻内の含有量が 2 番目に多い元素で，地殻の全質量の 28 パーセント近くを占める。

解法　この文のように，カンマの後に接続詞や主語を用いず，現在分詞形や過去分詞形の動詞を使って分詞構文にすることがよくある。「〜を構成している」という能動の意味を表すので，make は現在分詞 making になる。

重要語　□ **abundant**「豊富な」　　□ **make up**「〜を構成する」
　　　　　□ **crust**「地殻」　　　　□ **mass**「質量，かたまり」

⚠ チェックポイント

□ 述語動詞，準動詞，助動詞の脱落や重複がないかどうかなど，文構造を確認する。

□ 述語動詞が正しい時制で用いられているかどうかを確認する。

□ 現在分詞と過去分詞の混同がないかどうかを確認する。

133

7. 形容詞・副詞

最重要ストラテジー ▶▶▶

　形容詞は名詞を修飾し，副詞は動詞，形容詞，副詞，文全体などを修飾する。形容詞・副詞の出題ポイントは，品詞の混同（140 ページ）と比較表現である。比較問題の難度は低く，原級，比較級，最上級の基本的な変化と定型表現を覚えておくことで解答できる場合が多い。

練習問題 ▶▶▶

19. The drainage basin of the Mississippi River is <u>greatest</u> than that of

A   B

<u>any other</u> river <u>in</u> North America.

C   D

ⒶⒷⒸⒹ

20. Bacteria are the ------- living organisms.

(A) small

(B) small as

(C) smaller

(D) smallest

ⒶⒷⒸⒹ

21. In most media, the longer the wavelength of light, ------- it travels.

(A) the fast

(B) the faster

(C) faster

(D) fast

ⒶⒷⒸⒹ

練習問題　解答・解説 ▶▶▶

19. 解答：B　greatest を greater にする

The drainage basin of the Mississippi River is **greater** than that of any other river in North America.

訳 ミシシッピ川流域は北米の河川の中で最大である。

解法 《比較級 + than + any other +単数名詞》で最上級の意味を表すので，greatest を greater にする必要がある。

重要語 □ **drainage basin**「流域，集水域」

20. 解答：D

Bacteria are the **smallest** living organisms.

訳 バクテリアは最小の有機体である。

解法 この文では，the の後には形容詞の最上級が適切であるため，正解は (D) smallest になる。原級の (A) small は，前に the が不要のため正解にならない。

重要語 □ **organism**「有機体」

21. 解答：B

In most media, the longer the wavelength of light, **the faster it travels.**

訳 ほとんどの媒体では，光の波長が長ければ長いほど通過速度は速い。

解法 「～すればするほど…」を意味するのは，《the +比較級～, the +比較級 ...》で，(B) the faster が正解である。

重要語 □ **media**「媒質，媒体」(単数形：medium)

⚠ チェックポイント

□ 形容詞や副詞がどの語を修飾しているかを確認し，それぞれの混同がないかどうかを確認する。形容詞は名詞を修飾し，副詞は動詞，形容詞，副詞，文全体などを修飾する。

□ 文の構成や意味を考え，原級，比較級，最上級の形が正しいかどうかを確認する。

比較級と結びつく語：far, much, ever, still, a lot
最上級と結びつく語：in ..., of ..., among ..., up to ..., ever, by far, much, yet など

◆ 比較級+ than + any other +単数名詞「最も～である」
◆ the +比較級～, the +比較級 ...「～すればするほど…」
◆ 比較級+ and +比較級「どんどん～」

135

8. 接続詞・前置詞

最重要ストラテジー ▶▶▶

接続詞は語と語，句と句，節と節を結びつける語で，対等の関係にあるものを結びつける等位接続詞（and, or, but など）と，主となる節に別の節を結びつける従位接続詞（if, when, though など）がある。前置詞は，1 語の前置詞（at, in, under など）と 2 語以上の群前置詞（because of ..., in front of ..., in addition to ... など）があり，名詞，代名詞，名詞相当語句（動名詞など）の前に置く。接続詞と前置詞の混同を避けて正しい語を選ぶ，またはそのように訂正しなければならない。

練習問題　▶▶▶

22. To achieve its peak growing potential, the corn plant needs both
　　　　　A　　　 B　　　　　　　　　　　　　　　　　　　　　　C

adequate water or abundant sunlight.
　　　　　　　 D
　　　　　　　　　　　　　　　　　　　　　　　Ⓐ Ⓑ Ⓒ Ⓓ

23. At 1855, the American poet Walt Whitman published his famous book
　　　 A　　　　　　　　　　　　　　　　　 B　　　　 C

of poems *Leaves of Grass* at his own expense.
　　　　　　　　　　　　　　　　　 D
　　　　　　　　　　　　　　　　　　　　　　　Ⓐ Ⓑ Ⓒ Ⓓ

24. ------- ancient astronomers considered Venus to be a star, medieval
scientists discovered that it was actually a planet.

(A) Although

(B) Despite

(C) Because

(D) For
　　　　　　　　　　　　　　　　　　　　　　　Ⓐ Ⓑ Ⓒ Ⓓ

練習問題　解答・解説　▶▶▶

22.　　　　　　　　　　　　　　　　　　　　　　　　　解答：D　　or を and にする

To achieve its peak growing potential, the corn plant needs both adequate water **and** abundant sunlight.

訳　トウモロコシの成長能力を最大限引き出すためには，十分な水と豊富な日光の両方が必要である。

解法　both は and とともに both *A* and *B*「*A* も *B* も」の形を作る。or を用いた表現には，either *A* or *B*「*A* か *B* か」がある。他に否定の表現として，neither *A* nor *B*「*A* も *B* も〜ない」がある。

重要語　□ **potential**「潜在能力，可能性」　　□ **adequate**「十分な，適当な」

23.　　　　　　　　　　　　　　　　　　　　　　　　　解答：A　　At を In にする

In 1855, the American poet Walt Whitman published his famous book of poems *Leaves of Grass* at his own expense.

訳　1855 年，アメリカの詩人ウォルト・ホイットマンは有名な詩集『草の葉』を自費出版した。

解法　年を表すには，前置詞は at ではなく in を用いる。年，季節，月など比較的長い時間には in，曜日や日付には on，時刻など時の一点を表すには at を使う。

重要語　□ **expense**「費用」

24.　　　　　　　　　　　　　　　　　　　　　　　　　　　　　　解答：A

Although ancient astronomers considered Venus to be a star, medieval scientists discovered that it was actually a planet.

訳　古代天文学者は金星を恒星だと考えていたが，中世の科学者は，実際には惑星であることを発見した。

解法　文の意味から，空所には「〜だが」を表す接続詞 although を用いる。despite は「〜にもかかわらず」を意味する前置詞で，後ろには名詞や名詞相当語句がくるため，ここでは不適切。

重要語　□ **ancient**「古代の」　　　　□ **medieval**「中世の」
　　　　　□ **astronomer**「天文学者」　□ **planet**「惑星」

⚠ チェックポイント

□ 接続詞や前置詞が文法的に正しく使われているかどうかを確認する。

接続詞　等位接続詞（and，or など）：語，句，節を導く
　　　　　従位接続詞（if，when など）：節を導く

前置詞　名詞，代名詞，名詞相当語句（動名詞など）を導く

□ 接続詞や前置詞が文脈で正しく使われているかどうかを確認する。

137

9. 冠詞

最重要ストラテジー ▶▶▶

冠詞の使い分けは難しい文法項目だが，TOEFL ITP に出題されるのは基本的な a/an の使い分け，不定冠詞と定冠詞の混同，必要な冠詞の脱落や不要な冠詞の削除など，基礎的な事項に限られる。不定冠詞と定冠詞の基本的な違いは次のとおりである。

不定冠詞 不特定なものであることを表す。初めて話に出る（＝新情報）か，任意のひとつを指す場合である。原則として可算名詞の単数形に付く。

定冠詞 特定のものであることを表す。すでに話に出ている（＝旧情報）か，状況から何を指すか明らかである場合，ひとつしかないものの場合である。可算／不可算，単数／複数にかかわらず付けることができる。

練習問題 ▶▶▶

25. Grandma Moses, <u>a</u> American primitive painter, <u>did</u> not begin her
            A   B

<u>public</u> career <u>until</u> the age of eighty.
  C   D

Ⓐ Ⓑ Ⓒ Ⓓ

26. The New Stone Age <u>is</u> also called the Neolithic Revolution <u>because of</u>
                  A   B

the great increase in technology and <u>a</u> great changes in the social and
                                    C

political <u>organizations</u> of humans.
       D

Ⓐ Ⓑ Ⓒ Ⓓ

27. <u>A</u> dancing has been done <u>for many</u> purposes, <u>including</u> religious,
  A   B   C

social, and <u>artistic</u> ones.
       D

Ⓐ Ⓑ Ⓒ Ⓓ

練習問題　解答・解説　▶▶▶

25.
解答：A　a を an にする

Grandma Moses, **an** American primitive painter, did not begin her public career until the age of eighty.

訳　グランマ・モーゼスはアメリカのプリミティブアートの画家であるが，彼女は 80 歳になって初めて公的な職業生活を開始した。

解法　American は母音で始まる語であるから，その前につく不定冠詞は a ではなく an が正しい。until は否定語とともに用いると，「～して初めて…する，～するまで…しない」という意味になる。

26.
解答：C　a を the にする

The New Stone Age is also called the Neolithic Revolution because of the great increase in technology and **the** great changes in the social and political organizations of humans.

訳　新石器時代は新石器革命とも呼ばれるが，それは大幅な技術進歩があったことと，人間の社会的，政治的な組織に大きな変化があったためである。

解法　changes は複数形であるから，単数形と結びつく不定冠詞 a とともに使えない。ここでは，increase と一緒に定冠詞 the が用いられているように，great changes の前にも the が必要である。

重要語　□ **Neolithic**「新石器時代の」　　□ **organization**「組織，機構」

27.
解答：A　A を削除して Dancing とする

Dancing has been done for many purposes, including religious, social, and artistic ones.

訳　踊りは宗教，社会，芸術などさまざまな目的のために行われてきた。

解法　dancing は総称的な名詞であり，数えられない。したがって，dancing の前の不定冠詞 a を削除する必要がある。

重要語　□ **religious**「宗教の」

⚠ チェックポイント

□ 不定冠詞と定冠詞の使い分けが正しいかどうかを確認する。

□ 不要な冠詞，必要な冠詞の脱落がないかどうかを確認する。

□ a と an の使い分けが正しいかどうかを確認する。原則として子音で始まる語の前に a，母音で始まる語の前に an を用いる。ただし，次の場合に注意。

◈ 母音字で始まっていても発音が子音で始まる語には a を用いる（例：a university, a one-day trip）

◈ つづりが子音字から始まっていても発音が母音で始まる場合は an をつける（例：an hour, an SOS）

10. 品詞

選択肢から正しい品詞の語を選ぶ，または下線の語を正しい品詞に訂正する問題は，TOEFL ITP 頻出項目のひとつである。それぞれの品詞の用法，特に，形容詞と副詞の区別，名詞と動詞の使い分けが正しくできるようにしよう。

練習問題 ▶▶▶

28. Henry Ford's innovation of assembly-line <u>production</u> of automobiles led to
　　　　　　　　　　　　　　　　　　　　　　A

<u>dramatic</u> manufacturing increases <u>and</u> made automobiles <u>wide</u> available.
　B　　　　　　　　　　　　　　　　　C　　　　　　　　　　　　　D
　　　　　　　　　　　　　　　　　　　　　　　　　　　　Ⓐ Ⓑ Ⓒ Ⓓ

29. Never a <u>successfully</u> author <u>during</u> his lifetime, Nathanael West's fame and
　　　　　　　A　　　　　　　B

popularity <u>rose</u> greatly after <u>his</u> premature death.
　　　　　　C　　　　　　　　D
　　　　　　　　　　　　　　　　　　　　　　　　　　　　Ⓐ Ⓑ Ⓒ Ⓓ

30. An increase in interest rates typically has the ------- of reducing the value of bonds.

(A) effective

(B) effect

(C) effecting

(D) effected
　　　　　　　　　　　　　　　　　　　　　　　　　　　　Ⓐ Ⓑ Ⓒ Ⓓ

練習問題　解答・解説　▶▶▶

28.　　　　　　　　　　　　　　　　　　　　　　　解答：D　　wide を widely にする

Henry Ford's innovation of assembly-line production of automobiles led to dramatic manufacturing increases and made automobiles **widely** available.

訳　組立ラインを用いて自動車を製造するというヘンリー・フォードの革新的な手法により，生産台数は飛躍的に増え，車は広く流通するようになった。

解法　形容詞 available を修飾するのは形容詞 wide ではなく，副詞 widely である。(D) が正解。

> **重要語**　□ **innovation**「革新」　　　　□ **available**
> 　　　　　□ **assembly-line**「組立ライン」　「入手可能な，利用できる」

29.　　　　　　　　　　　　　　　　　　解答：A　　successfully を successful にする

Never a **successful** author during his lifetime, Nathanael West's fame and popularity rose greatly after his premature death.

訳　生前のナサニエル・ウェストは作家として成功しなかったものの，若くして他界した後，彼の名声と人気は大いに高まった。

解法　冠詞 a と名詞 author の間に入るのは，author を修飾する形容詞 successful であって，副詞 successfully ではない。

> **重要語**　□ **fame**「名声」　　　　□ **premature**「早すぎる」
> 　　　　　□ **popularity**「人気」

30.　　　　　　　　　　　　　　　　　　　　　　　　　　　　解答：B

An increase in interest rates typically has the **effect** of reducing the value of bonds.

訳　金利の上昇は一般的に債券の価値を下げる結果となる。

解法　冠詞 the と前置詞 of の間には，形容詞 (A) effective「効果的な」，動名詞 (C) effecting「実施すること」，動詞の過去形 (D) effected「もたらした」は入らない。「結果」を意味する名詞 (B) effect が入る。

> **重要語**　□ **bond**「債券」

🎵 チェックポイント

空所補充問題の場合

□ 空所以外の部分に，文に必要な主語，述語動詞，目的語，補語などが欠けていないかどうかを確認する。

□ 空所を除いても文が成立している場合には，どの修飾語を当てはめるのが適切かを確認する。

誤文訂正問題の場合

□ 下線の引かれた形容詞，副詞の修飾関係が正しいかどうかを確認する。

□ 文に必要な主語，述語動詞，目的語，補語などの要素が欠けていないかどうかを確認する。欠けている場合は，下線の引かれた語の品詞を変えることで正しい文構造になるかどうかを確認する。

11. 語順

語順で特に注意すべきポイントは次のとおりである。

■ 倒 置

ある語句を強調する目的や文法上の慣習から，《主語＋動詞》ではなく，《動詞＋主語》，《助動詞＋主語＋本動詞》の語順にする。特に注意すべきは，文頭に not, never などの否定語や only などの限定語を置いて強調を表す倒置である。

■ 形容詞に関する語順

形容詞は基本的に修飾する名詞の前に置く（例：形容詞 good ＋名詞 books）。しかし，-thing, -one, -body で終わる代名詞を修飾する場合，形容詞は名詞の後に置く（例：代名詞 something ＋形容詞 cold）。

■ 副詞に関する語順

副詞が形容詞を修飾する場合は，通常副詞を前に置く（例：副詞 very ＋形容詞 good）。ただし，副詞 enough は形容詞の後に置く。

練習問題 ▶▶▶

31. The atomic clock <u>located in</u> Boulder, Colorado, is <u>enough accurate</u> to
       A   B

<u>measure even</u> the <u>most minute</u> quantities of time.
 C   D   Ⓐ Ⓑ Ⓒ Ⓓ

32. The asthenosphere is the soft, ------- of the mantle on which the rigid plates
of the Earth's surface rest.

 (A) partially molten layer

 (B) layer partially molten

 (C) molten layer partially

 (D) partially layer molten   Ⓐ Ⓑ Ⓒ Ⓓ

33. Not until 1923 ------- able to verify the theory that nebulae were separate
galaxies located far outside our own Milky Way.

 (A) that scientist were

 (B) were scientists

 (C) scientists were

 (D) when were scientists   Ⓐ Ⓑ Ⓒ Ⓓ

練習問題　解答・解説　▶▶▶

31.
解答：B　　語順を accurate enough にする

The atomic clock located in Boulder, Colorado, is **accurate enough** to measure even the most minute quantities of time.

訳　コロラド州ボールダーに設置された原子時計は非常に正確で，時間の最小単位まで測ることができる。

解法　通常，副詞は修飾する形容詞や副詞の前に置くが，enough は修飾する形容詞・副詞の後に置く。語順は enough accurate ではなく accurate enough が正解。

重要語　□ **minute** [mainjúːt]「微小の」　　□ **quantity**「量，数量」

32.
解答：A

The asthenosphere is the soft, **partially molten layer** of the mantle on which the rigid plates of the Earth's surface rest.

訳　岩流圏とは，一部が溶解したやわらかいマントル層のことで，その上は堅い地表のプレートである。

解法　partially は副詞，molten は動詞 melt の過去分詞から転化した形容詞，layer は名詞である。副詞は通常，修飾する形容詞や副詞の前にくるので，副詞 partially は形容詞 molten の前につく。名詞は形容詞の後につくので，(A) partially molten layer が正解。

重要語　□ **molten**「溶解した」　　□ **rigid**「堅い，固定した」
　　　　□ **layer**「層」

33.
解答：B

Not until 1923 **were scientists** able to verify the theory that nebulae were separate galaxies located far outside our own Milky Way.

訳　星雲は我々の銀河系からはるかに離れた場所に位置する独立した銀河である，という理論を科学者は 1923 年に初めて証明することができた。

解法　強調のための倒置である。否定語 not が文頭にくると，その後の主語と動詞は倒置されるので，(B) were scientists が正しい。

重要語　□ **verify**「～を証明する」　　□ **nebulae**「星雲の集団」
　　　　　　　　　　　　　　　　　　　（単数形：nebula）

🔬 チェックポイント

□ 主語の前に動詞や助動詞がくる倒置の文でないかどうかを確認する。

□ 空所や下線部にある形容詞，副詞，名詞，イディオムなどの語順が正しいかどうかを確認する。

12. 脱落

最重要ストラテジー ▶▶▶

　脱落とは，あるべき必要な語が抜けていることである。誤文訂正問題では，下線部に必要な語が脱落していないかどうかを確認しなければならない。特に2語以上にまたがって下線が引かれている場合には注意が必要である。

練習問題 ▶▶▶

34. Jute used principally in the manufacture of textiles and various forms
　　　 ─────── A　　　　　　　 ──── B　　　 ──────────── C　　 ──────── D
of fiber.　　　　　　　　　　　　　　　　　　　　　　　　　Ⓐ Ⓑ Ⓒ Ⓓ

35. Anything which occupies space and has mass be regarded as a form of
　　　 ──────── A　 ──── B　　　　　　　 ──── C　　　 ──────── D
matter.　　　　　　　　　　　　　　　　　　　　　　　　　Ⓐ Ⓑ Ⓒ Ⓓ

36. Freedom of expression is guaranteed as basic right by the First
　　　 ──────── A　　　　　　　 ──────── B　　　 ──── C
Amendment to the United States Constitution.
　　　　　　　 ──── D
　　　　　　　　　　　　　　　　　　　　　　　　　　　　Ⓐ Ⓑ Ⓒ Ⓓ

練習問題　解答・解説　▶▶▶

34.　　　　　　　　　　　　　　　　　　　　　　解答：A　　**is** を入れて **Jute is used** とする

Jute is used principally in the manufacture of textiles and various forms of fiber.

訳　ジュートは主に，布地やいろいろなタイプの繊維の製造に使われる。

解法　主語 jute は「使う」のではなく「使われる」ものなので，受動態《be 動詞＋過去分詞》の形が必要である。be 動詞が脱落しているので，正しくは is を入れて (A) を Jute is used とする。

重要語　□ **textile**「布地，織物」　　　　　□ **fiber**「繊維」

35.　　　　　　解答：C　　should, can, must のいずれかを入れて **mass should [can/must] be** とする

Anything which occupies space and has **mass should [can/must] be** regarded as a form of matter.

訳　空間的な広がりを有して質量を持つものは，物質と見なされる。

解法　問題文の主語は Anything ... mass までで，それに対応する動詞は原形 be だけでは不十分である。be の前に助動詞 can, should, must などを補う必要がある。または単に mass is と現在形にしてもよい。

重要語　□ **occupy**「～を占める」　　　　□ **mass**「質量」

36.　　　　　　　　　　　　　　　　　　　　　　解答：B　　**a** を入れて **as a basic** とする

Freedom of expression is guaranteed **as a basic** right by the First Amendment to the United States Constitution.

訳　表現の自由は，アメリカ合衆国憲法修正第 1 条で基本的権利として保障されている。

解法　不定冠詞の脱落。basic right は数えられる名詞の単数形であるため，(B) as basic を as a basic にしなければならない。

重要語　□ **the First Amendment**　　　□ **constitution**「憲法」
　　　　　　「アメリカ合衆国憲法修正第 1 条」

⚠ チェックポイント

□ 下線部に脱落があるかどうか，次の点に注意して確認する。

　◆ be 動詞の脱落（特に受動態や進行形）

　◆ 助動詞の脱落

　◆ 関係代名詞の脱落

　◆ 前置詞の脱落（特に自動詞のあと）

　◆ 不定冠詞（a, an）や定冠詞（the）の脱落

13. 重複

誤文訂正問題では，下線部に不要な語が含まれている場合がある。よく見られるのが代名詞の重複（Mr. Olimar *he* did ... など）や，同じものを表す指示詞の重複（in Osaka *there* など），同じ意味の形容詞や副詞の重複（a *fine good* book など）である。

練習問題 ▶▶▶

37. Colds <u>are</u> <u>typically</u> infections of the nasal passages <u>caused by</u> a large
      A   B   C

number of <u>various different</u> viruses.
             D

Ⓐ Ⓑ Ⓒ Ⓓ

38. <u>The rising increase</u> of inflation <u>during</u> the 1970s <u>caused</u> the consumer price
          A   B   C

index to nearly triple <u>by</u> 1980.
              D

Ⓐ Ⓑ Ⓒ Ⓓ

39. One <u>out of</u> eight Americans, <u>around</u> 40 million people, <u>lives</u> in
      A   B   C

California <u>there</u>.
      D

Ⓐ Ⓑ Ⓒ Ⓓ

練習問題　解答・解説　▶▶▶

37.　　　　　　　　　　　　　　　解答：D　　different または various を削除する

Colds are typically infections of the nasal passages caused by a large number of **various** [**different**] viruses.

訳　風邪は通常，多くのいろいろなウイルスによって引き起こされる鼻腔内の感染症である。

解法　形容詞 various と different は意味上重複している。どちらか一方を削除する必要がある。

> **重要語**　□ **infection**「感染（症）」　　□ **various**「種々の，いろいろな」
> 　　　　　□ **nasal**「鼻の」

38.　　　　　　　　　　　　　　　解答：A　　rising を削除して The increase とする

The increase of inflation during the 1970s caused the consumer price index to nearly triple by 1980.

訳　1970 年代にインフレが進行したため，1980 年までに消費者物価指数はほぼ 3 倍になった。

解法　形容詞 rising「増大している」と名詞 increase「増大」が意味のうえで重複している。主語である名詞 increase は必要であり，rising を削除するべきである。

> **重要語**　□ **consumer price index**　　□ **triple**「3 倍になる」
> 　　　　　「消費者物価指数」

39.　　　　　　　　　　　　　　　解答：D　　there を削除する

One out of eight Americans, around 40 million people, lives in **California**.

訳　アメリカ人の 8 人にひとり，すなわちおよそ 4,000 万人がカリフォルニア州に住んでいる。

解法　in California の後に「そこに」を表す there は不要である。

⚠ チェックポイント

□ 不要な語があるかどうか，次の点を確認する。

◆ 不要な代名詞の重複

　　例：Biology <u>it</u> is the scientific study of living organisms.

◆ 同じものを表す指示詞の重複

　　例：Many famous modern paintings are in <u>New York there</u>.

◆ 同じ意味の形容詞や副詞の重複

　　例：Very <u>tall high</u> buildings are often found in big cities.

◆ その他の例（文法的に不要な要素など）

　　例：Jet planes fly <u>more faster</u> than helicopters.（不要な more/less）

BURST ONE

1. Eudora Welty, -------, created fictional characters in her work that were both charming and eccentric.

   (A) she was the Southern novelist and short-story writer

   (B) the Southern novelist and short-story writer she was

   (C) being the Southern novelist and short-story writer

   (D) the Southern novelist and short-story writer   Ⓐ Ⓑ Ⓒ Ⓓ

2. ------- of contemporary urban planning is that it encourages a neighborhood community while allowing individual privacy.

   (A) Characteristically

   (B) The characteristics

   (C) One characteristic

   (D) It was the characteristic   Ⓐ Ⓑ Ⓒ Ⓓ

3. The president of the United States serves as the head of state, -------, and of the civil service.

   (A) military forces

   (B) of the military

   (C) of forces of the military

   (D) military head   Ⓐ Ⓑ Ⓒ Ⓓ

---

4. The theme of Henry David Thoreau's *Walden* <u>is</u> that people should lead
A

<u>sincere</u> and joyous lives rather <u>than</u> artificial and weary <u>one</u>.
B　　　　　　　　　　　　　　　C　　　　　　　　　　　　D

Ⓐ Ⓑ Ⓒ Ⓓ

5. <u>The</u> pressure in the Earth's atmosphere <u>decrease</u> <u>about</u> 11 percent for each
A　　　　　　　　　　　　　　　　　　　B　　　　C

kilometer of higher <u>altitude</u>.
D

Ⓐ Ⓑ Ⓒ Ⓓ

6. <u>Verse it is the</u> general name given <u>to</u> metrical or poetic <u>works</u>.
　A　　B　　　　　　　　　　　　C　　　　　　　　　D

Ⓐ Ⓑ Ⓒ Ⓓ

7. Each <u>cell</u> is a biochemical factory <u>capable</u> of producing its own food,
A　　　　　　　　　　　　　　B

<u>it repairs</u> its own tissue, and expelling its own <u>waste</u>.
C　　　　　　　　　　　　　　　　　　　D

Ⓐ Ⓑ Ⓒ Ⓓ

8. Edith Wharton's novels can <u>be divided</u> into those <u>about</u> farmers in a
A　　　　　　　　　　B

rural setting, those about people <u>in</u> World War I, and <u>the novels</u> about
C　　　　　　　　　　　　　D

aristocrats in New York and Europe.

Ⓐ Ⓑ Ⓒ Ⓓ

Section I Part A/B | Section I Part C | Section 2 | Section 3 | 総合模試 | 総合模試 解答・解説

集中練習問題 ❶ 解答・解説

1. 解答：D

Eudora Welty, **the Southern novelist and short-story writer,** created fictional characters in her work that were both charming and eccentric.

> **訳** ユードラ・ウェルティは南部の小説家であり短編作家だが，魅力的かつ風変わりな登場人物を作品の中で作り上げた。

> **解法** 空所の前は主語 Eudora Welty，空所の後は述語動詞 created である。したがって，空所には同格で主語を説明する名詞相当語句が入るので，(D) が適切。
>
> > **重要語** □ **eccentric**「風変わりな」

2. 解答：C

One characteristic of contemporary urban planning is that it encourages a neighborhood community while allowing individual privacy.

> **訳** 現代都市計画のひとつの特徴は，個人のプライバシーを尊重しつつ地域コミュニティを奨励していることである。

> **解法** 述語動詞 is に適した主語が必要である。of の前には名詞が入るため，(A) 副詞 Characteristically，(D) 主語＋動詞＋補語は不適切。(B) The characteristics は複数形だから動詞 is と合わない。正解は単数形の (C) である。
>
> > **重要語** □ **contemporary**「現代の」　　□ **encourage**「～を奨励する」

3. 解答：B

The president of the United States serves as the head of state, **of the military,** and of the civil service.

> **訳** 合衆国大統領は国家，軍隊，および行政の長として務める。

> **解法** 空所は，その前後にある of state と of the civil service と並列している。形が一致しているのは (B) of the military である。
>
> > **重要語** □ **civil service**「行政事務」

4. 解答：D　　one を ones にする

The theme of Henry David Thoreau's *Walden* is that people should lead sincere and joyous lives rather than artificial and weary **ones.**

> **訳** ヘンリー・デイヴィッド・ソローの『ウォールデン』のテーマは，人は偽りの退屈な人生ではなく，正直で楽しい人生を送るべきだ，ということである。

150

Section I Part A/B　Section I Part C　Section 2　Section 3　総合模試　総合模試 解答・解説

解法 (D) の代名詞 one は lives の繰り返しを避けるために用いられている。lives に合わせて複数形 ones にしなければならない。

> **重要語**　□ **theme**「テーマ」　　□ **weary**「退屈な」
> 　　　　　□ **artificial**「偽りの，人為的な」

5.　　　　　　　　　　　　　　　　　　　　　解答：B　　decrease を decreases にする

- -

The pressure in the Earth's atmosphere **decreases** about 11 percent for each kilometer of higher altitude.

訳　地球の大気圧は高度が 1 キロ増すごとに約 11 パーセント減少する。

解法　主語 pressure は単数形，文は現在形なので，それに一致させて述語動詞は decrease ではなく decreases となる。

> **重要語**　□ **pressure**「気圧」　　□ **altitude**「高度」
> 　　　　　□ **atmosphere**「大気」

6.　　　　　　　　　　　　　　　　　　　　　解答：A　　it を削除して Verse とする

- -

Verse is the general name given to metrical or poetic works.

訳　ヴァースとは，韻文や詩文を総括した名称である。

解法　(A) の名詞 verse と代名詞 it を併用すれば主語が 2 つになるので，it を削除する。

> **重要語**　□ **metrical**「韻文の」

7.　　　　　　　　　　　　　　　　　　　　解答：C　　it repairs を repairing にする

- -

Each cell is a biochemical factory capable of producing its own food, **repairing** its own tissue, and expelling its own waste.

訳　細胞はひとつひとつが自ら栄養物を作り，組織を修復し，老廃物を排出することのできる生化学工場である。

解法　producing および expelling と並列させるには，(C) it repairs を動名詞 repairing にする。

> **重要語**　□ **cell**「細胞」　　　　□ **tissue**「組織」
> 　　　　　□ **biochemical**「生化学の」　□ **expel**「〜を排出する」

8.　　　　　　　　　　　　　　　　　　　解答：D　　the novels を those にする

- -

Edith Wharton's novels can be divided into those about farmers in a rural setting, those about people in World War I, and **those** about aristocrats in New York and Europe.

訳　イーディス・ウォートンの小説は，田舎を舞台にした農夫の物語，第一次世界大戦下の人々の物語，ニューヨークやヨーロッパにいる上流社会の人々の物語に分類することができる。

解法　小説は 3 種類に分類されており，3 つが正しく並列される必要がある。最初と 2 番目が those で始まっているので，3 番目も the novels ではなく those にする。

> **重要語**　□ **aristocrat**「貴族（的な人），上流階級の人」

集中練習問題 ❷ 16 問

BURST TWO

1. Division is the process ------- reproduces itself.

   (A) which an ameba

   (B) that ameba

   (C) in that the ameba

   (D) by which an ameba   Ⓐ Ⓑ Ⓒ Ⓓ

2. The more oxygen is present in a compound, ------- is likely to be.

   (A) the more reactive it

   (B) it produces a reaction

   (C) the most reaction

   (D) its reactive   Ⓐ Ⓑ Ⓒ Ⓓ

3. Zinc has been used as a component of brass since the Bronze Age, ------- it was not recognized as a separate metal until 1746.

   (A) whereas

   (B) yet

   (C) moreover

   (D) then   Ⓐ Ⓑ Ⓒ Ⓓ

4. Lake Erie, one of the Great Lakes, ------- to the Hudson River by the New York State Barge Canal.

   (A) is linked

   (B) linked

   (C) linking

   (D) are linked   Ⓐ Ⓑ Ⓒ Ⓓ

Go on to the next page ➡

5. Some bacteria have evolved such that they are able to live in hot springs with temperatures ------- 175°F.

(A) as high as

(B) high as

(C) as high

(D) high

Ⓐ Ⓑ Ⓒ Ⓓ

6. The <u>precision</u> of a homeostatic system depends <u>upon</u> the quality and
　　　　A　　　　　　　　　　　　　　　　　　　B

amount of <u>informations</u> it <u>can</u> process.
　　　　　　C　　　　　D

Ⓐ Ⓑ Ⓒ Ⓓ

7. <u>The</u> woolly mammoth, roughly <u>a size</u> of <u>an</u> Indian elephant, had <u>long fur</u>
　　　A　　　　　　　　　　　B　　　C　　　　　　　　　　　D

and large inward-curving tusks.

Ⓐ Ⓑ Ⓒ Ⓓ

8. Embankment dams, <u>constructing</u> of earth and rock, <u>are</u> the largest <u>of</u> all
　　　　　　　　　　　A　　　　　　　　　　　　B　　　　　　C

dams in <u>the world</u>.
　　　　　　D

Ⓐ Ⓑ Ⓒ Ⓓ

9. The arthropod genus is by far <u>the large</u> group of animals in terms of the
　　　A　　　　　　　　　　　　B

number <u>of</u> species it <u>contains</u>.
　　　　　C　　　　　D

Ⓐ Ⓑ Ⓒ Ⓓ

10. Mass <u>transportation</u> changed more <u>dramatically</u> <u>in</u> 1900 and 1950 <u>than</u>
　　　　　　A　　　　　　　　　　　　B　　　C　　　　　　　　　D

during any other period of history.

Ⓐ Ⓑ Ⓒ Ⓓ

11. Sherwood Anderson's *Winesburg, Ohio* is a group of interconnected
                                                                   A

story dealing with the inhabitants of a fictional American town.
  B   C   D

Ⓐ Ⓑ Ⓒ Ⓓ

12. Esperanto, invented by L.L. Zamenhof in 1887, was intended to become
                   A   B   C

an universal language.
D

Ⓐ Ⓑ Ⓒ Ⓓ

13. Until the 1980s, it was thought that there are only three or four major ice
                                     A   B

ages, but recent research indicates there may have been as many as twenty.
           C   D

Ⓐ Ⓑ Ⓒ Ⓓ

14. Dinosaurs are traditionally classified as reptiles, but it is now believed that
             A

themselves may have been highly active and warm-blooded.
  B   C   D

Ⓐ Ⓑ Ⓒ Ⓓ

15. A change in velocity can be either a change in speed and a change in
                        A   B   C

direction.
D

Ⓐ Ⓑ Ⓒ Ⓓ

16. Few public transportation is as economical and efficient in urban areas
    A   B   C

as the trolley car.
D

Ⓐ Ⓑ Ⓒ Ⓓ

集中練習問題 ❷ 解答・解説

1. 解答：D

- -

Division is the process **by which an ameba** reproduces itself.

訳 分裂がアメーバの自己増殖の方法である。

解法 「分裂という方法によって，アメーバは自己増殖する」ことを表しているので，先行詞 process の後には，関係代名詞 which とともに「〜によって」を表す by が必要である。

> **重要語** □ **division** 「分裂，分割」　□ **reproduce** 「〜を増殖させる」
> □ **process** 「過程，方法」

2. 解答：A

- -

The more oxygen is present in a compound, **the more reactive it** is likely to be.

訳 化合物に酸素が多く含まれているほど，その反応性は大きくなる傾向にある。

解法 《the ＋比較級〜, the ＋比較級 ...》は「〜すればするほど…」を意味する。(A) が正解。

> **重要語** □ **oxygen** 「酸素」　□ **reactive** 「反応(性)の」
> □ **compound** 「化合物」

3. 解答：B

- -

Zinc has been used as a component of brass since the Bronze Age, **yet it was not recognized as a** separate metal until 1746.

訳 亜鉛は青銅器時代から真ちゅうの材料として使われてきたが，1746 年まで独立した金属元素とは認められなかった。

解法 最初の節「亜鉛は青銅器時代から使われてきた」に対して，次の節「1746 年まで独立した金属元素とは認められなかった」は反意的であるので，「しかし，それにもかかわらず」を表す接続詞 yet を用いる。

> **重要語** □ **zinc** 「亜鉛」　□ **the Bronze Age** 「青銅器時代」
> □ **component** 「成分，構成要素」　□ **metal** 「金属 (元素)」

4. 解答：A

- -

Lake Erie, one of the Great Lakes, **is linked** to the Hudson River by the New York State Barge Canal.

訳 エリー湖は五大湖のひとつであるが，ニューヨーク州バージ運河でハドソン川と連結されている。

解法 動詞 link は link *A* to *B* で「AをBに連結する」を表す。主語 Lake Erie は単数形で，「ハドソン川と連結されている」を表すには，受動態で現在形を表す is linked を用いる。link には自動詞もあり，link up with ... は「〜と連結する」を表すが，(B) は形が異なり適切ではない。

> **重要語** □ **the Great Lakes** 「五大湖」　□ **barge** 「はしけ，平底荷船」
> ＊米国とカナダの国境にある 5 つの大きな湖

Section Ⅰ Part A/B　Section Ⅰ Part C　Section 2　Section 3　総合模試　総合模試 解答・解説

5.

Some bacteria have evolved such that they are able to live in hot springs with temperatures **as high as** 175°F.

> **訳** バクテリアの中には，進化して華氏175度の温泉でも生存できるようになった種類もある。

> **解法** 原級を使った比較 as ... as は「〜もの」という程度を表す表現に使われる。ここでは as high as で「〜もの高温で」のニュアンスとなる。正解は (A)。

> **重要語** □ **evolve**「進化する」　　　□ **hot spring**「温泉」

6.

解答：C　informations を information にする

The precision of a homeostatic system depends upon the quality and amount of **information** it can process.

> **訳** 恒常性機能の正確さは処理できる情報の質と量による。

> **解法** information は不可算名詞なので，複数にはならない。information にする必要がある。

> **重要語** □ **precision**「正確さ」　　　□ **process**「〜を処理する」

7.

解答：B　a size を the size にする

The woolly mammoth, roughly **the size** of an Indian elephant, had long fur and large inward-curving tusks.

> **訳** ウーリーマンモスはおよそインド象ほどの大きさで，長い毛と内側にカーブした大きな牙を持っていた。

> **解法** size of an Indian elephant「インド象の大きさ」は特定のサイズを表すから，不定冠詞 a を定冠詞 the にする必要がある。

> **重要語** □ **fur**「毛衣，毛皮」　　　□ **inward**「内側に」

8.

解答：A　constructing を constructed にする

Embankment dams, **constructed** of earth and rock, are the largest of all dams in the world.

> **訳** 築堤ダムは土石で構築されており，世界のダムのなかで最も大きい。

> **解法** ダムは自ら土石で「構築する」のではなく「構築される」ものなので，分詞は現在分詞 constructing ではなく，受身を表す過去分詞 constructed を用いる。

> **重要語** □ **embankment**「堤防，土手」

9.　　　　　　　　　　　　　　解答：B　　the large を the largest にする

The arthropod genus is by far **the largest** group of animals in terms of the number of species it contains.

訳　種の数に関して言えば，節足動物は他をはるかにしのぐ最大の動物群である。

解法　by far は，最上級や比較級を強めて「はるかに，断然」を意味する。the large は the largest にする。

重要語　□ **arthropod**「節足動物」　□ **by far**「はるかに」
　　　　　□ **genus**「種，属」　　　□ **species**「種」

10.　　　　　　　　　　　　　　解答：C　　in を between にする

Mass transportation changed more dramatically **between** 1900 and 1950 than during any other period of history.

訳　大量輸送は，歴史的時期の中で 1900 年から 1950 年までの間に最も劇的に変化した。

解法　前置詞 in は「1900 年に」という特定の年を表すが，期間を表す場合には between *A* and *B* を用いる。in は between にする。

重要語　□ **transportation**「輸送（機関）」　□ **dramatically**「劇的に」

11.　　　　　　　　　　　　　　解答：B　　story を stories にする

Sherwood Anderson's *Winesburg, Ohio* is a group of interconnected **stories** dealing with the inhabitants of a fictional American town.

訳　シャーウッド・アンダーソンの『ワインズバーグ・オハイオ』は，アメリカの架空の町に住む人々を扱って相互に結びついた連作である。

解法　a group of ... の後には複数名詞がつくので，(B) は story ではなく stories が正しい。a number of ... や a bunch of ... も同様に複数名詞を従える。

重要語　□ **interconnect**「相互に結びつく」　□ **inhabitant**「住人」

12.　　　　　　　　　　　　　　解答：D　　an を a にする

Esperanto, invented by L.L. Zamenhof in 1887, was intended to become **a** universal language.

訳　エスペラント語は 1887 年 L.L. ザメンホフによって考案され，世界共通言語になるように意図された。

解法　形容詞 universal は母音字で始まっているが発音は子音で始まる。不定冠詞は an ではなく a を用いる。an hour, a university など，綴り字と一致しないものに注意。

13.

Until the 1980s, it was thought that there **were** only three or four major ice ages, but recent research indicates there may have been as many as twenty.

> **訳**　大きな氷河時代は 3，4 度しかなかったと 1980 年代までは考えられていたが，最近の研究では 20 回もあった可能性が示されている。

> **解法**　「大きな氷河時代は 3，4 度しかなかった」と考えられていたのは 1980 年代までだったので，動詞 are は過去形 were にする必要がある。

> > **重要語**　□ **ice age**「氷河時代」　　　　□ **as many as ...**「〜ほど多数の」

14.

Dinosaurs are traditionally classified as reptiles, but it is now believed that **they** may have been highly active and warm-blooded.

> **訳**　恐竜は昔からは虫類に分類されているが，現在はきわめて活動的な温血動物だったと考えられている。

> **解法**　that 以下の名詞節における主語は，再帰代名詞 themselves ではなく主格 they となる。再帰代名詞は，主語ではなく，動詞や前置詞の目的語として用いられたり，主語・補語・目的語の意味を強調するため独立して用いられたりする。

> > **重要語**　□ **dinosaur**「恐竜」　　　　□ **reptile**「は虫類」
> > 　　　　　　□ **classify**「〜を分類する」

15.

A change in velocity can be either a change in speed **or** a change in direction.

> **訳**　速度（ベロシティ）の変化とは，速さの変化か方向の変化のことである。

> **解法**　either は等位接続詞 or とともに用いて either A or B「A か B のどちらか」を表す。and を or に変える。and は both A and B「A も B も」に用いられる。

> > **重要語**　□ **velocity**「速度」

16.

Little public transportation is as economical and efficient in urban areas as the trolley car.

> **訳**　都市部において，路面電車ほど経済的で効率的な交通機関はほとんどない。

> **解法**　transportation は不可算名詞であるから，修飾する語は可算名詞に用いられる few ではなく，不可算名詞に使われる little である。

> > **重要語**　□ **transportation**「交通機関」　　□ **efficient**「効率的な」
> > 　　　　　　□ **economical**「経済的な」　　　　□ **trolley car**「路面電車」

Section 2

集中練習問題 ❸　16問

BURST THREE

1. As a general rule, only after an experiment has been replicated ------- that its results are reliable.

(A) a scientist should conclude

(B) a scientist conclude

(C) can conclude a scientist

(D) should a scientist conclude　　　　　Ⓐ Ⓑ Ⓒ Ⓓ

2. A ------- with an asteroid some 65 million years ago is thought to have been the cause of the extinction of the dinosaurs.

(A) collide

(B) colliding

(C) collisions

(D) collision　　　　　Ⓐ Ⓑ Ⓒ Ⓓ

3. Synthetic rubber, -------, was not widely used until the 1940s.

(A) it was invented in 1893

(B) invented in 1893

(C) in 1893 invented

(D) being invented in 1893　　　　　Ⓐ Ⓑ Ⓒ Ⓓ

4. Matthew Vassar, a wealthy <u>and rich</u> entrepreneur, was one of the <u>most vocal</u>

　　　　　　　　　　　A　　　　　　　　　　　　　　　B

19th-century proponents of <u>higher</u> education <u>for</u> American women.

　　　　　　　　　　　　　C　　　　　　　D

Ⓐ Ⓑ Ⓒ Ⓓ

Section I Part A/B　Section I Part C　**Section 2**　Section 3　総合模試　総合模試 解答・解説

5. A robot is <u>any</u> computerized machine which <u>can programmed</u> <u>to work</u>
            A   B   C

in place of <u>human labor</u>.
                D

Ⓐ Ⓑ Ⓒ Ⓓ

6. <u>Severe</u> heat <u>exhaustion</u> most <u>common</u> strikes infants <u>and</u> the elderly.
     A   B   C   D

Ⓐ Ⓑ Ⓒ Ⓓ

7. In <u>the field</u> of biology, the most <u>significant important</u> contribution <u>to</u>
       A   B   C

the <u>understanding</u> of the genetic make-up of humans has been the
         D

GENOME project.

Ⓐ Ⓑ Ⓒ Ⓓ

8. When debtors <u>officially</u> declare they are either insolvent <u>or</u> unable to
                   A   B

<u>repay</u> a loan, <u>they</u> be regarded as bankrupt.
  C   D

Ⓐ Ⓑ Ⓒ Ⓓ

9. Cermets, <u>combinations</u> of ceramics and metals, <u>behave</u> like <u>much</u> metals
                A   B   C

but have the <u>heat-resistant</u> qualities of ceramics.
               D

Ⓐ Ⓑ Ⓒ Ⓓ

10. An <u>allergic</u> occurs when the body's <u>immune</u> system overreacts to the
       A   B

<u>introduction</u> of a <u>normally</u> harmless foreign substance.
    C   D

Ⓐ Ⓑ Ⓒ Ⓓ

11. Until the <u>completion</u> of the first transcontinental railway in 1869, <u>West Coast</u>
                A   B

of the United States was <u>sparsely</u> settled by ranchers, <u>farmers</u>, and miners.
                                C   D

Ⓐ Ⓑ Ⓒ Ⓓ

12. <u>Originally</u> a Spanish fort, St. Augustine, Florida, <u>there</u> is <u>the oldest</u>
      A   B   C

community <u>in</u> the United States.
          D

Ⓐ Ⓑ Ⓒ Ⓓ

13. It is <u>estimation</u> that the ear of a young child can <u>typically</u> <u>detect</u> sounds
         A   B   C

in <u>the</u> range of 18 to 18,000 Hz.
    D

Ⓐ Ⓑ Ⓒ Ⓓ

14. <u>Until</u> about 10,000 years ago, humans lived in <u>villages small</u>, wandering
     A   B

from place to place <u>to obtain</u> food by hunting, <u>fishing</u>, and gathering.
                    C   D

Ⓐ Ⓑ Ⓒ Ⓓ

15. <u>During</u> a hyperinflationary cycle, consumer prices <u>climb</u> and currency
     A   B

<u>additionally also</u> loses <u>value</u>.
         C   D

Ⓐ Ⓑ Ⓒ Ⓓ

16. The American colonial period <u>generally regarded</u> as <u>beginning</u> with the
                                  A   B

establishment of Jamestown in 1607 and ending with the <u>recognition</u>
                                                  C

of independence <u>in</u> 1783.
         D

Ⓐ Ⓑ Ⓒ Ⓓ

集中練習問題 ❸ 解答・解説

1. 解答：D

As a general rule, only after an experiment has been replicated **should a scientist conclude** that its results are reliable.

> **訳** 一般的に，実験が再現されて初めて，その結果が信頼できると科学者は結論を下す。

> **解法** 強調のための倒置では，only を前に出して，主節の語順は《動詞＋主語》，または《助動詞＋主語＋動詞》にする。空所には《助動詞 (should) ＋主語 (a scientist) ＋動詞 (conclude)》の順である (D) が入る。

> **重要語** □ **replicate**「〜を繰り返す」 □ **reliable**「信頼できる」
> □ **experiment**「実験」

2. 解答：D

A **collision** with an asteroid some 65 million years ago is thought to have been the cause of the extinction of the dinosaurs.

> **訳** 約 6,500 万年前の小惑星との衝突が恐竜絶滅の原因だったと考えられている。

> **解法** 不定冠詞 a の後の空所には主語になる名詞が入るので，単数形の名詞である (D) collision「衝突」が正解。(A) collide「衝突する」は動詞，(C) collisions は名詞の複数形なので誤り。(B) colliding は動名詞で，前に不定冠詞の a をとらない。

> **重要語** □ **collision**「衝突」 □ **extinction**「絶滅」
> □ **asteroid**「小惑星」

3. 解答：B

Synthetic rubber, **invented in 1893,** was not widely used until the 1940s.

> **訳** 合成ゴムは 1893 年に発明されたが，1940 年代までは広く使われなかった。

> **解法** 主語 synthetic rubber と述語動詞 was の間の空所には，synthetic rubber に補足的説明を加える同格語句が入る。「1893 年に発明された」を表すには which was invented in 1893 の語順となるが，which was は省略できるので (B) invented in 1893 が正解。

> **重要語** □ **synthetic**「人造の，合成の」

4.　　　　　　　　　　　　　　　　　　解答：A　　and rich を削除する

Matthew Vassar, a **wealthy** entrepreneur, was one of the most vocal 19th-century proponents of higher education for American women.

> **訳**　裕福な起業家のマシュー・ヴァッサーは，19 世紀のアメリカで女性の高等教育を最も声高に唱えた提唱者のひとりであった。

> **解法**　wealthy と rich は同意語なので一方は不要。下線部 (A) の and rich を削除する。

> > **重要語**　□ **wealthy**「裕福な」　　　　□ **proponent**「提唱者，支持者」

5.　　　　　　　　　　　　　　　　解答：B　　be を入れて can be programmed とする

A robot is any computerized machine which **can be programmed** to work in place of human labor.

> **訳**　ロボットとは，人間の代わりに労働するようプログラムされることが可能なコンピュータ制御の機械のことである。

> **解法**　machine は自ら「プログラムする」のでなく「プログラムされる」ので，受動態を用いる。(B) には be 動詞が脱落しているため，can programmed を can be programmed にする。

> > **重要語**　□ **in place of ...**「～の代わりに」

6.　　　　　　　　　　　　　　　　　解答：C　　common を commonly にする

Severe heat exhaustion most **commonly** strikes infants and the elderly.

> **訳**　激しい熱疲労の犠牲に最もなりやすいのは幼児と高齢者である。

> **解法**　動詞 strikes を修飾するのは (C) の形容詞 common ではなく，「一般に，通例は」を意味する副詞 commonly である。

> > **重要語**　□ **heat exhaustion**「熱疲労」　　□ **infant**「幼児」

7.　　　　　　　　　　　　　解答：B　　important または significant を削除する

In the field of biology, the most **significant [important]** contribution to the understanding of the genetic make-up of humans has been the GENOME project.

> **訳**　生物学の分野で，ヒトの遺伝子構造の解読に最も重要な貢献を果たしたのはゲノム計画である。

> **解法**　(B) の形容詞 significant および important はどちらも「重要な」を意味する語であり，意味が重複している。どちらか一方を削除する。

> > **重要語**　□ **genetic**「遺伝子の」　　　□ **make-up**「構造，組織」

163

8.

When debtors officially declare they are either insolvent or unable to repay a loan, **they can be** [**they are**] regarded as bankrupt.

訳　債務者が支払い不能であること，またはローンの返済が不可能であることを公に宣言したとき，破産者と認められる。

解法　主節内の述語動詞として原形動詞 be は単独では使われない。助動詞 can を補って they can be にするか，be 動詞の形を変えて they are にする必要がある。

重要語　□ **debtor**「債務者」　　　　　　□ **bankrupt**「破産した」
　　　　　□ **insolvent**「支払い不能の」

9.

Cermets, combinations of ceramics and metals, behave **much like** metals but have the heat-resistant qualities of ceramics.

訳　サーメットはセラミックスと金属の複合材料で，金属とだいたい同じ性質だが，セラミックスの耐熱性も有している。

解法　(C) の副詞 much は「だいたい，およそ」を表して like を修飾する。語順は much like metals が正しく，「金属とだいたい同じように」を意味する。

重要語　□ **behave**「作用する，ふるまう」　　□ **heat-resistant**「耐熱性の」

10.

An **allergy** occurs when the body's immune system overreacts to the introduction of a normally harmless foreign substance.

訳　体内に入った通常は無害な異物に免疫システムが過剰反応すると，アレルギーが起こる。

解法　不定冠詞 an と述語動詞 occurs の間には，主語になる名詞が入る。(A) allergic は形容詞で「アレルギーの，アレルギーにかかった」を意味するので，名詞 allergy に変えなければならない。

重要語　□ **immune**「免疫」　　　　　□ **foreign substance**「異物」

11.

Until the completion of the first transcontinental railway in 1869, **the West Coast** of the United States was sparsely settled by ranchers, farmers, and miners.

訳　1869 年に最初の大陸横断鉄道が完成するまで，アメリカの西海岸地域は牧場主，農民，鉱山労働者がまばらに住んでいるだけだった。

解法　固有名詞は原則無冠詞だが，山脈，河川，海洋，海岸線などは慣用的に the を伴うのが普通である。(B) は定冠詞を付け，the West Coast とする。

重要語　□ **transcontinental**「大陸横断の」　□ **rancher**「牧場主」
　　　　　□ **sparsely**「まばらに」　　　　□ **miner**「鉱山労働者」

12.　　　　　　　　　　　　　　　　解答：B　　there を削除する

Originally a Spanish fort, St. Augustine, **Florida**, is the oldest community in the United States.

訳　元々はスペインの砦だったフロリダ州セント・オーガスティンは，米国で最も古いコミュニティである。

解法　a Spanish fort と同格の St. Augustine, Florida は場所を示す名詞であり，副詞 there を伴う必要はない。(B) を削除する。

重要語　□ **fort**「砦，城砦」

13.　　　　　　　　　　　　　　解答：A　　estimation を estimated にする

It is **estimated** that the ear of a young child can typically detect sounds in the range of 18 to 18,000 Hz.

訳　幼児の耳は通常 18 〜 1 万 8,000 ヘルツの音を聞き分けることができると考えられている。

解法　「〜と評価されている，考えられている」を表すには，受動態を用いる。(A) の名詞 estimation「評価」を動詞の過去分詞形 estimated に変える。

重要語　□ **estimate**　　　　　　□ **detect**「〜を感知 [検知] する」
　　　　　「〜を評価する，見積もる」

14.　　　　　　　　　　　　　解答：B　　語順を small villages にする

Until about 10,000 years ago, humans lived in **small villages**, wandering from place to place to obtain food by hunting, fishing, and gathering.

訳　1 万年ほど前まで人間は小さな村落に住み，狩猟，釣り，採集で食料を得るために各地を転々としていた。

解法　「小さな村落」を表す (B) の語順は，《形容詞＋名詞》が正しいので，small villages に変える必要がある。

重要語　□ **wander**「さすらう，放浪する」

15.　　　　　　　　　　　　解答：C　　also または additionally を削除する

During a hyperinflationary cycle, consumer prices climb and currency **additionally [also]** loses value.

訳　ハイパーインフレーション期には，消費者物価は上昇し，それに加えて貨幣の価値は下落する。

解法　副詞 additionally と also は「そのうえ，〜も」を表す同意語なので，also または additionally を削除する。

重要語　□ **consumer price**「消費者物価」　□ **currency**「貨幣」

16.

The American colonial period **generally is [is generally] regarded** as beginning with the establishment of Jamestown in 1607 and ending with the recognition of independence in 1783.

訳　アメリカ植民地時代とは，一般的に 1607 年のジェームズタウン建設から 1783 年の独立認定までの間と認識されている。

解法　(A) の動詞 regard は「～を認識する」という能動的な意味を持つ。主語の American colonial period は「(～と) 認識される」対象であるべきなので，be 動詞 is を補い，is regarded と受動態にする。原則的には動詞を修飾する副詞の位置は be 動詞の後とされるが，この場合は generally is regarded の語順でも問題ない。

III

Section 3
Reading Comprehension

攻略ストラテジー＋練習問題

Section 3 の概要

Reading Comprehension セクションは以下の構成になっている。

Reading Comprehension（50問：55分）

主な特徴

◇ 全問とも四肢択一形式。

◇ 大学レベルの多様な短いパッセージ5編または6編を読んで理解する能力を測定する。

◇ パッセージを読み，その内容あるいは語彙についての質問に答える。

Reading Comprehension のストラテジー

　本章では Reading Comprehension セクションで頻出の設問タイプを **1**〜**9** に分類し，それぞれについて学習する。

---

1 頻出設問タイプ **1** **2**

1 パッセージ／パラグラフの主要なポイントを問う設問

2 パッセージの構成に関する設問

　　前後の段落の内容を推測する設問

　　構成パターンを問う設問

---

2 頻出設問タイプ **3** **4** **5**

3 パッセージに記述されている情報を問う設問

4 パッセージに記述されていない情報を問う設問

5 指定された内容を表すパラグラフを選ぶ設問

---

3 頻出設問タイプ **6** **7**

6 推測に関する設問

7 著者の論調・立場・態度に関する設問

---

4 頻出設問タイプ **8** **9**

8 語彙に関する設問

9 語法に関する設問

　　単語・フレーズが指す対象を問う設問

　　修辞上の効果を問う設問

1.　頻出設問タイプ 🄵 🄶

【設問タイプ 🄵】　パッセージ／パラグラフの主要なポイントを問う設問

◆ 「パッセージの主題は何ですか」

　「次のうち，パラグラフ～のポイントはどれですか」

　パッセージの主要なポイントを問う問題は，最初の設問としてよく出題されるが，まず他の設問に答え，全体に関する設問は後に回すほうが効率的である。事実を問う設問を先に解くことで，後で全体に関する設問を解くときに役立つ情報を得られるからである。

設問例

☐ What is the main topic of the passage?

☐ What is the author's main point?

☐ What does the passage [paragraph 3] mainly discuss?

☐ What is the main purpose of the passage?

☐ The passage answers which of the following questions?

☐ With which of the following subjects is the passage mainly concerned?

☐ In paragraph 2, the author primarily discusses ...

☐ Which of the following is most extensively discussed in the last paragraph?

☐ What aspect of *physical science* does the author discuss [mention] in the first paragraph?

最重要ストラテジー▶▶▶

【設問タイプ❷】　パッセージの構成に関する設問

◆　前後の段落の内容を推測する設問

「パッセージの前後では何が述べられていますか」

◆　構成パターンを問う設問

「パッセージはどのような構成ですか —— 時系列か，列挙か，原因と結果か」

設問例

🐾 前後の段落の内容を推測する設問

☐ What does the paragraph following [preceding] the passage probably discuss?

🐾 構成パターンを問う設問

☐ Which of the following statements best describes [characterizes] the organization of the passage?

☐ The author organizes the passage according to which principle?

☐ Which of the following best expresses the relationship between the first and second paragraph?

☐ What types of organization does the author use to illustrate the two kinds of *breeding processes* mentioned in paragraph 3?

171

1.-6.

Line

(1)　　　Just as in other vertebrates, the human liver is essential to life and may be considered the master "chemistry laboratory" of the body. It is the largest human organ, making up between 2 to 3 percent of a healthy adult's body weight. Reddish-brown in color, it has the consistency of foam rubber and is shaped like a three-sided pyramid.

(5)　It is located on the right side of the abdominal cavity, covered by the rib cage. The gall bladder, a small pouch that stores bile, is partially embedded in the base at the back of the liver. Also, in contact with the liver are the large and small intestines, as well as the stomach. The liver is divided into two lobes, with the right lobe being approximately six times larger than the left.

(10)　　　The liver has a double blood supply. The *portal vein* brings venous blood from the stomach, the intestines, and the spleen. The *hepatic artery* brings oxygenated blood from the heart. These two blood vessels supply the liver with somewhere in the neighborhood of 1.2 liters of blood every minute. Blood leaves the liver through the *hepatic veins*, which empty into the inferior *vena cava*, a major vein leading

(15)　back to the heart. Both the portal vein and the hepatic artery branch side by side sequentially into smaller and smaller channels. At the very smallest level, they connect with each other forming capillaries known as *sinusoids*.

　　　The function of the liver can be divided into five categories: storing food substances and changing fat and protein into glucose sugar; regulating the amounts

(20)　of certain necessary substances in the bloodstream; removing poisons and other harmful materials from the body; manufacturing bile, the digestive juice needed for removing those unwanted materials; and renewing the liver, replacing the approximately 50 percent of all liver cells that die each six months. Considering all the functions it performs, the liver is indeed one of the most indispensable human

(25)　organs.

1. What is the main topic of the passage?

   (A)　The replacement of cells

   (B)　The human liver

   (C)　Important human organs

   (D)　The function of the liver　　　　Ⓐ Ⓑ Ⓒ Ⓓ

2. What aspect of the human liver does the author mainly discuss in the first paragraph?

   (A)　Its various operations

   (B)　Its physical description

   (C)　Its value for survival

   (D)　Its location within the body　　　Ⓐ Ⓑ Ⓒ Ⓓ

3. In paragraph 2, the author primarily discusses which of the following?

   (A)　The shape of the blood vessels in the liver

   (B)　The liver's circulation system

   (C)　The amount of blood pumped within the liver

   (D)　The liver's capacity to regenerate itself　　Ⓐ Ⓑ Ⓒ Ⓓ

4. Which of the following questions does paragraph 3 answer?

   (A)　How many parts does the liver have?

   (B)　What is the purpose of the liver?

   (C)　How does the body function without a liver?

   (D)　Where does blood flow within the liver?　　Ⓐ Ⓑ Ⓒ Ⓓ

5. Which of the following best characterizes the organization of paragraph 3?

   (A)　A generalization followed by specific examples

   (B)　A cause followed by its effects

   (C)　A list of definitions

   (D)　A classification scheme　　　　　Ⓐ Ⓑ Ⓒ Ⓓ

173

6. What does the paragraph preceding the passage probably discuss?

    (A) The human skeletal structure

    (B) Internal organs of invertebrates

    (C) The liver in other vertebrate species

    (D) Chemical reactions within the liver   Ⓐ Ⓑ Ⓒ Ⓓ

練習問題　解答・解説　▶▶▶

問題文訳

パラグラフ1　他の脊椎動物と同様，ヒトの肝臓は生命維持に不可欠であり，体内ではすぐれた「化学工場」と考えることができる。肝臓はヒトの臓器の中で最大で，健康な成人の体重の2%から3%を占める。色は赤茶色で気泡ゴム程度の堅さを有し，形は三側面のピラミッド型である。肝臓は腹腔の右側に位置し，胸郭に包まれている。胆汁を貯蔵する小さな袋状組織である胆のうは，部分的に肝臓の底面の裏に埋め込まれた形になっている。同様に大腸と小腸，胃もまた肝臓に接触している。肝臓は2つの葉に分かれており，右葉は左葉の約6倍の大きさである。

パラグラフ2　肝臓には血液供給源が2つある。「門脈」は胃，腸，脾臓から静脈血を運ぶ。「肝動脈」は心臓から酸素を含んだ血液を運んでくる。これら2つの血管が肝臓に毎分約1.2リットルの血液を供給している。血液は「肝静脈」を通って肝臓を離れ，心臓に戻る大静脈である「下大静脈」に流れていく。門脈と肝動脈は隣り合い，どちらもさらに細かく枝分かれしている。最小レベルでは，それらは互いに結びつき，「類洞（シヌソイド）」の名で知られる毛細血管を形成する。

パラグラフ3　肝臓の機能は5つに分類することができる。その機能とは，食物から得た物質の貯蔵および脂肪とタンパク質からのブドウ糖生成，血中における必要な物質の量の調整，毒素や他の有害な物質の排出，好ましくない物質を取り除くために必要な消化液である胆汁の生成，6か月ごとに死滅する約50%の肝細胞の入れ替えである。その全機能を考えると，ヒトの器官のなかで，肝臓は欠くことのできないもののひとつであると言える。

1.

訳 このパッセージの主なトピックは何ですか。

(A) 細胞の入れ替え　　　　　　　　　　(C) 重要なヒトの諸器官

(B) ヒトの肝臓　　　　　　　　　　　　(D) 肝臓の機能

解法 パッセージの主要なポイントを問う問題。主な話題は冒頭から示されているように，the human liver「ヒトの肝臓」であり，正解は (B)。肝臓の機能だけではなく，構造も述べているので，(D) は正解ではない。

2.

訳 パラグラフ 1 で著者はヒトの肝臓のどのような点を主に論じていますか。

(A) その多様な働き　　　　　　　　　　(C) 生存するために果たす価値

(B) その物質的描写　　　　　　　　　　(D) 体内のその位置

解法 パラグラフの主要なポイントを問う問題。パラグラフ 1 では肝臓の大きさ，色，堅さ，形状，位置などを述べているので，正解は (B)。

3.

訳 パラグラフ 2 で著者は次のどれを主に論じていますか。

(A) 肝臓内の血管の形　　　　　　　　　(C) 肝臓内に送り込まれる血液量

(B) 肝臓の循環系　　　　　　　　　　　(D) 肝臓の自己再生能力

解法 パラグラフの主要なポイントを問う問題。パラグラフ 2 は肝臓の血液循環系について述べているので，正解は (B)。

4.

訳 パラグラフ 3 は次のどの質問に答えていますか。

(A) 肝臓にはいくつの部分があるか。　　(C) 体は肝臓なしにいかに機能するか。

(B) 肝臓の目的は何か。　　　　　　　　(D) 血液は肝臓内のどこを流れるか。

解法 パラグラフの主要なポイントを問う問題。パラグラフ 3 は肝臓の 5 つの機能について述べているので，正解は (B)。

5.

訳 パラグラフ 3 の構成を最もよく特徴づけているのは次のどれですか。

(A) 概括とその具体例　　　　　　　　　(C) 定義の列挙

(B) ある原因とその結果　　　　　　　　(D) 分類体系

解法 パラグラフの構成に関する問題。パラグラフ 3 は，「肝臓の機能は 5 つに分類することができる」という文で始まり，その後に各機能を解説しているので，正解は (D)。

6.

訳 このパッセージの前のパラグラフではおそらく何を論じていますか。

(A) ヒトの骨格構造　　　　　　　　　(C) 他の脊椎動物の肝臓

(B) 非脊椎動物の内部器官　　　　　　(D) 肝臓内の化学反応

解法 前パラグラフの内容を推測する問題。このパッセージの最初に Just as in other vertebrates, the human liver is essential to life「他の脊椎動物と同様，ヒトの肝臓は生命維持に不可欠である」とあるので，その前には他の脊椎動物の肝臓について述べていることが推測できる。正解は (C)。

重要語
- □ **vertebrate**「脊椎動物」
- □ **liver**「肝臓」
- □ **organ**「器官，臓器」
- □ **consistency**「堅さ，濃度，密度」
- □ **foam rubber**「気泡ゴム」
- □ **abdominal**「腹部の」
- □ **rib cage**「胸郭」
- □ **pouch**「嚢，小袋」

- □ **bile**「胆汁」
- □ **intestine**「腸」
- □ **venous blood**「静脈血」
- □ **spleen**「脾臓」
- □ **blood vessel**「血管」
- □ **capillary**「毛細血管」
- □ **digestive**「消化の；消化剤」
- □ **indispensable**
  「欠かすことのできない，不可欠な」

2.　頻出設問タイプ ③④⑤

【設問タイプ ③】　パッセージに記述されている情報を問う設問

◆　「パッセージ [パラグラフ] によれば～はいつ [何・どこ] ですか」

　文中で述べている情報を問う設問。該当する情報がパッセージのどこにあるのかをすばやく把握することで，解答時間を短縮することができる。

　このタイプの設問に答えるには，設問中のキーワードと同じ語または同意語をパッセージから探し出し，その前後を読み，必要な情報を得て答えを選ぶ，いわゆる「スキャニング」が有効である。たとえば According to the passage, where did the blues begin? という設問の場合，キーワードである the blues，begin に注目してパッセージをすばやくスキャンし，the blues や begin，同意語の start，originate などを探し出すことで解答時間を短縮し，効率よく答えることができる。

設問例

□ When did *the most drastic innovation occur in the printing industry*?

□ Which of the following does the author mention was *the main reason for the decline in the national economy during the 1930s*?

□ According to the passage, what is *unusual about the way a raptorial bird captures its prey*?

□ According to the passage [paragraph 2], *chimpanzee society resembles that of humans* in which of the following ways?

□ In paragraph 3, the author compares a *genome* to which of the following?

□ The main difference between *the male and female mouse* is ...

最重要ストラテジー ▶▶▶

【設問タイプ 4】　パッセージに記述されていない情報を問う設問

◆ 「次のうち，パッセージ［パラグラフ］で述べられていないのはどれですか」
....
　【設問タイプ 3】 とは逆に，文中に記述されていない選択肢を選ぶ設問で，多くは NOT
や EXCEPT を設問中に含む。

　このタイプの設問では，"A, B, and C" のような並列構文に情報が集まっていれば，記述
されていない点を探すのは容易である。まずは and や or など列挙の表現に注目し，その前後
を重点的に確認するとよい。並列構文に情報が列挙されていない場合は簡単に答えが見つか
らないので，答えるのは後回しにして，先に他の問題を解答し，情報を収集してから解くよ
うにする。

**　設問例**

　□ Which of the following is NOT mentioned *as a major characteristic of vertebrates*?

　□ The author mentions all of the following *attributes of minerals* EXCEPT ...

　□ Which of the following is NOT referred to as *being one purpose of propaganda*?

　□ According to the author, which is the LEAST *effective method of preventing
the common cold*?

最重要ストラテジー ▶▶▶

【設問タイプ 5】　指定された内容を表すパラグラフを選ぶ設問

◆ 「著者が〜を述べているのはどのパラグラフですか」
....
　ある内容がパッセージのどこに述べられているかを探し出す設問。

　【設問タイプ 3】 と同様に，設問中のキーワードと同じ語，または同意語を文中から探すこ
とで解答できる。

**　設問例**

　□ Where in the passage does the author classify *the changes that matter
undergoes*?

　□ In which paragraph does the author point out *the importance of journalism*?

Line

(1)   A very long and bitter scientific battle over one of the world's most important food crops, ordinary corn, has finally been resolved. Recent genetic analysis has solved the contentious riddle of where corn came from. Although most people don't fret much over where and how corn originated, among archaeologists and plant *(5)* scientists the history of maize—one ancient form of corn—has been an important, long-standing, and tangled mystery. The results of the genetic testing suggest that corn's direct ancestor is a weedy type of grass called "teosinte," which can still be found growing wild in remote areas of Mexico.

   Before the genetic evidence at last put the feud to rest, the argument raged for *(10)* more than half a century, with one camp arguing in teosinte's favor, and another camp, led by Harvard researchers, contending that corn's ancestors were in fact varieties of early domesticated maize. The Harvard researchers found old samples of primitive corncobs and pollen in remote Mexican caves and concluded that these were the earliest versions of domesticated corn, dating from around 7,000 years ago. The *(15)* scenario they constructed was that corn's direct and immediate ancestor was a very primitive corn plant that disappeared into extinction from two to five thousand years ago, never to be found. In other words, it turns out that corn was corn, not an offspring of teosinte.

   For agriculture, the outcome of the argument over the origin of corn is more *(20)* important than one might assume. Today's corn breeders, for example, need to study corn's ancient ancestors to search for additional genes that might improve the plant's hardiness and resistance to drought and disease. Such genes, if they exist, are most likely present in corn's ancient and stronger progenitors.

   In addition to helping plant scientists improve future breeds of corn, the *(25)* tracing of corn to its origin in teosinte also gives archaeologists an interesting piece to an ancient puzzle; that is, how such large civilizations were able to flourish in antiquity in Central America. They now suspect that people began harvesting grain from wild teosinte as early as 10,000 years ago.

7. What form of research solved the riddle of corn's origin?

 (A) Genetic testing

 (B) Plant breeding

 (C) Archaeological fieldwork

 (D) Comparative botany   Ⓐ Ⓑ Ⓒ Ⓓ

8. According to the passage, which of the following is corn's direct ancestor?

 (A) Primitive corncobs

 (B) An early domesticated grain

 (C) Maize found in Mexico

 (D) A type of wild grass   Ⓐ Ⓑ Ⓒ Ⓓ

9. According to the passage, when did the early American people likely first consume corn-like grain?

 (A) 2,000 years ago

 (B) 5,000 years ago

 (C) 7,000 years ago

 (D) 10,000 years ago   Ⓐ Ⓑ Ⓒ Ⓓ

10. Which of the following is NOT mentioned in the passage as an improvement plant scientists hope to make in future varieties of corn?

 (A) Overall strength

 (B) Need for water

 (C) Disease resistance

 (D) Grain yield   Ⓐ Ⓑ Ⓒ Ⓓ

Section I Part A/B　Section I Part C　Section 2　Section 3　総合模試　総合模試 解答・解説

11. Where in the passage does the author refer to the length of the dispute over the origin of corn?

(A) Paragraph 1

(B) Paragraph 2

(C) Paragraph 3

(D) Paragraph 4   Ⓐ Ⓑ Ⓒ Ⓓ

12. Why are archaeologists interested in the origin of corn?

(A) Corn cultivation may have influenced the political structure of early civilizations.

(B) The adoption of agriculture may have changed early peoples' religious beliefs.

(C) The consumption of corn may explain how some ancient societies prospered.

(D) The breeding of corn may have first been undertaken in Central America.

Ⓐ Ⓑ Ⓒ Ⓓ

13. In which paragraph does the author most fully discuss the competing theories for the origin of corn?

(A) Paragraph 1

(B) Paragraph 2

(C) Paragraph 3

(D) Paragraph 4   Ⓐ Ⓑ Ⓒ Ⓓ

14. The passage answers which of the following questions?

(A) Where did corn come from?

(B) What farming methods were used to grow corn?

(C) How reliable is corn as a crop?

(D) Why did primitive corn die out?   Ⓐ Ⓑ Ⓒ Ⓓ

練習問題　解答・解説　▶▶▶

問題文訳

パラグラフ1　世界で最も重要な食用農作物のひとつであるトウモロコシに関するとても長く辛辣な科学論争は，ついに決着した。最近の遺伝子解析が，トウモロコシがどこから来たのかという議論を呼ぶ謎を解いたのである。ほとんどの人は，トウモロコシがどこでどのように生まれたかについてそれほど悩みはしないが，考古学者や植物学者の間では，古いトウモロコシの一種であるメイズの歴史は重要で，長年にわたって紛糾した謎であった。遺伝子テストの結果，トウモロコシの直系の祖先は「ブタモロコシ」という雑草の一種であることがわかり，それはまだメキシコの人里離れた場所で自生している。

パラグラフ2　遺伝学的に証明されて争いに区切りがつくまで，議論は半世紀以上にわたって白熱した。その中であるグループはブタモロコシ説を唱え，ハーバード大学の研究者たちによる別の一派は，トウモロコシの祖先は早期に栽培化したメイズ種だと論じた。ハーバード大学の研究者は，原始的なトウモロコシの穂軸や花粉のサンプルをメキシコの人里離れた洞窟で発見し，これが栽培種になったトウモロコシの最初の種類で，7,000年ほど前のものであると結論づけた。彼らの書いたシナリオは，トウモロコシの直系直近の祖先は非常に原始的なトウモロコシで，2,000年から5,000年前に絶滅したため発見できないというものだった。言い換えれば，トウモロコシはもともとトウモロコシであって，ブタモロコシの子孫ではないということである。

パラグラフ3　農業にとって，トウモロコシの起源に関する論争の結論は思いのほか重要である。例えば，現在のトウモロコシ栽培者は，トウモロコシの強さや，干ばつ，病気に対する抵抗力を改善する追加遺伝子を探すために，トウモロコシの祖先の研究をしなければならない。そうした遺伝子がもし存在するのなら，それは古くてもっと強いトウモロコシの原種の中に見つかる可能性が最も高い。

パラグラフ4　トウモロコシを祖先のブタモロコシまでさかのぼって追跡することは，植物学者がこの先トウモロコシの品種改良をする際に役立つばかりでなく，考古学者が古代の謎を解き明かす興味深いヒントにもなる。すなわちそれは，いかにして古代中央アメリカであれほど大きな文明が栄えることができたのかということである。人類は1万年も前に，野生のブタモロコシから穀物の収穫を始めたのではないかと，学者たちは現在考えている。

7.　　　　　　　　　　　　　　　　　　　　　　　　　　　　　　　　　　解答：A

訳　トウモロコシの起源の謎を解き明かしたのはどのようなタイプの研究でしたか。

(A) 遺伝子テスト　　　　　　　　　　　　(C) 考古学的フィールドワーク
(B) 植物栽培　　　　　　　　　　　　　　(D) 比較植物学

解法　記述されている情報を問う問題。パラグラフ1に Recent genetic analysis has solved the contentious riddle of where corn came from. 「最近の遺伝子解析が，トウモロコシがどこから来たのかという議論を呼ぶ謎を解いた」とあるので，正解は (A)。設問中のキーワード solve, riddle に注目して，文中に類似表現を探すことで，すばやく解答できる。

183

8.　　　　　　　　　　　　　　　　　　　　　　　　　　　　　　　　　　　　　　　解答：D

訳　パッセージによれば，次のうちトウモロコシの直系の祖先はどれですか。

(A) 原始的なトウモロコシの穂軸　　　　　(C) メキシコで見つかったメイズ
(B) 早くから栽培植物化された穀物　　　　(D) 雑草の一種

解法　記述されている情報を問う問題。設問中のキーワード direct ancestor に注目してパッセージを
スキャンすると，パラグラフ 1 に The results of the genetic testing suggest that corn's direct
ancestor is a weedy type of grass called "teosinte," 「トウモロコシの直系の祖先はブタモロコ
シという雑草の一種」の一文が見つかる。正解は (D)。

9.　　　　　　　　　　　　　　　　　　　　　　　　　　　　　　　　　　　　　　解答：D

訳　パッセージによれば，初期のアメリカ人が最初にトウモロコシに似た穀物を食べたのはいつだ
と思われますか。

(A) 2,000 年前　　　　　　　　　　　　(C) 7,000 年前
(B) 5,000 年前　　　　　　　　　　　　(D) 1 万年前

解法　推測に関する問題。パラグラフ 4 に「人類は 1 万年も前に，野生のブタモロコシから穀物の収
穫を始めたのではないかと，学者たちは現在考えている」とあるので，このときに人類がトウ
モロコシの祖先を食べたのではないかと考えられる。正解は (D)。

10.　　　　　　　　　　　　　　　　　　　　　　　　　　　　　　　　　　　　　解答：D

訳　植物学者が将来トウモロコシの品種改良で改善したいと考えている点として，パッセージの中
で述べられていないものは次のどれですか。

(A) 総合的な強さ　　　　　　　　　　　(C) 病気に対する抵抗力
(B) 水の必要性　　　　　　　　　　　　(D) 穀物の収穫量

解法　記述されていない情報を問う問題。パラグラフ 3 に品種改良の可能性のある項目として the
plant's hardiness and resistance to drought and disease の 3 点が述べられており，それぞれ
(A)(B)(C) に対応している。ここに収穫量は含まれていない。正解は (D)。

11.　　　　　　　　　　　　　　　　　　　　　　　　　　　　　　　　　　　　　解答：B

訳　パッセージのどこで著者はトウモロコシの起源についての論争の長さを述べていますか。

(A) パラグラフ 1　　　　　　　　　　　(C) パラグラフ 3
(B) パラグラフ 2　　　　　　　　　　　(D) パラグラフ 4

解法　指定された内容を表すパラグラフを選ぶ問題。設問の dispute をキーワードとして，類似の表
現と議論の「長さ」を表す文をすばやくスキャンする。パラグラフ 2 最初の argument, for
more than half a century を含み，「遺伝学的に証明されて争いに区切りがつくまで，議論は半
世紀以上にわたって白熱した」を表す文が該当するので，正解は (B)。

》Before the genetic evidence at last put the feud to rest, the argument raged for more than half a
century, with one camp arguing in teosinte's favor, and another camp, led by Harvard
researchers, contending that corn's ancestors were in fact varieties of early domesticated maize.

12. 解答：C

訳 なぜ考古学者はトウモロコシの起源に興味を持つのですか。

(A) トウモロコシ栽培は古代文明の政治構造に影響を与えたかもしれない。
(B) 農業を取り入れたことが古代人の宗教信仰を変えたかもしれない。
(C) トウモロコシの消費は古代社会がどのように繁栄したかを説明するかもしれない。
(D) トウモロコシの栽培は中央アメリカで始まったのかもしれない。

解法 記述されている情報を問う問題。考古学者 archaeologists に関する記述はパラグラフ 4 にある。how such large civilizations were able to flourish in antiquity in Central America「いかにして古代中央アメリカであれほど大きな文明が栄えることができたのか」を知るヒントは，トウモロコシをさかのぼって追跡することで得られるので，(C) が正解となる。

13. 解答：B

訳 トウモロコシの起源についての競合する理論を著者が最も詳しく論じているのは，どのパラグラフですか。

(A) パラグラフ 1
(B) パラグラフ 2
(C) パラグラフ 3
(D) パラグラフ 4

解法 指定された内容を表すパラグラフを選ぶ問題。パラグラフ 2 で with one camp ... and another camp ...「あるグループは～また別の一派は～」と競合する理論を対比形で述べている。feud, argument などの語もヒントとなる。正解は (B)。

14. 解答：A

訳 パッセージは次のどの問いに答えていますか。

(A) トウモロコシはどこから来たのか。
(B) トウモロコシを栽培するのにどのような農法が使われたか。
(C) トウモロコシは穀物としてどの程度信頼性があるのか。
(D) 昔のトウモロコシはなぜ絶滅したのか。

解法 パッセージの主要なポイントを問う問題。最初に「トウモロコシがどこから来たのかという議論を呼ぶ謎を解いたのである」とあり，以下にその経緯と内容を述べている。正解は (A)。

重要語
- **genetic**「遺伝子の，発生の」
- **contentious**「議論を起こす」
- **fret**「やきもきする，いらいらする」
- **originate**「起源となる，起こる，生じる」
- **archaeologist**「考古学者」
- **tangled**「もつれた，紛糾した」
- **remote**「人里離れた，遠方の」
- **feud**「確執，争い」
- **camp**「グループ」
- **pollen**「花粉」
- **offspring**「子孫，成果」
- **progenitor**「原種，祖先」
- **antiquity**「古代」

3.　頻出設問タイプ 6 7

【設問タイプ 6】　推測に関する設問

◆　「パッセージから何が推測できますか」

　　「次のうち，著者が賛成すると思われる意見はどれですか」

　　解答が直接パッセージ中には述べられておらず，推測が必要となる設問。

　推測や含みに関する設問は【設問タイプ 3】と重複する部分もあるが，いっそう総合的な読解力が必要である。解答にはパッセージの適切な部分を見つけ，ポイントを総合的に理解するよう注意して読む。パッセージ全体に関係する推測問題は，他の問題に答えてから取り組むとよい。それにより追加の情報を得ることができ，推測問題の答えを探し出すことができる場合がある。

設問例

　□ It can be inferred from the passage that ...

　□ The author implies that ...

　□ It can be concluded from the passage that ...

　□ Which of the following generalizations is supported by the passage?

　□ Which of the following statements best reflects *the author's impression of the Hudson River School artists*?

　□ With which of the following statements would the author most likely agree?

　□ The passage supports which of the following statements?

　□ In which paragraph does the author most clearly express an opinion?

最重要ストラテジー▶▶▶

【設問タイプ 7 】　著者の論調・立場・態度に関する設問

◆　「著者はどのような立場で論じていますか」

「次のうち，著者の論調・立場・態度を最もよく表すのはどれですか」

パッセージから読みとれる，主題に対する著者の論調・立場・態度を問う設問。

　この種の設問に答えるためには，文中に見られる著者の態度を表す形容詞や副詞がヒントとなる。たとえば文中に without doubt，definitely など断定的な表現が使われていれば，著者は強くその事実を肯定，主張していることがわかり，態度も熱心であることが読みとれるだろう。逆にそうした論調を表す表現が見られない場合には，客観的で中立的な立場をとっていると考えられる。

設問例

☐ The tone of this passage could best be described as ...

☐ Which of the following best describes the author's tone in the passage?

☐ What is the author's attitude toward *the claim that gender is correlated with mathematical ability*?

☐ Where would this passage most likely appear?（まれ）

☐ To which profession does the author probably belong?（まれ）

Line

(1)　　The nations of Europe that colonized the Western Hemisphere attempted to replicate the educational institutions in their homelands. The first universities in the Americas, regardless of whether they were located in French, British, or Spanish colonies, had as their main curriculum a focus on the classics, without neglecting the

(5)　study of emerging new sciences. They were based on the assumption of residential living for undergraduates and comprised a pattern of structured courses of study leading to examinations and the conferring of recognized degrees.

　　In what was to become the United States, nine colonial colleges had been founded by the time of the Revolutionary War. All of these were religious in

(10)　orientation. Even though not all graduates were destined for the ministry, the extracurricular life of students was governed by strict Christian principles of behavior—mandatory attendance at chapel services, rigorous study of the Bible, and corporal punishment for infractions of the code of conduct.

　　The president of the college was almost always a member of the clergy, as were

(15)　the vast majority of his top administrative officials, and all faculty members felt their duty was to educate both the mind and the soul, doing so in the spirit of *in loco parentis*, the notion that to a great extent educators were required to serve as surrogate parents during the young person's university years.

　　Yet the early universities were not simply religious training grounds. A

(20)　combination of secular and religious studies was thought in those days to be the best preparation for the future colonial elite. And it is in this "elite" sense that colonial colleges were not popular institutions—they touched the daily lives of very few average colonists, though they did train a disproportionate number of those who eventually governed the new nation which emerged from the colonial period.

15. What is the main purpose of this passage?

(A) To outline the creation of the first North American university

(B) To show how much the colonial powers valued higher education

(C) To describe the system of higher education during the colonial period

(D) To explain the role of colonial universities in the American Revolution

Ⓐ Ⓑ Ⓒ Ⓓ

16. It can be inferred from the passage that universities in the French colonies of North America would have been

(A) substantially different from their counterparts in British colonies

(B) mainly concerned with the study of the newly developed sciences

(C) primarily intended for those who would pursue degrees in theology

(D) essentially modeled after universities in their mother country

Ⓐ Ⓑ Ⓒ Ⓓ

17. Where in the passage does the author mention the number of universities prior to America's War of Independence?

(A) Paragraph 1

(B) Paragraph 2

(C) Paragraph 3

(D) Paragraph 4

Ⓐ Ⓑ Ⓒ Ⓓ

18. During colonial times, which would NOT be assumed to be part of university students' experience?

(A) They would be required to go to church on a regular basis.

(B) Their teachers would occasionally administer physical punishment.

(C) They would be obliged to reside on the university campus.

(D) Their classmates would be representative of colonial society as a whole.

Ⓐ Ⓑ Ⓒ Ⓓ

19. It can be inferred from the passage that most colonial university administrators

   (A) had been ordained as Christian ministers

   (B) were appointed to their positions by the Church

   (C) believed in the separation of Church and State

   (D) advocated the establishment of secular colleges   Ⓐ Ⓑ Ⓒ Ⓓ

20. What aspect of colonial university education does the author discuss in paragraph 3?

   (A) The philosophy of the teachers

   (B) The practicality of the courses

   (C) The accomplishments of the students

   (D) The funding of the institutions   Ⓐ Ⓑ Ⓒ Ⓓ

21. How can the author's view of colonial universities best be described?

   (A) Sarcastic

   (B) Objective

   (C) Provocative

   (D) Offensive   Ⓐ Ⓑ Ⓒ Ⓓ

練習問題　解答・解説　▶▶▶

問題文訳

（ パラグラフ1 ）　西半球を植民地化したヨーロッパ諸国は，自国の教育機関を複製しようと試みた。アメリカ大陸における初期の大学は，フランス，イギリス，スペインのいずれの植民地にあったかにかかわらず，主要なカリキュラムとして古典を取り入れていたし，新しい学問の研究を怠ることもなかった。これらの大学では学部生は宿舎に住むこととされ，体系化された学習の後，試験を行い，認定学位の授与という形式になっていた。

（ パラグラフ2 ）　のちにアメリカ合衆国となった場所では，独立戦争までに9つの植民地大学が設立された。これらはすべて宗教的な色合いが濃かった。卒業生全員が聖職者になったわけではないが，学生の課外生活は，義務づけられた礼拝出席，厳しい聖書の学習，行動規範を破った際の体罰など，厳格なキリスト教的行動規範により管理されていた。

（ パラグラフ3 ）　大学の学長はほとんどの場合聖職者で，役員の大多数も同様であった。全教員は，「親代わり」の精神で，心と魂の両方を教育することが自分たちの義務であると感じていた。親代わりの精神とは，若者が大学にいる間，教育者は代理親としての役目を十分に果たす必要があるという考えであった。

（ パラグラフ4 ）　しかし初期の大学は，ただ単に宗教的な鍛錬の場所であったわけではない。非宗教的学問と宗教的学問を学ぶことが植民地で将来エリートになるためには最善だと当時は考えられていた。この「エリート」養成の意味で，植民地大学は一般的ではなかった。大学は，ほとんどの平均的入植者の日常生活に関係なかったのである。そうは言っても大学は，植民地時代後の新国家をやがて治めた人々を数多く教育する結果となった。

15.　　　　　　　　　　　　　　　　　　　　　　　　　　　　　　　　　　　　　解答：C

訳　このパッセージの主な目的は何ですか。
(A) 北米における最初の大学の創立について概略を述べること
(B) 植民地支配者がどれだけ高等教育を重視していたかを示すこと
(C) 植民地時代における高等教育体制を述べること
(D) アメリカ独立革命での植民地大学の役割を説明すること

解法　パッセージの主要なポイントを問う問題。このパッセージでは，植民地時代の大学のカリキュラム，宗教に基礎を置いた大学の行動規範，大学教員の背景などを述べている。植民地時代の高等教育体制に関する文章なので，正解は (C)。最初の問題ではあるが，読み進めないと答えを見つけにくいので，最後に答えることが望ましい。

16.   解答：D

パッセージから，北米にあったフランス植民地の大学はどうだったと推測できますか。

(A) イギリス植民地の大学とは大きく異なっていた

(B) 主に新しく発展した学問を扱っていた

(C) 本来は神学の学位を取りたい人向きだった

(D) 本質的に本国の大学をモデルに作られた

解法 推測に関する問題。パラグラフ 1 の初めに regardless of whether they were located in French, British, or Spanish colonies としたうえで，「自国の教育機関を複製しようと試みた」と述べている。フランスも植民地である北米の大学を本国のそれと同じようにしようと試みたと推測できるので，正解は (D)。

---

17.   解答：B

訳 パッセージのどこで著者はアメリカ独立戦争前の大学数について述べていますか。

(A) パラグラフ 1   (C) パラグラフ 3

(B) パラグラフ 2   (D) パラグラフ 4

解法 指定された内容を表すパラグラフを選ぶ問題。アメリカ独立戦争前の大学数は，パラグラフ 2 の In what was to become the United States, nine colonial colleges had been founded by the time of the Revolutionary War. の中の nine colonial colleges，Revolutionary War を見つけることができれば，正解は (B) であることがわかる。

---

18.   解答：D

訳 植民地時代に大学生が経験しなかったと思われるものはどれですか。

(A) 定期的に教会へ行くことを求められた。

(B) 教師はときどき体罰を加えた。

(C) 大学のキャンパス内に住まなければならなかった。

(D) 同級生は植民社会全体を代表するような人々であった。

解法 推測に関する問題。学生の経験したこととして，パラグラフ 1 では① residential living for undergraduates，パラグラフ 2 では② mandatory attendance at chapel services，③ corporal punishment が述べられており，それぞれ (C) (A) (B) に対応している。しかし，パラグラフ 4 では「大学は，ほとんどの平均的な入植者の日常生活に関係なかった」とあるので，同級生は植民社会の平均的な人々ではなかったと推測される。正解は (D)。

19.

訳 パッセージから，ほとんどの植民地大学管理者はどうだったと推測できますか。

(A) キリスト教聖職者として聖職位を授けられていた

(B) 教会から大学での役職の任命を受けていた

(C) 政教分離を支持していた

(D) 非宗教的な大学の設立を唱えた

解法 推測に関する問題。パラグラフ3の最初に「大学の学長はほとんどの場合聖職者で，役員の大多数も同様であった」とある。聖職者は通常聖職位を授けられるので，大学管理者も聖職位を授けられていたことが暗に示されている。正解は (A)。

20.

訳 パラグラフ3で著者は植民地大学教育のどのような点を論じていますか。

(A) 教員の哲学　　　　　　　　　　(C) 学生の業績

(B) 科目の実用性　　　　　　　　　(D) 大学の資金

解法 パラグラフの主要なポイントを問う問題。全教員は「親代わり」の精神で，心と魂の両方を教育することが自分たちの義務であるとの考えを持っていたので，正解は (A)。

21.

訳 植民地大学に対する著者の立場を最もよく表しているのはどれですか。

(A) 皮肉っぽい　　　　　　　　　　(C) 挑発的

(B) 客観的　　　　　　　　　　　　(D) 攻撃的

解法 著者の立場に関する問題。著者は，植民地大学に関して賞賛や皮肉など自らの立場を示す語句を使わず，客観的に大学について述べている。正解は (B)。

重要語
- **replicate**「〜を複製する，繰り返す」
- **emerging**「新生の，現れた」
- **on the assumption of** ...「〜という仮定のもとで」
- **undergraduate**「(大学の) 学部学生」
- **the Revolutionary War**「アメリカ独立戦争」
- **be destined for** ...「〜することになっている，〜する運命にある」
- **ministry**「聖職者」
- **extracurricular**「課程外の」
- **mandatory**「強制的な，義務的な」
- **rigorous**「厳格な」
- **corporal**「肉体の」
- **infraction**「違反」
- **code**「規約，規範」
- **clergy**「聖職者，牧師」
- **faculty**「教員，学部教授」
- *in loco parentis*「親代わりに」
- **surrogate**「代理」
- **secular**「非宗教的な，世俗の」
- **disproportionate**「不釣り合いな」

4.　頻出設問タイプ 8 9

【設問タイプ 8 】　語彙に関する設問

◆　「〜行目の＊＊という単語に最も意味の近い語はどれですか」

　語彙問題のわからない語については，文脈から推測し，接頭辞，接尾辞，語幹に関する知識を使うなどの工夫が必要である。意味だけでなく，コロケーションや文脈における適切さを考えて答えを選ばなければならない。

設問例

- ☐ The word "*ranged*" in line 16 is closest in meaning to
- ☐ What does "*impel*" in line 7 mean?
- ☐ In line 10, the phrase "*this notion*" suggests that ...
- ☐ In line 13, the term "*colonial period*" implies that ...
- ☐ In line 15, the word "*stringent*" could best be replaced with which of the following?

Section I Part A/B　Section I Part C　Section 2　Section 3　総合模試　総合模試 解答・解説

最重要ストラテジー ▶▶▶

【設問タイプ ❾】　語法に関する設問

◆　単語・フレーズが指す対象を問う設問

「次のうち，～行目の it が指しているのはどれですか」

◆　修辞上の効果を問う設問

「著者はなぜ "＊＊" という語に引用符を用いているのですか」

代名詞や名詞，指示詞が文中のどの語を指しているかを問う設問。また，特殊な問題として，引用符などの修辞上の効果を問う設問もある。

パッセージを読みながら，代名詞なら数や性別が一致している語を探し，代名詞の代わりに当てはめて正しいかどうかを確認する必要がある。代名詞はそれが指す語より前に置かれることもあるので注意が必要である。

設問例

🐾 単語・フレーズが指す対象を問う設問

☐ In line 15, to which of the following does the word "It" refer?

☐ In line 10, the word "there" [they/them/their/other/another/one] refers to ...

☐ The phrase *"the task"* in line 4 refers to ...

🐾 修辞上の効果を問う設問

☐ The word *"instinct"* is put in quotation marks because ...

☐ The phrase *"the facts"* is put in quotation marks for which of the following reasons?

Line

(1)　　　Anthropomorphism is the assigning of human attributes to beings that are not human or to objects in nature or to abstract phenomena. Examples of this can be found in the phrases "wise old owls," "cunning foxes," "furious storms," and "fickle fate." Anthropomorphism is used as a technical term in anthropology, psychology,

(5)　intercultural communication, linguistics, and the study of literature. It is an important term in theology and mythology as well because people often speak of gods as having human traits. The ancient Greeks and Romans depicted their gods and goddesses as having human form and carrying on many human activities, including feasting, feuding with one another, and intervening in wars. The

(10)　characteristics of gods often reflected human interests and needs. For instance, the Greek goddess Demeter was often portrayed as a matronly woman associated with the cycle of the seasons and the growth of crops that the people needed for food. Such anthropomorphism can be considered a response to the human need to explain mysterious forces and events in terms of the human experience. Anthropomorphic

(15)　symbols are frequently found in secular literature as well. An author may write of the "wrathful sea," or the "rosy-fingered dawn." Animals with human qualities have been the main characters in fables and fairy tales for thousands of years, all the way from the fables of Aesop down to the animation of Disney. The popularity of animated cartoons, such as Mickey Mouse, gives a clear example of the willingness of the

(20)　public to accept anthropomorphic figures.

　　　The phenomenon of anthropomorphism is of great interest to specialists as an illustration of the way humans view the world which exists around them. By examining which entities and phenomena are imbued with which human traits, researchers can gain insight into the perception of reality by members of a given

(25)　culture. In fact, this tendency to interpret animal behavior in human terms sometimes constitutes a problem in the conducting of psychological experiments in which animals are the subjects, since even the investigators themselves are not immune from this powerful force.

22. The word "attributes" in line 1 is closest in meaning to

   (A)　merits

   (B)　problems

   (C)　qualities

   (D)　vices   Ⓐ Ⓑ Ⓒ Ⓓ

23. In line 5, the word "It" refers to

   (A)　fickle fate

   (B)　anthropomorphism

   (C)　anthropology

   (D)　study of literature   Ⓐ Ⓑ Ⓒ Ⓓ

24. The word "feuding" in line 9 is closest in meaning to which of the following?

   (A)　Fighting

   (B)　Laughing

   (C)　Talking

   (D)　Eating   Ⓐ Ⓑ Ⓒ Ⓓ

25. In line 11, the word "portrayed" could best be replaced with which of the following?

   (A)　Criticized

   (B)　Admired

   (C)　Concealed

   (D)　Represented   Ⓐ Ⓑ Ⓒ Ⓓ

26. It can be inferred from the passage that because of anthropomorphism, scientific investigators

(A) may be reluctant to examine the results of animal experiments

(B) may lack objectivity in some of their experiments

(C) should avoid psychological experimentation

(D) should recognize that animals also exhibit cultural behavior

Ⓐ Ⓑ Ⓒ Ⓓ

27. The word "them" in line 22 refers to

(A) specialists

(B) humans

(C) entities

(D) human traits

Ⓐ Ⓑ Ⓒ Ⓓ

28. The word "given" in line 24 is closest in meaning to

(A) particular

(B) obtained

(C) allocated

(D) insular

Ⓐ Ⓑ Ⓒ Ⓓ

練習問題　解答・解説 ▶▶▶

問題文訳

パラグラフ1　擬人化とは，人間の特質を人間以外の生き物や自然界の事物，抽象的な事象に当てはめることである。この例は「賢い老フクロウ」「ずる賢い狐」「怒り狂う嵐」「気まぐれな運命」といった言葉に見られる。擬人化は人類学，心理学，異文化間コミュニケーション，言語学，そして文学研究において専門用語として使われる。それは神学や神話学においても同様に重要な用語だが，その理由は神が人間の特性を持っているかのようにしばしば語られるからである。古代ギリシャ人や古代ローマ人は，神や女神は人間の形をしており，祝宴を行ったり，互いに争ったり，戦争の調停をしたりと人間の多くの行動をとる存在として描写した。神々の特徴はしばしば人間の興味や欲求を反映した。例えばギリシャ神話の女神デメテルは，季節や人間に必要な食料である穀物の成長周期と結びつけて考えられ，品のある女性としてしばしば描写された。こうした擬人化は，人間が自分たちの経験において，不可思議な力や出来事を説明する必要性から生じた反応だと考えることもできる。擬人化表現は世俗的な文学でも頻繁に見られる。作家は「激怒した海」や「ばら色の指をした夜明け」のように書くこともある。人間の特徴を持った動物は，イソップ童話からディズニー映画に至るまで，寓話や童話の中で何千年もの間主役を務めてきた。ミッキーマウスのようなアニメの人気は，擬人化された姿を大衆は喜んで受け入れるということを示す明快な例である。

パラグラフ2　人間が自分の周りの世界をどのように見ているかを示すものとして，擬人化現象は専門家にとって非常に興味深いものである。研究者は，どのような事物や現象にどのような人間の特質が吹き込まれているかを調べることで，ある特定の文化に属する人々の現実認識について知見を得ることができる。実際，動物の行動を人間の世界に置き換えるこうした傾向は，研究者自身でさえもこの大きな影響力から免れられないため，動物を対象とした心理学実験を行う際，時々問題を引き起こすことがある。

22.

訳 1行目のattributesという語に最も意味が近い語はどれですか。

(A) 長所 　　　　　　　　　　　　　 (C) 特質

(B) 問題 　　　　　　　　　　　　　 (D) 悪

解法 語彙問題。「特質」を意味するattributesに近い意味の語はqualities「質，特質，性質」である。正解は(C)。

23.

訳 5行目のItは何を指していますか。

(A) 気まぐれな運命 　　　　　　　　 (C) 文化人類学

(B) 擬人化 　　　　　　　　　　　　 (D) 文学研究

解法 代名詞が指す対象を問う語法問題。Itは「それは神学や神話学においても同様に重要な用語」の中の「それ」であり，その前の文で述べられているさまざまな分野の専門用語として用いられている「擬人化」であることがわかる。正解は(B)。

24.

訳 次のうちで，9行目のfeudingという語に最も意味が近い語はどれですか。

(A) 戦うこと 　　　　　　　　　　　 (C) 話すこと

(B) 笑うこと 　　　　　　　　　　　 (D) 食べること

解法 語彙問題。「争い」を意味するfeudingに近い意味の語を選ぶ。feudingの意味がわからない場合，前後の語句に注意する。ここでは次に続く語句がintervening in wars「戦争の調停をする」であり，feudingは戦争に関係があるかもしれないと考えることができる。またwith one anotherもヒントになる。正解は(A)。

25.

訳 11行目のportrayedという語は次のどの語と最も適切に入れ換えることができますか。

(A) 批判された 　　　　　　　　　　 (C) 隠された

(B) 賞賛された 　　　　　　　　　　 (D) 描かれた

解法 語彙問題。「描写された」を意味するportrayedに近い意味の語はrepresented「描かれた，表された」である。正解は(D)。

26.　　　　　　　　　　　　　　　　　　　　　　　　　　　　　　解答：B

訳　パッセージから，擬人化があるため科学者について何が推測できますか。

(A) 動物実験の結果を考察したがらないかもしれない
(B) 実験の中には客観性を欠くものがあるかもしれない
(C) 心理学的な実験は避けるべきである
(D) 動物も文化的な行動をするということを認識するべきである

解法　推測に関する問題。パラグラフ 2 で，擬人化により ... sometimes constitutes a problem in the conducting of psychological experiments in which animals are the subjects, since even the investigators themselves are not immune from this powerful force.「研究者自身でさえもこの大きな影響力から免れられないため，動物を対象とした心理学実験を行う際，時々問題を引き起こすことがある」ことが指摘されている。研究者が動物の行動を人間の世界に置き換えることで，実験を客観的に考察できなくなるという問題が生じる可能性が推測されるので，正解は (B)。

27.　　　　　　　　　　　　　　　　　　　　　　　　　　　　　　解答：B

訳　22 行目の them は何を指していますか。

(A) 専門家
(B) 人間
(C) 実在するもの
(D) 人間の特質

解法　代名詞が指す対象を問う語法問題。the way humans view the world which exists around them「人間が自分の周りの世界をどのように見ているか」の中の them は，その前にある humans を指している。正解は (B)。

28.　　　　　　　　　　　　　　　　　　　　　　　　　　　　　　解答：A

訳　24 行目の given という語に最も意味が近い語はどれですか。

(A) 特定の
(B) 広く行われた
(C) 割り当てられた
(D) 島国の

解法　語彙問題。given には多くの意味があるが，ここでは culture を修飾する形容詞で「特定の」という意味になる。正解は (A)。

重要語

- **anthropomorphism**「擬人化」
- **assign**「〜を割り当てる」
- **attribute**「特質」
- **phenomena**「事象，現象」
- **technical term**「専門用語」
- **linguistics**「言語学」
- **mythology**「神話」
- **trait**「特質，特徴」

- **depict**「〜を描写する」
- **feast**「祝宴（を行う），ごちそう（を食べる）」
- **feud**「争う；争い」
- **matronly**「落ち着いた，品のある」
- **wrathful**「怒りに満ちた」
- **entity**「存在物，実体」
- **imbue**「〜を吹き込む」
- **immune**「免疫のある，免れる」

集中練習問題 **❶** 1題9問

BURST ONE

Line

(1)   Because of its close proximity to the Earth, the Moon is second only to the Sun in apparent size and brilliance. In astronomical terms, however, it is a common, small, and insignificant body. It generates no heat or radiance. Its only light is actually reflected sunlight.

(5)   The Moon's immense dark areas—easily seen by the naked eye—are called "maria" or "seas." They are huge flat plains made of fine, dark lava debris mixed with glass fragments and rocks. One theory for their existence is that they are the remains of terrific meteorite collisions billions of years ago when the Moon's interior was hot. The explosive impact would have caused great heat, melted the Moon's surface, and *(10)* released molten rock from the interior, forming the maria from lava. Another more recent theory, however, maintains that a meteorite collision would be more likely to pulverize rock than to melt it. Three probes which photographed the Moon in 1964 and 1965 increased speculation among scientists about whether the Moon's maria are composed primarily of volcanic ash, lava flows, dust, or some unknown material. In *(15)* the 1970s, however, analyses of rocks brought back to the Earth during manned United States space missions seemed to confirm the earlier theory.

    The Moon's brighter areas are mountains and craters. Tens of thousands of craters are scattered over the Moon's surface, often overlapping one another, and ranging in size from a single meter to 240 kilometers. As with the maria, astronomers *(20)* have long debated their origin. They may have been created by volcanoes, now extinct for billions of years. A more widely accepted current theory holds that they were caused both by showers of meteorites and by volcanic activity.

    For years scientists believed there was no trace of an atmosphere on the Moon. Astonishingly, there is now some evidence of an atmosphere, though it may be almost *(25)* too thin to measure. During an occultation of the Crab nebula, astronomers using a radio telescope at Cambridge University detected a slight bending of the rays of the nebula. This deflection could have been due to a thin lunar atmosphere.

The Moon does not follow a perfect circle in its path around the Earth, rather its orbit is a moderate ellipse. At perigee—when the Moon is nearest the Earth—its
(30) distance from the Earth's center is about 222,000 miles; when it reaches the opposite point—its apogee—the Moon is about 253,000 miles from the Earth's center. Recent high-tech measurements of the Moon's orbit have revealed an interesting fact—each year it is moving slightly farther away from us.

1. What is the main topic of the passage?

(A) The features of the Moon
(B) The Moon's interior
(C) The movement of the Moon
(D) The origin of the Moon   Ⓐ Ⓑ Ⓒ Ⓓ

2. According to the passage, the Moon appears to be an important heavenly body when viewed from the Earth because of

(A) its large size
(B) its nearness
(C) the light it produces
(D) the maria on its surface   Ⓐ Ⓑ Ⓒ Ⓓ

3. Which of the following is NOT mentioned as a quality of the Moon's maria?

(A) Their large size
(B) Their flatness
(C) Their brightness
(D) Their dustiness   Ⓐ Ⓑ Ⓒ Ⓓ

4. The word "primarily" in line 14 can best be replaced with which of the following?

(A) Completely
(B) Exclusively
(C) Principally
(D) Presumably   Ⓐ Ⓑ Ⓒ Ⓓ

5. To which of the following ideas does the phrase "the earlier theory" in line 16 refer to?

(A) That maria were caused by eruptions from the Moon's volcanoes

(B) That maria were created when the Moon's surface became liquefied

(C) That maria were one of the original natural features of the Moon

(D) That maria were formed through explosions in the interior of the Moon

Ⓐ Ⓑ Ⓒ Ⓓ

6. The word "extinct" in line 21 is closest in meaning to

(A) dead

(B) dormant

(C) erupting

(D) explosive

Ⓐ Ⓑ Ⓒ Ⓓ

7. What does the author imply is the most unusual recent discovery about the Moon?

(A) Its craters were formed by both meteorites and volcanic activity.

(B) Its surface temperature varies dramatically from day to night.

(C) It may possess a slight atmosphere.

(D) It has an erratic orbit around the Earth.

Ⓐ Ⓑ Ⓒ Ⓓ

8. Which of the following is the best description of the Moon's orbit?

(A) An extreme ellipse

(B) A modest oval

(C) An erratic spiral

(D) A perfect circle

Ⓐ Ⓑ Ⓒ Ⓓ

9. Where in the passage does the author refer to the number of craters on the Moon?

(A) Paragraph 1

(B) Paragraph 2

(C) Paragraph 3

(D) Paragraph 4

Ⓐ Ⓑ Ⓒ Ⓓ

Section 3

集中練習問題 ❶　解答・解説

1.-9.　　　　　　　　　　　　　　　　　　　　　　　　　　　　　　　　**Astronomy: Moon**

（パラグラフ 1）　Because of its close proximity to the Earth, the Moon is second only to the Sun in apparent size and brilliance. In astronomical terms, however, it is a common, small, and insignificant body. It generates no heat or radiance. Its only light is actually reflected sunlight.

（パラグラフ 2）　The Moon's immense dark areas—easily seen by the naked eye—are called "maria" or "seas." They are huge flat plains made of fine, dark lava debris mixed with glass fragments and rocks. One theory for their existence is that they are the remains of terrific meteorite collisions billions of years ago when the Moon's interior was hot. The explosive impact would have caused great heat, melted the Moon's surface, and
(10)　released molten rock from the interior, forming the maria from lava. Another more recent theory, however, maintains that a meteorite collision would be more likely to pulverize rock than to melt it. Three probes which photographed the Moon in 1964 and 1965 increased speculation among scientists about whether the Moon's maria are composed primarily of volcanic ash, lava flows, dust, or some unknown material. In
(15)　the 1970s, however, analyses of rocks brought back to the Earth during manned United States space missions seemed to confirm the earlier theory.

（パラグラフ 3）　The Moon's brighter areas are mountains and craters. Tens of thousands of craters are scattered over the Moon's surface, often overlapping one another, and ranging in size from a single meter to 240 kilometers. As with the maria, astronomers
(20)　have long debated their origin. They may have been created by volcanoes, now extinct for billions of years. A more widely accepted current theory holds that they were caused both by showers of meteorites and by volcanic activity.

（パラグラフ 4）　For years scientists believed there was no trace of an atmosphere on the Moon. Astonishingly, there is now some evidence of an atmosphere, though it may be almost
(25)　too thin to measure. During an occultation of the Crab nebula, astronomers using a radio telescope at Cambridge University detected a slight bending of the rays of the nebula. This deflection could have been due to a thin lunar atmosphere.

（パラグラフ 5）　The Moon does not follow a perfect circle in its path around the Earth, rather its orbit is a moderate ellipse. At perigee—when the Moon is nearest the Earth—its
(30)　distance from the Earth's center is about 222,000 miles; when it reaches the opposite point—its apogee—the Moon is about 253,000 miles from the Earth's center. Recent high-tech measurements of the Moon's orbit have revealed an interesting fact—each year it is moving slightly farther away from us.

（パラグラフ1） 地球への距離的な近さから，月は太陽に次いで大きく明るく見える。しかし天文学的に言えば，月はごくふつうの小さな，取るに足りない天体である。熱も光も発しない。月の光は実際には反射した太陽光である。

（パラグラフ2） 月の広大な暗い部分は肉眼で容易に見られるが，これは maria（海）や seas（海）と呼ばれる。これらは巨大な平地で，ガラスのかけらや岩が混じり合った，細かな黒い溶岩の破片でできている。海の存在は，数十億年前，月の内部が高温だった時期の大規模な隕石衝突の名残だという説がある。爆発の衝撃で温度が上がり，その熱で月の地表が溶け，内部から融解した岩石が流れ出し，溶岩から海ができたというのである。しかし別のもっと新しい説では，隕石の衝突は岩を溶かしたのではなく，粉砕した可能性が高いとされている。1964 年と 1965 年に月を撮影した 3 回の探査により，月の海の主成分は火山灰，溶岩流，塵，または何か未知の物質なのかという考えが科学者の間に広まった。しかし 1970 年代にはアメリカの有人宇宙探査で地球に持ち帰られた岩石の分析により，前者の説が確認されたようである。

（パラグラフ3） 月の明るいほうの地帯は山とクレーターである。月の表面には数万のクレーターが散在しており，重なり合っていることもしばしばで，大きさも 1 メートルから 240 キロメートルまでさまざまである。天文学者は，海と同様長い間クレーターの起源について議論してきた。それらは数十億年前に活動をやめた火山によって作られたのかもしれない。より広く受け入れられている現在の説では，クレーターは多くの隕石の衝突と火山活動の両方によってできたとされている。

（パラグラフ4） 長い間科学者は月に大気の痕跡はないと信じていた。驚くべきことに，観測できないほどかすかなものではあるが大気があるという証拠は現時点で存在している。かに星雲の星食の間，ケンブリッジ大学で電波望遠鏡を使用していた天文学者は，星雲の光にわずかな屈折を発見した。この屈折は月のかすかな大気のせいだったかもしれない。

（パラグラフ5） 地球の周りを回るとき，月は正円をたどるのではなく，軌道はやや楕円である。近地点，すなわち月が地球に最も近いとき，地球の中心からの距離は約 22 万 2,000 マイルである。逆の地点，遠地点においては，月は地球の中心から 25 万 3,000 マイルの距離にある。近年の先端技術で月の軌道を測定したところ，興味深い事実が明らかになった。年々月は少しずつ私たちから遠ざかっているのである。

---

1. 解答：A

What is the main topic of the passage?	このパッセージの主なトピックは何ですか。
(A) The features of the Moon	(A) 月の特徴
(B) The Moon's interior	(B) 月の内部
(C) The movement of the Moon	(C) 月の動き
(D) The origin of the Moon	(D) 月の起源

解法 パッセージの主要なポイントを問う問題。このパッセージでは，月にある海，山，クレーター，大気，軌道などについて述べている。これらは月の特徴であり，正解は (A)。

2.　　　　　　　　　　　　　　　　　　　　　　　　　　　　　　　解答：B

According to the passage, the Moon appears to be an important heavenly body when viewed from the Earth because of	パッセージによれば，月はなぜ地球から眺めると重要な天体に見えるのですか。
(A)　its large size	(A)　大きさのため
(B)　its nearness	(B)　近さのため
(C)　the light it produces	(C)　自ら作り出す光のため
(D)　the maria on its surface	(D)　地表にある海のため

> **解法**　記述されている情報を問う問題。パラグラフ 1 の最初の一文 Because of its close proximity … から，地球に近いため，大きく明るく見えて重要に思えることがわかる。正解は (B)。

3.　　　　　　　　　　　　　　　　　　　　　　　　　　　　　　　解答：C

Which of the following is NOT mentioned as a quality of the Moon's maria?	次のうち，月の海の特性として述べられていないものはどれですか。
(A)　Their large size	(A)　大きいこと
(B)　Their flatness	(B)　平らであること
(C)　Their brightness	(C)　明るいこと
(D)　Their dustiness	(D)　ちり状であること

> **解法**　記述されていない情報を問う問題。パラグラフ 2 に They are <u>huge</u> <u>flat</u> plains made of <u>fine, dark lava debris</u> mixed with glass fragments and rocks. とあり，下線部はそれぞれ選択肢 (A)(B)(D) に対応している。(C) の「明るい」は dark という記述に反するので，正解は (C)。

4.　　　　　　　　　　　　　　　　　　　　　　　　　　　　　　　解答：C

The word "primarily" in line 14 can best be replaced with which of the following?	14 行目の primarily という語は次のどの語と最も適切に入れ換えることができますか。
(A)　Completely	(A)　完全に
(B)　Exclusively	(B)　もっぱら
(C)　Principally	(C)　主に
(D)　Presumably	(D)　たぶん

> **解法**　語彙問題。primarily は「主に」という意味なので，「主に，主として」を表す (C) Principally を選ぶ。

Section Ⅰ Part A/B　Section Ⅰ Part C　Section 2　Section 3　総合模試　総合模試 解答・解説

5.

To which of the following ideas does the phrase "the earlier theory" in line 16 refer to?

(A) That maria were caused by eruptions from the Moon's volcanoes

(B) That maria were created when the Moon's surface became liquefied

(C) That maria were one of the original natural features of the Moon

(D) That maria were formed through explosions in the interior of the Moon

16 行目の「前者の説」とは次のどの考えを指していますか。

(A) 海は月の火山噴火によって作られた
(B) 海は月の表面が融解した際にできた
(C) 海は月の自然地形のひとつであった
(D) 海は月内部の爆発で形成された

> **解法** 記述されている情報を問う問題。パラグラフ2では One theory ... Another more recent theory ... と2つの説が述べられている。前者，すなわち先に述べられている説の記述に「隕石衝突の名残だという説がある。爆発の衝撃で温度が上がり，その熱で月の地表が溶け，内部から融解した岩石が流れ出し，溶岩から海ができた」とあるため，正解は (B)。

6.

The word "extinct" in line 21 is closest in meaning to

(A) dead
(B) dormant
(C) erupting
(D) explosive

21 行目の extinct という語に最も意味が近い語はどれですか。

(A) 死んだ
(B) 休止した
(C) 噴火している
(D) 爆発性の

> **解法** 語彙問題。extinct は「活動をやめた，死滅した」の意味であり，(A) dead が最も意味の近い語である。

7.

What does the author imply is the most unusual recent discovery about the Moon?

(A) Its craters were formed by both meteorites and volcanic activity.

(B) Its surface temperature varies dramatically from day to night.

(C) It may possess a slight atmosphere.

(D) It has an erratic orbit around the Earth.

月について最も珍しい最近の発見は何であると著者は示唆していますか。

(A) クレーターは隕石と火山活動の両方によってできた。
(B) 地表の温度は昼から夜にかけて劇的に変わる。
(C) かすかに大気がある可能性がある。
(D) 地球の周りを不規則な軌道で回る。

> **解法** 記述されている情報を問う問題。著者が考える最も珍しい最近の発見は，パラグラフ4の Astonishingly「驚くべきことに」という副詞を伴う「観測できないほどかすかなものではあるが大気があるという証拠は現時点で存在している」点である。正解は (C)。

8.

Which of the following is the best description of the Moon's orbit?

(A) An extreme ellipse
(B) A modest oval
(C) An erratic spiral
(D) A perfect circle

次のうち，月の軌道を最もよく描写しているのはどれですか。

(A) 極度の楕円形
(B) やや楕円形
(C) 不規則ならせん形
(D) 正円形

解法　記述されている情報を問う問題。パラグラフ5で its orbit is a moderate ellipse と述べていて，月の軌道はやや楕円形であることがわかる。正解は (B)。

9.

Where in the passage does the author refer to the number of craters on the Moon?

(A) Paragraph 1
(B) Paragraph 2
(C) Paragraph 3
(D) Paragraph 4

著者はパッセージのどこで月のクレーターの数を述べていますか。

(A) パラグラフ1
(B) パラグラフ2
(C) パラグラフ3
(D) パラグラフ4

解法　記述されている情報を問う問題。パラグラフ3で Tens of thousands of craters are scattered over the Moon's surface, often overlapping one another, and ranging in size from a single meter to 240 kilometers. と述べており，月には数万のクレーターが散在していることがわかる。正解は (C)。

重要語
- **proximity**「近接，近いこと」
- **astronomical**「天文（学上）の」
- **generate**「～を発生させる，生み出す」
- **lava**「溶岩」
- **debris**「破片」
- **meteorite**「隕石」
- **collision**「衝突」
- **pulverize**「～を砕く，粉々にする」
- **probe**「調査，探測機」
- **speculation**「推測」
- **crater**「噴火口，クレーター」
- **trace**「痕跡，記録」
- **occultation**「星食」
- **nebula**「星雲」
- **radio telescope**「電波望遠鏡」
- **ray**「光線，放射線」
- **deflection**「屈折」
- **path**「軌道」
- **orbit**「軌道」
- **ellipse**「楕円，長円」

集中練習問題 ❷ 1 題 9 問

BURST TWO

Line

(1)   In contrast to those who went before her, Eleanor Roosevelt broke the mold of what had been considered proper for the wife of a sitting president. Active in social issues, she had a considerable influence on national policy toward the poor, the youth population, and the eventual creation of the United Nations. Without doubt, Roosevelt

(5) was one of the most significant public figures of early 20th-century America.

    Born into a prominent family of great wealth, the young Eleanor Roosevelt had an unhappy childhood. Her mother, known for her beauty, often teased her less attractive offspring. Her father, whom she adored and who adored her in turn, was banished from the family because of alcoholism. After her parents died while she

(10) was still young, Roosevelt was raised by her strict and conservative grandmother. Forced to attend elite private secondary schools, she further became disenchanted with the "ivory tower" existence of the wealthy upper classes. In her late teens, she sought temporary escape from her privileged existence by working with the city's poor at a settlement house.

(15)   Ultimately, though, she cleverly made use of her family connections. In 1905, at the age of 21, she married her distant cousin Franklin D. Roosevelt. Another distant relative, then President Theodore Roosevelt, walked her down the aisle at the marriage ceremony. During the next 11 years Eleanor Roosevelt gave birth to six children and dutifully performed her expected role as the devoted wife of a rising

(20) public official. Her work with the Red Cross during World War I was particularly noteworthy. She became active in the League of Women Voters, the Women's Trade Union League, and the women's faction of the Democratic Party. When her husband was stricken with polio in 1921, her emancipation was complete. Resolved to keep his interest in politics alive, she became the driving force behind his career, often

(25) serving as his stand-in. His successful run for governor of New York in 1928 was followed by his election to the White House in 1932.

Go on to the next page ➡

At first, Eleanor feared the move to the White House would make her a prisoner in a gilded cage. But, in fact, the opposite was true. Using her position as First Lady as a springboard, she broke many established precedents, establishing weekly press
(30)　conferences with women reporters, lecturing throughout the country, having her own radio program, and writing a syndicated newspaper column. Not only did she serve as her husband's eyes and ears, but she also became a major voice within his administration for measures to aid the underprivileged, women, and racial minorities.

1. With which of the following subjects is the passage mainly concerned?

(A)　Important 20th-century politicians
(B)　The life and deeds of Eleanor Roosevelt
(C)　Eleanor Roosevelt and the United Nations
(D)　The wives of important American presidents　Ⓐ Ⓑ Ⓒ Ⓓ

2. It can be inferred from the passage that Eleanor Roosevelt's father was

(A)　not interested in raising his children
(B)　the most respected member of his family
(C)　the product of a disadvantaged upbringing
(D)　extremely fond of his daughter　Ⓐ Ⓑ Ⓒ Ⓓ

3. The author organizes paragraph 2 according to which principle?

(A)　Chronology
(B)　Classification
(C)　Comparison
(D)　Spatial Orientation　Ⓐ Ⓑ Ⓒ Ⓓ

4. In line 23, the word "stricken" can best be replaced with

(A)　compensated
(B)　occupied
(C)　afflicted
(D)　distracted　Ⓐ Ⓑ Ⓒ Ⓓ

Go on to the next page ➡

5. What does the phrase "established precedents" in line 29 mean?

    (A) Contemporary laws

    (B) Unexpected roles

    (C) Longstanding conventions

    (D) Meaningless rules   Ⓐ Ⓑ Ⓒ Ⓓ

6. The last paragraph most extensively discusses how Eleanor Roosevelt

    (A) felt trapped by her position as the president's wife

    (B) helped her husband to become elected president

    (C) opposed a number of her husband's policies

    (D) redefined the post of America's First Lady   Ⓐ Ⓑ Ⓒ Ⓓ

7. With which of the following statements about Eleanor Roosevelt would the author most likely agree?

    (A) She grew up in a supportive and emotionally secure home.

    (B) She mainly devoted herself to her children during her later years.

    (C) She was one of the most important factors in her husband's success.

    (D) She gave up involvement in politics upon moving into the White House.

                                      Ⓐ Ⓑ Ⓒ Ⓓ

8. What is the author's attitude toward the accomplishments of Eleanor Roosevelt?

    (A) Relatively indifferent

    (B) Distinctly favorable

    (C) Rather critical

    (D) Largely hostile   Ⓐ Ⓑ Ⓒ Ⓓ

9. What does the paragraph following the passage most likely discuss?

    (A) The traditional role for the wife of an American president

    (B) Eleanor Roosevelt's own campaign for elective office

    (C) Eleanor Roosevelt's influence within her husband's administration

    (D) The establishment of regular press conferences with female reporters

                                      Ⓐ Ⓑ Ⓒ Ⓓ

Section 3　集中練習問題 ❷　解答・解説

1.-9.　　　　　　　　　　　　　　　　　　　　　　　　　　Eleanor Roosevelt

（パラグラフ 1）In contrast to those who went before her, Eleanor Roosevelt broke the mold of what had been considered proper for the wife of a sitting president. Active in social issues, she had a considerable influence on national policy toward the poor, the youth population, and the eventual creation of the United Nations. Without doubt, Roosevelt
(5) was one of the most significant public figures of early 20th-century America.

（パラグラフ 2）Born into a prominent family of great wealth, the young Eleanor Roosevelt had an unhappy childhood. Her mother, known for her beauty, often teased her less attractive offspring. Her father, whom she adored and who adored her in turn, was banished from the family because of alcoholism. After her parents died while she
(10) was still young, Roosevelt was raised by her strict and conservative grandmother. Forced to attend elite private secondary schools, she further became disenchanted with the "ivory tower" existence of the wealthy upper classes. In her late teens, she sought temporary escape from her privileged existence by working with the city's poor at a settlement house.

（パラグラフ 3）Ultimately, though, she cleverly made use of her family connections. In 1905, at the age of 21, she married her distant cousin Franklin D. Roosevelt. Another distant relative, then President Theodore Roosevelt, walked her down the aisle at the marriage ceremony. During the next 11 years Eleanor Roosevelt gave birth to six children and dutifully performed her expected role as the devoted wife of a rising
(20) public official. Her work with the Red Cross during World War I was particularly noteworthy. She became active in the League of Women Voters, the Women's Trade Union League, and the women's faction of the Democratic Party. When her husband was stricken with polio in 1921, her emancipation was complete. Resolved to keep his interest in politics alive, she became the driving force behind his career, often
(25) serving as his stand-in. His successful run for governor of New York in 1928 was followed by his election to the White House in 1932.

（パラグラフ 4）At first, Eleanor feared the move to the White House would make her a prisoner in a gilded cage. But, in fact, the opposite was true. Using her position as First Lady as a springboard, she broke many established precedents, establishing weekly press
(30) conferences with women reporters, lecturing throughout the country, having her own radio program, and writing a syndicated newspaper column. Not only did she serve as her husband's eyes and ears, but she also became a major voice within his administration for measures to aid the underprivileged, women, and racial minorities.

(パラグラフ1)　先人たちとは対照的に，エレノア・ルーズベルトはそれまで現職大統領の妻にふさわしいと考えられてきたことの常識を破った。彼女は社会問題に積極的に取り組み，貧しい人々や若年層に対する国策，ひいては国連の創設にも多大な影響を与えた。間違いなくルーズベルトは，20世紀初頭のアメリカで最も重要な公人のひとりであった。

(パラグラフ2)　有名な大富豪の一家に生まれたエレノア・ルーズベルトは不幸な少女時代を送った。美しいことで知られた彼女の母親は，魅力では劣る自分の子どもをしばしばいじめた。父親のことは大好きで，彼も彼女を愛していたが，アルコール依存症のため彼は家を追放された。まだ幼いうちに両親が亡くなると，ルーズベルトは厳格で保守的な祖母の手で育てられた。彼女は強制的にエリートの私立中学校に入学させられ，裕福な上流階級の「象牙の塔」の存在にさらに幻滅を感じた。彼女は十代後半に，市の貧しい人々とセツルメントハウスで働くことにより，特権を持った自分の立場から一時的に逃避しようと努めた。

(パラグラフ3)　しかし最終的に，彼女は自分の家族のコネクションを賢く利用した。1905年，彼女は21歳で遠縁のいとこであったフランクリン・D・ルーズベルトと結婚した。結婚式では，別の遠戚にあたる当時の大統領セオドア・ルーズベルトが，彼女とバージンロードを歩いた。その後の11年間でエレノア・ルーズベルトは6人の子供をもうけ，公職についている上り坂の男の献身的な妻として，期待される役割を忠実に演じた。第一次世界大戦中に彼女が行った赤十字の仕事は特に注目に値した。彼女は女性投票者連盟，女性労働組合連盟，民主党内の女性派閥で活躍を始めた。夫が1921年にポリオに倒れたとき，彼女の自己解放は完了した。夫が政治に興味を持ち続けるように努めようと彼女は心に決め，夫の影の駆動力となり，しばしば代役も務めた。彼は1928年ニューヨーク州知事に当選し，引き続き1932年の大統領選挙でホワイトハウス入りとなった。

(パラグラフ4)　エレノアは初めホワイトハウスへ引っ越すことで，華美な鳥かごに捕らわれるのではないかと恐れた。しかし実際は逆だった。ファーストレディとしての地位を足掛かりとして使い，彼女は多くの確立されていた慣例を打ち破った。彼女は女性記者との会見を毎週開き，全国で講演を行い，ラジオ番組を持ち，多くの新聞に配信されるコラムを書いた。彼女は夫の目や耳となっただけでなく，夫の政権内部において，恵まれない人々，女性，人種的少数派を援助する施策を求める重要な発言者にもなった。

1.　　　　　　　　　　　　　　　　　　　　　　　　　解答：B

With which of the following subjects is the passage mainly concerned?

(A)　Important 20th-century politicians

(B)　The life and deeds of Eleanor Roosevelt

(C)　Eleanor Roosevelt and the United Nations

(D)　The wives of important American presidents

次のうち，パッセージはどの題材を主に取り上げていますか。

(A)　20 世紀の重要な政治家たち

(B)　エレノア・ルーズベルトの人生と功績

(C)　エレノア・ルーズベルトと国連

(D)　重要なアメリカ大統領の妻たち

解法　パッセージの主要なポイントを問う問題。このパッセージの内容はエレノア・ルーズベルトの人生とその行動に絞られているので，正解は (B)。

2.　　　　　　　　　　　　　　　　　　　　　　　　　解答：D

It can be inferred from the passage that Eleanor Roosevelt's father was

(A)　not interested in raising his children

(B)　the most respected member of his family

(C)　the product of a disadvantaged upbringing

(D)　extremely fond of his daughter

パッセージから，エレノア・ルーズベルトの父親はどうだったと推測できますか。

(A)　子供を育てることに興味がなかった

(B)　家族の中で最も尊敬されていた

(C)　恵まれない幼少期の産物だった

(D)　娘のことがとても好きだった

解法　推測に関する問題。父親に関することはパラグラフ 2 に記述されている。Her father, whom she adored and who adored her in turn ...「父親のことは大好きで，彼も彼女を愛していた」とあるので，正解は (D)。

3.　　　　　　　　　　　　　　　　　　　　　　　　　解答：A

The author organizes paragraph 2 according to which principle?

(A)　Chronology

(B)　Classification

(C)　Comparison

(D)　Spatial Orientation

著者はどの原則に従ってパラグラフ 2 を組み立てていますか。

(A)　年代順

(B)　分類

(C)　比較

(D)　空間的配置

解法　パラグラフの構成に関する問題。幼いときから十代後半まで年代順に述べているので，正解は (A)。

4.

In line 23, the word "stricken" can best be replaced with	23 行目の stricken という語はどの語と最も適切に入れ換えることができますか。
(A)　compensated	(A)　補償された
(B)　occupied	(B)　占められた
(C)　afflicted	(C)　苦しめられた
(D)　distracted	(D)　気を散らされた

解法 語彙問題。her husband was stricken with polio の stricken は strike の過去分詞形で「苦しめられた，（病気に）かかった」の意味で，この語と置き換えられるのは with を伴うことのできる (C) afflicted である。選択肢のなかには意味が似ていても語法が合わない場合があるので，文脈のなかでどの語が正しいか判断する必要がある。

5.

What does the phrase "established precedents" in line 29 mean?	29 行目の established precedents は何を意味しますか。
(A)　Contemporary laws	(A)　現代の法律
(B)　Unexpected roles	(B)　意外な役割
(C)　Longstanding conventions	(C)　長年の慣習
(D)　Meaningless rules	(D)　無意味な規則

解法 語彙問題。established precedents とは「確立されていた先例，慣例」のことなので，正解は (C)。

6.

The last paragraph most extensively discusses how Eleanor Roosevelt	最後のパラグラフでは，エレノア・ルーズベルトがどうであることを最も詳しく論じていますか。
(A)　felt trapped by her position as the president's wife	(A)　大統領の妻という地位に捕らわれたように感じた
(B)　helped her husband to become elected president	(B)　夫が大統領になる手助けをした
(C)　opposed a number of her husband's policies	(C)　夫の政策の多くに反対した
(D)　redefined the post of America's First Lady	(D)　アメリカのファーストレディの地位を再定義した

解法 パラグラフの主要なポイントを問う問題。最終パラグラフには Using her position as First Lady as a springboard, she broke many established precedents「ファーストレディとしての地位を足掛かりとして使い，彼女は多くの確立されていた慣例を打ち破った」とあり，続いてその内容が述べられている。正解は (D)。

7.

解答：C

With which of the following statements about Eleanor Roosevelt would the author most likely agree?

(A) She grew up in a supportive and emotionally secure home.

(B) She mainly devoted herself to her children during her later years.

(C) She was one of the most important factors in her husband's success.

(D) She gave up involvement in politics upon moving into the White House.

エレノア・ルーズベルトについての次の意見のうち，著者が最も賛成しそうなものはどれですか。

(A) 彼女は支えてくれるような心安らぐ家庭で育った。

(B) 彼女は晩年，主として自分の子どもに尽くした。

(C) 彼女は夫の成功の最も重要な要因のひとつだった。

(D) 彼女はホワイトハウスに移るときに政治への関与を諦めた。

> **解法** 推測に関する問題。パラグラフ3に dutifully performed her expected role as the devoted wife「献身的な妻として期待される役割を忠実に演じた」とある。またパラグラフ4に Not only did she serve as her husband's eyes and ears, but she also became a major voice within his administration for measures「彼女は夫の目や耳となっただけではなく，夫の政権内部において，施策を求める重要な発言者にもなった」と記述され，夫を支えていたことがわかる。正解は (C)。

8.

解答：B

What is the author's attitude toward the accomplishments of Eleanor Roosevelt?

(A) Relatively indifferent

(B) Distinctly favorable

(C) Rather critical

(D) Largely hostile

エレノア・ルーズベルトの業績に対する著者の態度はどのようなものですか。

(A) 比較的無関心

(B) 明確に好意的

(C) かなり批判的

(D) おおむね敵対的

> **解法** 著者の立場に関する問題。パラグラフ1の Without doubt, Roosevelt was one of the most significant public figures of early 20th-century America.「間違いなくルーズベルトは，20世紀初頭のアメリカで最も重要な公人のひとりであった」という文から，著者がルーズベルトに好意的であることがわかる。without doubt に著者の語調の強さが現れている。正解は (B)。

9.

What does the paragraph following the passage most likely discuss?

(A) The traditional role for the wife of an American president

(B) Eleanor Roosevelt's own campaign for elective office

(C) Eleanor Roosevelt's influence within her husband's administration

(D) The establishment of regular press conferences with female reporters

このパッセージに続くパラグラフではおそらく何を論じていますか。

(A) アメリカ大統領の妻の伝統的な役割

(B) エレノア・ルーズベルト自身の選挙戦

(C) 夫の政権内でのエレノア・ルーズベルトの影響

(D) 女性記者との定例会見の実施

解法 パッセージの後を推測する問題。パラグラフ4では，エレノア・ルーズベルトがファーストレディとしての慣例を打ち破る行動をとったこと，また夫の政権内部において，恵まれない人々，女性，人種的少数派を支援する施策を求める重要な発言者になったことが述べられている。この後のパラグラフでは，さらに夫の政権内部における発言者としての彼女の活動やその影響が述べられていると推測される。正解は (C)。

重要語

- ☐ **in contrast to ...**「～とは対照的に」
- ☐ **mold**「型，枠組」
- ☐ **sitting**「現職の」
- ☐ **prominent**「著名な」
- ☐ **tease**「～をいじめる，悩ませる」
- ☐ **offspring**「子，子孫」
- ☐ **adore**「～を敬愛する」
- ☐ **disenchanted**「幻滅した」
- ☐ **privileged**「特権のある」
- ☐ **settlement house**「セツルメントハウス」
  *貧しい人々が住む地域に定住して改善事業を行う施設

- ☐ **make use of ...**「～を利用する」
- ☐ **faction**「派閥」
- ☐ **emancipation**「解放，釈放」
- ☐ **driving force**「強い影響を与える力」
- ☐ **stand-in**「代役」
- ☐ **gilded cage**「豪華だが窮屈な環境」
- ☐ **springboard**「出発点，踏み台」
- ☐ **precedent**「先例，慣例」
- ☐ **syndicated**「同時配信の」
- ☐ **underprivileged**「(社会的・経済的に) 恵まれない」
- ☐ **racial minority**「人種的少数派」

集中練習問題 ❸　1題8問

BURST THREE

Line

(1)　Water molecules remain as part of the water vapor in the air unless they are cooled below the point at which they will release their latent energy and join together. This temperature at which they begin to condense and fuse is called the dew point. At any temperature lower than the dew point, water vapor may begin to change into

(5)　liquid or solid form, resulting in clouds.

There are a number of ways this cooling of water vapor can take place. The most common way for clouds to form is that a body of air becomes warmer than the surrounding air and rises. This is especially visible on a clear day when direct rays of sunlight strike the ground and cause the air near it to warm. The heated parcel of air

(10)　will then climb and undergo cooling as it ascends into the cooler heights. As its moisture condenses below the dew point, it will begin to form a cloud. Air is also cooled as it is lifted in its passage over mountains, and it is for this reason that entire mountaintops are often covered with clouds.

Yet another way that clouds form is when currents of air moving against each

(15)　other in the sky force one to rise and reach its dew point. Large bodies of clouds connected with storms are typically created in this way when a mass of warm air is pushed up over a heavier body of cooler air.

Among the three types of high-level clouds, perhaps the most beautiful ones are the cirrus. Thin, feather-like, and delicate in appearance, they are frequently arranged

(20)　in bands across the sky called "mare's tails." Cirrocumulus clouds, by contrast, look like patches of fluffy cotton and they usually appear in groups. Because they resemble schools of fish, they are sometimes called "a mackerel sky." Cirrostratus are probably the most ghostly of clouds. They appear in whitish layers, like a sheet or a veil, giving the ceiling of the sky a milky appearance. They may produce a halo around the Sun or

(25)　Moon, which is a result of the bending of light by their high-altitude ice crystals.

1. What is the main purpose of the passage?

(A) To investigate the structure of water molecules
(B) To explain how clouds form
(C) To describe the beauty of clouds
(D) To show how clouds influence weather   Ⓐ Ⓑ Ⓒ Ⓓ

2. The word "fuse" in line 3 is closest in meaning to

(A) combine
(B) vanish
(C) collapse
(D) split   Ⓐ Ⓑ Ⓒ Ⓓ

3. In line 9, the word "it" refers to

(A) the surrounding air
(B) a clear day
(C) the ground
(D) the heated parcel of air   Ⓐ Ⓑ Ⓒ Ⓓ

4. What role do mountains play in cloud formation?

(A) They draw cold air towards the ground.
(B) They increase the humidity of the air.
(C) They cause air to rise and cool.
(D) They create high winds.   Ⓐ Ⓑ Ⓒ Ⓓ

5. What form of cloud sometimes causes a ring to form around the Moon?

(A) Storm
(B) Cirrus
(C) Cirrocumulus
(D) Cirrostratus   Ⓐ Ⓑ Ⓒ Ⓓ

6. Which of the following best characterizes the organization of the last paragraph?

(A) Division and classification of types
(B) Claim followed by supporting evidence
(C) Steps in a process
(D) Description of cause and effect　　　　　Ⓐ Ⓑ Ⓒ Ⓓ

7. Where in the passage does the author express an opinion about which type of clouds are most attractive?

(A) Paragraph 1
(B) Paragraph 2
(C) Paragraph 3
(D) Paragraph 4　　　　　Ⓐ Ⓑ Ⓒ Ⓓ

8. What does the paragraph following the passage probably discuss?

(A) Snow and ice
(B) Cloud movement
(C) The ways that storms form
(D) Types of mid-level clouds　　　　　Ⓐ Ⓑ Ⓒ Ⓓ

1.-8. How Clouds Form

パラグラフ1 Water molecules remain as part of the water vapor in the air unless they are cooled below the point at which they will release their latent energy and join together. This temperature at which they begin to condense and fuse is called the dew point. At any temperature lower than the dew point, water vapor may begin to change into (5) liquid or solid form, resulting in clouds.

パラグラフ2 There are a number of ways this cooling of water vapor can take place. The most common way for clouds to form is that a body of air becomes warmer than the surrounding air and rises. This is especially visible on a clear day when direct rays of sunlight strike the ground and cause the air near it to warm. The heated parcel of air (10) will then climb and undergo cooling as it ascends into the cooler heights. As its moisture condenses below the dew point, it will begin to form a cloud. Air is also cooled as it is lifted in its passage over mountains, and it is for this reason that entire mountaintops are often covered with clouds.

パラグラフ3 Yet another way that clouds form is when currents of air moving against each (15) other in the sky force one to rise and reach its dew point. Large bodies of clouds connected with storms are typically created in this way when a mass of warm air is pushed up over a heavier body of cooler air.

パラグラフ4 Among the three types of high-level clouds, perhaps the most beautiful ones are the cirrus. Thin, feather-like, and delicate in appearance, they are frequently arranged (20) in bands across the sky called "mare's tails." Cirrocumulus clouds, by contrast, look like patches of fluffy cotton and they usually appear in groups. Because they resemble schools of fish, they are sometimes called "a mackerel sky." Cirrostratus are probably the most ghostly of clouds. They appear in whitish layers, like a sheet or a veil, giving the ceiling of the sky a milky appearance. They may produce a halo around the Sun or (25) Moon, which is a result of the bending of light by their high-altitude ice crystals.

（パラグラフ1）　潜熱エネルギーを放出して結合する温度以下に冷却されなければ，水の分子は空気中の水蒸気成分としてとどまる。水の分子が凝結し，融合を始めるこの温度は露点と呼ばれる。露点を下回ると水蒸気は液体や固体に変化し始め，結果として雲を形成する。

（パラグラフ2）　こうした水蒸気冷却が起こる方法はいくつもある。雲が形成される最も一般的な過程では，ある空気が周囲の空気よりも温かくなり上昇する。直射日光が地面に当たり，その近くの空気が温かくなるような晴れた日に，これは特にはっきりと見ることができる。温められた空気の塊は上昇し，さらに低温の高度に上昇するにつれ冷却されていく。露点以下で水分は凝結し，雲を形成し始める。空気は山越えで上昇するときにも冷却され，山頂がよくすっぽりと雲に覆われているのはこのためである。

（パラグラフ3）　雲が形成される別の過程は，空中で空気の流れがぶつかって上昇し，露点に達する方法である。温かい空気の塊が冷たくて重い空気の塊の上に押し出されると，嵐につながるような大きな雲がよくこのようにして生まれる。

（パラグラフ4）　3タイプの上層雲の中で，おそらく最も美しい雲は「巻雲」である。巻雲は薄く，羽根のような形をしており，見た目も繊細で，しばしば帯状に空に広がり「馬尾雲」と呼ばれる。対照的に「巻積雲」はふわふわした綿の断片のようで，通常はいくつかまとまって現れる。魚群に似ているため，「さば雲」と呼ばれることもある。「巻層雲」はおそらく最もぼんやりした雲である。シーツかベールのような白っぽい層で，空の上層を乳白色に彩る。この雲は太陽や月の周りにかさをつくることがあるが，これは高空にある氷晶が光を屈折させることによってできるのである。

1.

What is the main purpose of the passage?	パッセージの主な目的は何ですか。
(A) To investigate the structure of water molecules	(A) 水の分子構造を調べること
(B) To explain how clouds form	(B) 雲がどのようにしてできるかを説明すること
(C) To describe the beauty of clouds	(C) 雲の美しさを描写すること
(D) To show how clouds influence weather	(D) 雲が天気にいかに影響するかを示すこと

解法 パッセージの主要なポイントを問う問題。パラグラフ 1 の resulting in clouds, パラグラフ 2 の The most common way for clouds to form is, パラグラフ 3 の Yet another way that clouds form is などから，雲の形成について説明しているパッセージであることがわかる。正解は (B)。

2.

The word "fuse" in line 3 is closest in meaning to	3 行目の fuse という語に最も意味が近い語はどれですか。
(A) combine	(A) 結合する
(B) vanish	(B) 消える
(C) collapse	(C) 崩れる
(D) split	(D) 分裂する

解法 語彙問題。fuse「融合する」に意味の近い語は combine である。正解は (A)。

3.

In line 9, the word "it" refers to	9 行目の it は何を指していますか。
(A) the surrounding air	(A) 周りの空気
(B) a clear day	(B) 晴れた日
(C) the ground	(C) 地面
(D) the heated parcel of air	(D) 温められた空気の塊

解法 代名詞が指す対象を問う語法問題。it を含む次の文「直射日光が地面に当たり，その近くの空気が温かくなるような晴れた日に，これは特にはっきりと見ることができる」の中で，「その近く」は「地面の近く」を指すので，正解は (C)。

4.

解答：C

What role do mountains play in cloud formation?	山は雲の形成にどのような役割を果たしますか。
(A) They draw cold air towards the ground.	(A) 地表面に冷たい空気を運ぶ。
(B) They increase the humidity of the air.	(B) 空気中の湿度を上げる。
(C) They cause air to rise and cool.	(C) 空気を上昇させ冷却する。
(D) They create high winds.	(D) 強い風を起こす。

解法 記述されている情報を問う問題。設問の mountains に関する記述はパラグラフ 2 にある。Air is also cooled as it is lifted in its passage over mountains「空気は山越えで上昇するときにも冷却される」から，正解は (C)。

5.

解答：D

What form of cloud sometimes causes a ring to form around the Moon?	月にかさがかかる状態を引き起こすことがある雲は何ですか。
(A) Storm	(A) 嵐雲
(B) Cirrus	(B) 巻雲
(C) Cirrocumulus	(C) 巻積雲
(D) Cirrostratus	(D) 巻層雲

解法 記述されている情報を問う問題。設問の causes a ring to form around the Moon はパラグラフ 4 最後の produce a halo around the Sun or Moon と類似している。ここで述べられているのは cirrostratus「巻層雲」なので，正解は (D)。

6.

解答：A

Which of the following best characterizes the organization of the last paragraph?	最後のパラグラフの構成を最もよく特徴づけているのは次のどれですか。
(A) Division and classification of types	(A) 種類の区分と分類
(B) Claim followed by supporting evidence	(B) 主張とその根拠
(C) Steps in a process	(C) 過程における段階
(D) Description of cause and effect	(D) 原因と結果の記述

解法 パラグラフの構成に関する問題。最後のパラグラフでは，雲が巻雲，巻積雲，巻層雲に分類されて説明されている。正解は (A)。

7.

Where in the passage does the author express an opinion about which type of clouds are most attractive?	パッセージのどこで著者はどの雲が最も魅力的かについて意見を述べていますか。
(A) Paragraph 1	(A) パラグラフ1
(B) Paragraph 2	(B) パラグラフ2
(C) Paragraph 3	(C) パラグラフ3
(D) Paragraph 4	(D) パラグラフ4

解法 指定された内容を表すパラグラフを選ぶ問題。パラグラフ4の最初で「3タイプの上層雲の中で，おそらく最も美しい雲は巻雲である」と述べているので，正解は (D)。

8.

What does the paragraph following the passage probably discuss?	このパッセージに続くパラグラフではおそらく何を論じていますか。
(A) Snow and ice	(A) 雪と氷
(B) Cloud movement	(B) 雲の動き
(C) The ways that storms form	(C) 嵐のできる過程
(D) Types of mid-level clouds	(D) 中層雲の種類

解法 パッセージの後を推測する問題。最後の段落は上層雲の種類について説明しているので，その次の段落では別の種類，おそらく中層雲の種類について述べることが推測できる。正解は (D)。

重要語 □ **molecule**「分子」	□ **cirrus**「巻雲」
□ **vapor**「蒸気」	□ **cirrocumulus**「巻積雲」
□ **latent**「隠れた，潜在の」	□ **patch**「断片，布」
□ **condense**「凝縮する，凝結する」	□ **fluffy**「綿毛の，ふわふわした」
□ **fuse**「融合する，融解する」	□ **cirrostratus**「巻層雲」
□ **dew point**「露点」	□ **veil**「ベール」
□ **parcel**「かたまり」	□ **halo**「円光，光輪」

IV

総合模試

Section 1—Listening Comprehension

The test directions for **Section 1: Listening Comprehension** have not been licensed for reprinting by ETS. They are available, however, on the Web. Please log on to **https://www.ets.org/toefl/itp.html** for the test directions and sample test questions.

Part A

The test directions for **Part A** have not been licensed for reprinting by ETS. They are available, however, on the Web. Please log on to **https://www.ets.org/toefl/itp.html** for the test directions and sample test questions.

Go on to the next page ➡

Section I Part A/B | Section I Part C | Section 2 | Section 3 | 総合模試 | 総合模試 解答・解説

1. What can be inferred about the printer?

    (A)   It probably cannot be fixed.

    (B)   It may be expensive to repair.

    (C)   It was costly to purchase.

    (D)   It is difficult to replace.

2. What does the man mean?

    (A)   The library probably opens at 1 o'clock.

    (B)   There is only one library on campus.

    (C)   He has plans to go study by himself.

    (D)   The library is not open on Sundays.

3. What does the woman say about Bob?

    (A)   He wants to take a history class.

    (B)   He no longer has a double major.

    (C)   He has stopped studying economics.

    (D)   He has not decided yet on a major.

4. What does the woman want the man to do?

    (A)   Make a doctor's appointment

    (B)   Sign up for a health class

    (C)   Work out in the gym

    (D)   Get an eye examination

◀)) 074

5. What does the woman mean?

   (A) She needs to leave for the airport soon.

   (B) Mail is delivered directly to the student center.

   (C) The man can look at the bus timetable himself.

   (D) They do not have time in their schedule to go running.

◀)) 075

6. What does the man imply?

   (A) He has yet to finish the report.

   (B) He has to hand in the essay by three.

   (C) He has written four different essays.

   (D) He has worked hard on his paper.

◀)) 076

7. What does the woman imply?

   (A) She did not get to hear the concert.

   (B) She sold her ticket to her friend.

   (C) The concert was not as good as she expected.

   (D) The concert started an hour late.

◀)) 077

8. What does the man imply?

   (A) He did not expect the woman to invite him.

   (B) He already has plans for Saturday.

   (C) He definitely wants to go to the game.

   (D) He assumed the woman did not like football.

Go on to the next page ➡ *231*

9. What does the woman imply about the chemistry course?

(A) It is often difficult to enroll in.

(B) It is extremely challenging.

(C) It is not being offered this term.

(D) It requires instructor permission.

10. What will the man probably do?

(A) Telephone the woman soon

(B) Prepare a meal for the woman

(C) Help the woman pick up her books

(D) Eat lunch with the woman

11. What does the woman imply?

(A) They have not been served any water.

(B) It was colder than she expected.

(C) There is now a water shortage.

(D) She was not able to take a break.

12. What does the man say about his research project?

(A) He lost some of the data he collected.

(B) He thought it would go better than it did.

(C) It is producing unexpected results.

(D) It is proceeding smoothly.

Go on to the next page ➡

🔊 082

13. What does the woman imply?

(A) She does not like to watch foreign language films.

(B) She thinks the man should focus on an assignment.

(C) She did not know that the man moved to a new place.

(D) She has to go to her English class this afternoon.

🔊 083

14. What does the man mean?

(A) The woman should be more patient.

(B) He regrets she cannot sit down.

(C) The woman should turn at the corner.

(D) He will be done in about an hour.

🔊 084

15. What does the woman mean?

(A) She is really busy right now.

(B) She thinks the man made a mistake.

(C) She is available at the present time.

(D) She will be back in a moment.

🔊 085

16. What does the man imply?

(A) The woman should start exercising.

(B) He needs to get some exercise himself.

(C) Exercise is good for your health.

(D) Sleeping too much can be bad for you.

Section Ⅰ Part A/B | Section Ⅰ Part C | Section 2 | Section 3 | 総合模試 | 総合模試 解答・解説

17. What had the man assumed?

(A) The information was not based upon fact.

(B) The university website was down.

(C) Everyone had already heard the announcement.

(D) He would not be eligible to stay in the dorm.

18. What does the man mean?

(A) The professor will have to cancel the appointment.

(B) The professor does not have much time to meet today.

(C) The woman should schedule another appointment.

(D) The woman should wait for the professor.

19. What will the man probably do?

(A) Tell the woman how to get to the pharmacy

(B) Get some medicine for the woman

(C) Pick up the woman at the drugstore

(D) Offer the woman some of his aspirin

20. What does the man imply?

(A) He wants to participate in a volunteer organization.

(B) He disagrees with the dean's proposal.

(C) He has more free time than he expected this term.

(D) He is thinking about changing his major.

◀) 090

21. What does the man want to do?

    (A)   Pay his student health insurance premium

    (B)   Petition to pay his fees after the deadline

    (C)   Register for additional courses

    (D)   Make an appointment with a doctor

◀) 091

22. How does the woman feel?

    (A)   Pleased

    (B)   Anxious

    (C)   Upset

    (D)   Disappointed

◀) 092

23. What had the woman assumed about the man?

    (A)   He would not attend the glee club concert.

    (B)   He would not be able to join the glee club.

    (C)   He was going to the concert with someone else.

    (D)   He did not know where the concert was being held.

◀) 093

24. What does the woman imply about the man and the study group?

    (A)   He should have attended the first meeting.

    (B)   He will probably enjoy taking part in it.

    (C)   He has been making a big contribution to it.

    (D)   He ought to be more punctual in attending it.

Section I Part A/B   Section I Part C   Section 2   Section 3   総合模試   総合模試 解答・解説

25. What can be inferred about the man from this conversation?

    (A) He will reduce the number of hours he works.

    (B) He will apply for another scholarship.

    (C) He will request permission to take extra classes.

    (D) He will meet his advisor later in the week.

26. What do we learn about the woman from this conversation?

    (A) She does not like to dance.

    (B) She enjoys writing research papers.

    (C) She started her essay about a month before.

    (D) She regrets not doing the assignment earlier.

27. What is the man's problem?

    (A) The television in the dorm is not working.

    (B) He was not able to go to the library to study.

    (C) The dorm is too noisy for him to concentrate.

    (D) He missed the TV program he wanted to see.

28. What do we learn about the man from this conversation?

    (A) He was unable to graduate on time.

    (B) He will conduct a survey with his boss.

    (C) He is looking for a new place to work.

    (D) He is recruiting new bank employees.

Go on to the next page ➡

098

29. What is the woman's problem?

(A) She has not attended class very often.

(B) She lost her copy of the syllabus.

(C) She put off doing her required reading.

(D) She does not understand the class assignment.

◀) 099

30. What does the woman imply?

(A) She would prefer to go to the cafeteria later.

(B) She was just at the cafeteria.

(C) She does not want to go to the cafeteria.

(D) She has not been at the cafeteria for a long time.

NO TEST MATERIAL ON THIS PAGE

Part B

The test directions for **Part B** have not been licensed for reprinting by ETS. They are available, however, on the Web. Please log on to **https://www.ets.org/ toefl/itp.html** for the test directions and sample test questions.

Go on to the next page ➡

Questions 31-34

31. Why are the two students discussing Professor Conrad?

(A) He is retiring.

(B) He just won an award.

(C) He was recently promoted.

(D) He suffers from poor health.

32. What field does Professor Conrad teach?

(A) Geography

(B) Ecology

(C) Chemistry

(D) Biology

33. What do the students say about Professor Conrad's class?

(A) It required a lot of work.

(B) It was unusually stimulating.

(C) It mainly attracted science majors.

(D) It focused on original research.

34. Where do the students plan to hold the party?

(A) In a lecture hall

(B) In a hotel

(C) In a conference center

(D) In a laboratory

Go on to the next page ➡

Questions 35-38

35. Why is the woman visiting the professor?

    (A)   To apply for a research assistantship

    (B)   To register for his literature course

    (C)   To get his approval for course registration

    (D)   To discuss the possibility of changing majors

36. What is the woman's area of study?

    (A)   Art

    (B)   Literature

    (C)   Music

    (D)   Women's Studies

37. What is the professor concerned about?

    (A)   The woman was absent from too many classes.

    (B)   The woman has not completed her required courses.

    (C)   The woman's plan of study may be too demanding.

    (D)   The woman missed the deadline for registration.

38. What advice does the professor give the woman?

    (A)   She should take a greater variety of courses.

    (B)   She should concentrate more on her major.

    (C)   She should consider taking an extra course.

    (D)   She should take a foreign language.

Section I Part A/B   Section I Part C   Section 2   Section 3   総合模試   総合模試 解答・解説

NO TEST MATERIAL ON THIS PAGE

Part C

The test directions for **Part C** have not been licensed for reprinting by ETS. They are available, however, on the Web. Please log on to **https://www.ets.org/ toefl/itp.html** for the test directions and sample test questions.

39. According to the professor, how large is Jupiter?

(A)   Larger than all of the other planets combined

(B)   Eleven times as large as all of its moons

(C)   Ten times as large as the Earth

(D)   Half as large as the Sun

40. According to the lecture, which of the following is a noteworthy feature of Jupiter?

(A)   It gives off heat.

(B)   It has few clouds.

(C)   Its magnetic fields are reversed.

(D)   Its surface is very dense.

41. What does the professor say about Jupiter's visibility?

(A)   It can typically be seen just after sunset.

(B)   It is usually the brightest object in the sky.

(C)   It increases when the planet approaches the Sun.

(D)   It varies depending upon atmospheric conditions.

42. What will the professor do next?

(A)   Show slides of Jupiter

(B)   Talk about Jupiter's moons

(C)   Conclude the class

(D)   Answer questions

108
109 **Questions 43-46**

43. When did the painters of the Ashcan School create their art?

(A) The late 19th century

(B) The early 20th century

(C) The mid-20th century

(D) The late 20th century

44. What does the professor say about the nature of art?

(A) Beauty is the basis of all art.

(B) Most artists strive to create beauty.

(C) Not all art is beautiful.

(D) Beauty is created by artistic truth.

45. Why were the Ashcan painters initially rejected by many viewers of art?

(A) They chose to paint barren scenes from city life.

(B) They depicted unrecognizable objects.

(C) Their painting technique was crude.

(D) The colors they used were extremely bright.

46. According to the lecture, what feeling did Edward Hopper's paintings often express?

(A) Excitement

(B) Elegance

(C) Poverty

(D) Loneliness

Section 1 Part A/B   Section 1 Part C   Section 2   Section 3   総合模試   総合模試 解答・解説

Questions 47-50

47. Which of the following were the students probably discussing in previous classes?

(A) Meteors
(B) Volcanoes
(C) Hurricanes
(D) Tides

48. What process is this lecture mainly about?

(A) Rock formation
(B) Storm creation
(C) Erosion
(D) Extinction

49. According to the professor, what human activity caused the Dust Bowl of the 1930s?

(A) The cutting of forests
(B) The damming of rivers
(C) Inadequate irrigation
(D) Poor farming practices

50. What example of a dramatic land feature created by water is mentioned by the professor?

(A) The Great Lakes
(B) Death Valley
(C) The Grand Canyon
(D) The Missouri River

This is the end of Section 1. Stop work on Section 1.

Section 2—Structure and Written Expression

Time: 25 minutes

The test directions for **Section 2: Structure and Written Expression** have not been licensed for reprinting by ETS. They are available, however, on the Web. Please log on to **https://www.ets.org/toefl/itp.html** for the test directions and sample test questions.

Structure

The test directions for **Structure** have not been licensed for reprinting by ETS. They are available, however, on the Web. Please log on to **https://www.ets.org/toefl/itp. html** for the test directions and sample test questions.

Go on to the next page ➡ *247*

1. ------- study of human interaction within a society, along with the rules and processes that both unite and separate people as members of associations, groups, and institutions.

(A) That sociology

(B) Sociology it is

(C) Sociology is the

(D) It is sociology which

2. A powerful hurricane can inflict massive damage and widespread loss of life with its high winds, -------, and storm surges.

(A) rains that are heavy

(B) heavily rain

(C) heavy rains

(D) the heaviness of its rain

3. The Erie Canal, -------, was an engineering marvel of the 19th century that connected the Hudson River to Lake Erie through a system of 57 locks.

(A) built from 1817 to 1825

(B) being built from 1817 to 1825

(C) from 1817 to 1825 it was built

(D) it was built from 1817 to 1825

Go on to the next page ➡

4. In upper Wisconsin, the northern pike and the walleyed pike are the two most popular game fish among anglers, ------- the large-mouth bass.

    (A) the third is

    (B) the third has been

    (C) the third which was

    (D) the third being

5. About 70 percent of all adults report ------- from back pain at some point in their lives.

    (A) having suffered

    (B) having been suffer

    (C) have suffered

    (D) are having suffering

6. In 1865, Robert E. Lee and Ulysses S. Grant ------- a treaty at Appomattox Courthouse ending the War Between the States.

    (A) signs

    (B) signing

    (C) were signed

    (D) signed

Go on to the next page ➡

7. In mammals, ------- the brain is in proportion to total body weight, the greater the intelligence of the animal.

(A) the larger

(B) larger

(C) largest

(D) the large

8. ------- the tomato is popularly regarded as a vegetable, it is biologically classified as a fruit.

(A) Although

(B) In spite of

(C) Even

(D) When

9. Ocean ridges are ------- on the floor of the ocean where tectonic plates meet and magma rises to the surface of the seabed.

(A) the mountain range

(B) mountain ranges

(C) a range of mountain

(D) a mountain ranges

10. Anne Marbury Hutchinson, ------- of the Massachusetts Bay Colony, was known for her sharp intellect and forceful personality.

(A) she leads early

(B) whose early leader

(C) the leader early

(D) an early leader

11. Being higher in nutrients but -------, the milk of goats may be better for human consumption than that of cows.

(A) with lower fat

(B) lower in fat

(C) low fat

(D) having low fat

12. In geology, ------- of one principal river and its tributaries.

(A) a drainage basin consisting

(B) a drainage basin consists

(C) a drainage basin it consists

(D) a drainage basin which consists

13. ------- the brain which coordinates muscular movements and balance, the cerebellum is rather large in birds since flight requires such precise coordination.

(A) It is part of
(B) Being the part of
(C) To be a part of
(D) By being a part

14. A catchment area, originally an area from which water is collected by a river, now also refers to the area ------- a school draws its students.

(A) which
(B) by that
(C) from which
(D) that from

15. Only if a society has abundant resources and a well-developed infrastructure ------- a rapid rise in population.

(A) it can support
(B) supports
(C) can it support
(D) will support it

Written Expression

The test directions for **Written Expression** have not been licensed for reprinting by ETS. They are available, however, on the Web. Please log on to **https://www.ets.org/ toefl/itp.html** for the test directions and sample test questions.

16. Two eco-systems are <u>considered</u> interdependent if alterations in one

                                        A

<u>causes</u> changes <u>in</u> the <u>other</u>.
  B   C   D

17. The raptor, comprising <u>a</u> large number of keen-sighted birds, hunts

                                 A

<u>for</u> food while <u>in</u> flight and catches <u>their</u> prey live.
 B   C   D

18. Lake Michigan, <u>the</u> only Great Lake located <u>entirely</u> within the United

                   A   B

States, <u>is</u> the fifth <u>large</u> freshwater body of water in the world.
     C   D

19. <u>Many</u> volcanic activity occurs in places <u>where</u> the Earth's tectonic

    A   B

plates meet, <u>such as</u> in the Ring of Fire <u>that</u> borders the Pacific Ocean.
          C   D

20. The 31st president Herbert C. Hoover, <u>who</u> economic policies

                                     A

<u>were considered</u> pro-business, <u>was</u> later blamed <u>for</u> the Great Depression.
     B   C   D

21. <u>Although</u> the first color <u>film marketed</u> in 1935, color photography
    A   B

did not become <u>widely</u> affordable <u>until</u> the 1960s.
                   C   D

22. A <u>falling decrease</u> in the purchasing power of <u>a</u> currency is the <u>most</u>
           A   B   C

immediate <u>indication</u> of inflation.
          D

23. <u>In addition</u> to pain, <u>swelling</u> around a joint is <u>a</u> obvious sign of <u>injury</u>.
    A   B   C   D

24. When people <u>experience</u> emotional stress, <u>their</u> respiration and heart
                A   B

rate rise <u>sharp</u>, <u>providing</u> them for a short time with increased
        C   D

strength and stamina.

25. The altitude displayed on an aircraft's altimeter <u>is</u> really a measurement
                                                  A

of air pressure, and <u>therefore</u> can also be influenced <u>by</u> such factors
                    B   C

as temperature and <u>humid</u>.
                 D

Section 1 Part A/B   Section 1 Part C   Section 2   Section 3   総合模試   総合模試 解答・解説

Go on to the next page ➡   *255*

26. International Falls, Minnesota, is <u>widely</u> <u>considered</u> the coldest <u>cities</u>
                                         A   B   C

in <u>the entire</u> continental United States.
     D

27. An affidavit is a <u>legally</u> document used in court proceedings <u>in which</u>
  A   B   C

a person swears that <u>certain</u> facts are true.
                    D

28. The dugong, perhaps <u>a</u> gentlest of large, sea-dwelling mammals, <u>is</u> now
                             A   B

in danger of extinction due to <u>human</u> encroachment on <u>its</u> natural habitat.
                                       C   D

29. Although a <u>rise</u> in temperature can sometimes be caused by <u>severe</u>
                 A   B

stress or strenuous exercise, fever <u>is</u> <u>often most</u> a sign of infection.
                                        C   D

30. Vermont was the first <u>initial</u> state to be permitted <u>to join</u> the union
                               A   B

in 1791, thus <u>gaining</u> admittance to the <u>newly formed</u> nation.
                   C   D

31. The early <u>researches</u> in behavioral psychology aimed <u>at</u> identifying
                A   B

<u>measurable</u> stimuli <u>and</u> responses.
    C   D

32. Ida Tarbell was <u>an</u> American journalist <u>whose</u> articles on corruption
                   A   B

made <u>herself</u> one of the most prominent newspaper writers of <u>her</u> time.
      C   D

33. The <u>main</u> industries of Waco, Texas, <u>includes</u> aircraft parts, <u>glass</u>,
    A   B   C

cement, tires, and <u>textiles</u>.
                   D

34. <u>Asparagus</u>, tulips, and green <u>onions all</u> plants included <u>in</u> the lily <u>family</u>.
      A   B   C   D

35. Considering <u>about</u> its size, South Dakota <u>is</u> one of <u>the least</u> populated
                A   B   C

of <u>all</u> of the fifty states.
    D

36. The Heisenberg uncertainty principle proposes that it is <u>possible</u> to

A

<u>accurately</u> specify either the position <u>and</u> the momentum of a particle,

B C

but not both <u>at</u> the same time.

D

37. Renewable resources are <u>that</u> which <u>can be</u> replaced <u>naturally</u> over

A B C

time, such as forests <u>or</u> fishing grounds.

D

38. Louisa May Alcott, <u>a</u> novelist, <u>she</u> lived in Boston and <u>served as a</u>

A B C

nurse with the Union Army <u>during</u> the Civil War.

D

39. <u>The</u> mosaic is <u>one of</u> the oldest and <u>most durable</u> forms of artistic <u>decorate</u>.

A B C D

40. Kinship forms <u>the</u> basis for <u>most</u> human societies and for <u>such</u> social

A B C

groupings as the family, clan, or <u>tribal</u>.

D

This is the end of Section 2. Stop work on Section 2.

Section 3—Reading Comprehension

Time: 55 minutes

The test directions for **Section 3: Reading Comprehension** have not been licensed for reprinting by ETS. They are available, however, on the Web. Please log on to **https://www.ets.org/toefl/itp.html** for the test directions and sample test questions.

Section Ⅰ Part A/B Section Ⅰ Part C Section 2 Section 3 総合模試 総合模試 解答・解説

Line

(1)   There are two major types of deserts in the world: deserts of dryness and deserts of cold. The former, what most people have in mind when they speak of the "desert," comprises areas with an arid climate, sparse or no vegetation, angular landforms, abundant sand, and an absence of full-flowing rivers. The latter type

(5) of desert can be found on the polar fringes of the continents of the Northern Hemisphere and the ice-covered wastelands of Greenland and Antarctica.

Deserts of dryness cover about 18 percent of the Earth's surface and deserts of cold cover 16 percent. All deserts, regardless of type, share two common attributes: any precipitation, whether in the form of rain or snow, is both meager

(10) and uncertain.

Any attempt to measure rainfall in the desert is almost meaningless, because the amount of precipitation does not necessarily correspond with the amount of water absorbed by the soil. At times, clouds form and one can see rain beginning to fall from them, only to be re-evaporated before it reaches the

(15) ground. Further, the small amount of rain that does reach the ground is subject to great variation from year to year. Finally, months or even years may pass between rains.

Water, therefore, is not the main agent of erosion as it is in other types of terrain where more precipitation falls. In humid lands with full-flowing streams,

(20) water sweeps away accumulated rock fragments. In the desert, though, only the wind and intermittent streams can transport them. Wind moves only the finest of dust, and streams seldom reach beyond the desert. Hence, little of the weathered rock material is removed. The result is an abundance of sharp, angular weathered landforms.

1. What does the passage mainly discuss?

   (A) Northern deserts

   (B) Rainfall in the desert

   (C) Characteristics of deserts

   (D) The origin of deserts

2. The word "arid" in line 3 is closest in meaning to

   (A) severe

   (B) dry

   (C) scorching

   (D) erratic

3. The phrase "The latter type" in lines 4 refers to

   (A) deserts of dryness

   (B) deserts of cold

   (C) areas

   (D) angular landforms

4. Which of the following qualities of a dry desert is NOT mentioned in the passage?

   (A) A shortage or absence of plants

   (B) A lack of year-round rivers

   (C) Frigid temperatures

   (D) Ample sand

5. Paragraph 3 mentions all of the follow limitations of measuring rainfall in the desert EXCEPT

   (A) failure of the soil to absorb water

   (B) lack of precise instruments

   (C) great variation in amounts of rainfall

   (D) long periods with no precipitation

Go on to the next page ➡

6. The word "agent" in line 18 is closest in meaning to

(A) representative

(B) solution

(C) resource

(D) cause

7. Paragraph 4 suggests that in non-desert terrain

(A) there is less wind than there is in desert regions

(B) precipitation is more sporadic than it is in the desert

(C) water is the main cause of changes in the shape of landforms

(D) streams tend to be intermittent depending on the season

8. In line 21, the word "them" refers to

(A) other types of terrain

(B) humid lands

(C) full-flowing streams

(D) rock fragments

9. Where in the passage does the author give a specific example of how evaporation can exceed precipitation?

(A) Paragraph 1

(B) Paragraph 2

(C) Paragraph 3

(D) Paragraph 4

10. Where would this text most likely appear?

(A) A geography textbook

(B) A research report

(C) A college bulletin

(D) A conference summary

Go on to the next page ➡

Questions 11-20

Line

(1)　　It's easy to forget that human technology is not new but in fact has evolved over about two-and-a-half million years since the first stone implements were used to extend and amplify human muscle and dexterity.

　　The first and most important jump occurred between 50,000 and 100,000 (5) years ago and is closely linked to physical changes in the human body. It was during this time that anatomical changes led to fully vocalized speech and modern brain function, which in turn led to the development of more specialized bone tools, single-purpose stone implements such as meat scrapers, and compound tools such as spears with shafts and axes with handles. Like all (10) technology, these better tools extended the reach and effectiveness of human activity and ingenuity, in this case, hunting and food preparation.

　　The second jump occurred 13,000 years ago in some parts of the world and still has not yet occurred in other parts of the world. It concerns, of course, the invention of agriculture. The growing of food, rather than the gathering and (15) hunting of it, revolutionized human societies since it required that humans remain in one place to care for fields and orchards, rather than migrating with the animals and the seasons. This transformed their societies, since it led to such practices as division of labor.

　　It is impossible to overestimate the effects of this shift which influenced (20) human society far more than the telephone, the TV, or the computer combined. When people settled down, it meant that they were able to amass non-transportable possessions and to further develop tools—that is, technology—eventually leading to the machine. Hunter-gatherers were limited to technology that could be carried with them, such as spears, stakes, ropes, and drinking (25) gourds. However, when people remained in one place, they could build permanent houses (and develop all of the technology needed to construct and maintain them effectively), fire pottery to store water and cook food, and spend their free time developing more technology which could be passed on to the next generation. Beyond its effect on humans' material lives, the shift from (30) hunting and gathering to specialized food-production—specifically to farming and to the raising of livestock—completely revised how humans conceived of themselves and led to new stories, myths, and religions.

Section I Part A/B　Section I Part C　Section 2　Section 3　総合模試　総合模試 解答・解説

11. What is the author's main point?

(A) The pace of technological change is very fast today.

(B) Humans have always been creative by nature.

(C) Technology continually improves human life.

(D) Some important technologies were invented long ago.

12. Which of the following does the author mention as the first technological invention?

(A) Weapons

(B) Tools

(C) Fire

(D) Pots

13. According to the author, when did the most significant advance in technology occur?

(A) Two-and-a-half million years ago

(B) Between fifty and one hundred thousand years ago

(C) Around thirteen thousand years ago

(D) In the 20th century

14. The word "amplify" in line 3 is closest in meaning to

(A) increase

(B) generate

(C) condense

(D) replace

Go on to the next page ➡

15. In paragraph 2, the author implies that

    (A) human technology and physiology evolved together

    (B) the earliest humans were unusually inventive

    (C) the first technology extended human life spans

    (D) some technologies spread rapidly among early societies

16. According to the passage, which of the following is probably the most significant result of the rise of agriculture?

    (A) Humans were able to increase their populations.

    (B) Villages began to trade with each other.

    (C) People accumulated possessions and passed on knowledge.

    (D) Families could construct safer and larger dwellings.

17. The word "livestock" in line 31 is closest in meaning to

    (A) farm animals

    (B) cultivated plants

    (C) staples

    (D) fruits

18. Which of the following statements best describes the organization of paragraph 4?

    (A) An extended definition

    (B) A comparison of viewpoints

    (C) A series of types

    (D) A claim followed by supporting points

19. With which of the following statements would the author most likely agree?

(A) Modern societies will continue to change radically.

(B) Many technologies can harm or even destroy their makers.

(C) The invention of agriculture has had the greatest effect on culture.

(D) Humans have remained fundamentally the same for thousands of years.

20. In which paragraph does the author refer to the relationship between technology and how people view themselves?

(A) Paragraph 1

(B) Paragraph 2

(C) Paragraph 3

(D) Paragraph 4

Questions 21-29

Line

(1)   One group of Native Americans who migrated much later to the Southwest than other tribes was the Navajo. While the ancestors of the Navajo likely crossed the land bridge between Asia and Canada some 20,000 years ago, archaeological evidence suggests that they first came to their present home

(5) approximately five centuries ago. Navajo folklore tells of emerging into this world from earlier worlds, which can be interpreted as a tale of migrations.

Although they have always lived in an extremely dry, harsh, and relatively remote desert of the Southwest, the Navajo have never been fully isolated from their neighbors. In fact, it is clear that they adopted many agricultural practices

(10) from the Pueblos who lived in the region prior to them. It was probably this association which contributed both to their economic development and to their sedentary tendencies. In general, the Navajo have been a far less nomadic people than has been portrayed in the popular literature, content to eke out an existence by farming land which is virtually barren.

(15)   In addition to borrowing from other cultures, the Navajo often staged raids on adjacent peoples, making them feared by other tribes and Europeans alike. However, it is misleading to think of the Navajo as a single tribe, at least until the arrival of the European Americans in the late 1840s. While united loosely by language and cultural tradition, the Navajo certainly were not one political

(20) body and never functioned as a single unit. A battle waged by one group would not necessarily be condoned or even known about by another. Moreover, an agreement made by one group would not bind all Navajo.

This changed with the introduction of the reservation system in the two decades after the American military occupied New Mexico in 1846 during the war

(25) between the United States and Mexico. Discovering to their dismay the reality of the dispersed Navajo population while attempting to exert their control over the region, the American authorities came into direct conflict with the Navajo and skirmishes were common for many years. It was decided in the middle of the 1860s that the Navajo must be converted to Christianity and forcibly moved to

(30) a reservation located some 300 miles to the east of their homeland. More than 2,000 Navajo died, but as a result of this experience the Navajo banded together politically and pressured the United States government to allow them to return

home. The government finally relented and in 1868 the Navajo were ceded a huge tract of their original homeland straddling the three states of Arizona, Utah, and *(35)* New Mexico, an area which serves as their primary reservation now. Today the Navajo population is second to none among all Native American tribes.

21. With what topic is this passage mainly concerned?

(A) The history of Native Americans
(B) The struggle of Native Americans in the Southwest
(C) The story of the Navajo peoples
(D) The new Navajo reservation

22. According to the author, how many years ago did the Navajo first appear in the American Southwest?

(A) 250 years
(B) 500 years
(C) 5,000 years
(D) 20,000 years

23. In line 2, the word "ancestors" could best be replaced with which of the following?

(A) Citizens
(B) Descendants
(C) Forbearers
(D) Rulers

24. Paragraph 3 implies that prior to the arrival of the European Americans in the late 1840s the Navajo were

(A) little concerned with agriculture
(B) hostile towards outsiders
(C) linguistically diverse
(D) politically fragmented

Go on to the next page ➡

25. The word "waged" in line 20 is closest in meaning to

(A) finished

(B) reported

(C) planned

(D) conducted

26. The Navajo homeland can be described as all of the following EXCEPT

(A) fertile

(B) vast

(C) rugged

(D) remote

27. The word "their" in line 25 refers to

(A) American military

(B) United States

(C) dispersed Navajo population

(D) American authorities

28. What aspect of Navajo experience does the last paragraph mainly discuss?

(A) Physical relocation

(B) Cultural origins

(C) Agricultural practices

(D) Population growth

29. It can be concluded from the passage that the Navajo

(A) taught farming techniques to their neighbors

(B) are essentially a tribe of nomads

(C) constitute the largest Native American tribe

(D) have a higher level of education than other tribes

Go on to the next page ➡

Questions 30-39

(1)   Drugs have traditionally been prescribed according to the estimated dose needed and the optimal period between doses. However, it is well-known that the human body's daily cycle, known as the circadian rhythm, has a significant influence on the body's physical state as well as its receptivity to drugs. Focusing on this day-night

(5) cycle, scientists have come up with the following hypothesis: If some diseases also follow cyclical patterns during the course of a single day and night, it may be possible both to pinpoint the most effective times of the day for administering drugs and to take advantage of the rhythms to minimize their undesirable side effects.

In general, body temperature and blood pressure start to increase after people

(10) wake up and they start to decline from early to late evening. This general cycle helps to promote activity during the daytime while allowing the body to rest at night. However, there are individual differences in circadian rhythm—not everyone runs according to the same exact biological cycle—and as a result, some people are more energetic in the daytime while others are more energetic at night. Scientists and

(15) doctors know that irregular lifestyles, such as working the night shift every third week, jet lag after a long trip, and even surgery can affect the circadian cycle. One interesting physiological discovery is that the body's circadian rhythm is regulated by a particular part of the brain known as the "biological clock." When some diseases occur, this inner clock not only affects a patient's activity levels but also affects the

(20) state of the disease during the course of the day.

Among the significant influences of the biological clock on those suffering from particular medical syndromes is that strokes and heart attacks tend to occur in the morning since they are typically associated with an increase in blood pressure. By contrast, bronchial asthma attacks occur mainly between the evening and the

(25) early morning due to changes in the rhythm of the respiratory system during that period. Already a treatment has been devised for bronchial asthma sufferers: they take special drugs before going to bed, and these drugs are slowly released into the patient's system so that they are effective during the patient's most vulnerable hours.

In the future, it is likely that medicines currently labeled with instructions such as

(30) "To be taken three times a day after meals" will instead read "To be taken according to your particular biological clock."

30. What topic does the passage mainly discuss?

(A) Scientists' discovery of circadian rhythms

(B) Drugs that work better at night

(C) How body rhythms influence medicine

(D) Resetting the biological clock

31. How long does the circadian rhythm last?

(A) 12 hours

(B) 24 hours

(C) During the daylight hours

(D) For the duration of one night

32. The word "optimal" in line 2 is closest in meaning to

(A) ideal

(B) extended

(C) fixed

(D) assumed

33. In line 8, the word "their" refers to

(A) some diseases

(B) drugs

(C) rhythms

(D) cyclical patterns

34. According to the passage, what happens to blood pressure in the evening?

(A) It is stable.

(B) It rises.

(C) It falls.

(D) It rises then falls.

35. What part of the human body appears to regulate the circadian rhythm?

(A) The heart

(B) The optic nerves

(C) The glandular system

(D) The brain

36. It can be inferred from paragraph 2 that

(A) regular working hours may be harmful to health

(B) not all people have the same circadian rhythm

(C) most people experience higher bodily temperature in the evening

(D) morning is seldom the best time for physical activity

37. The word "syndromes" in line 22 could best be replaced by which of the following?

(A) Accelerations

(B) Adaptations

(C) Afflictions

(D) Aggravations

38. With which of the following statements would the author probably agree?

(A) In the future, the administration of medication may be carefully timed.

(B) All diseases have a specific relationship to the body's biological clock.

(C) Drugs should be prescribed only as a last resort for serious illness.

(D) The instructions for taking prescriptive medicines are highly inaccurate.

39. Which of the following best describes the author's tone in the passage?

(A) Skeptical

(B) Optimistic

(C) Sarcastic

(D) Outspoken

Go on to the next page ➡

Questions 40-50

Line

(1) The Treaty of Paris in 1763 concluded the French and Indian War and ended any direct French influence in what was to become the United States, thus assuring British title to the area south of the Ohio River comprising Kentucky and Tennessee. Soon, the so-called "long hunters," including the legendary Daniel Boone, returned

(5) from expeditions to Tennessee with glowing reports about the richness of the land and the opportunities present there. Despite the fact that the British government formally barred any settlement west of the Appalachian Mountains, hundreds of English, Scotch-Irish, and German inhabitants of the Virginia and North Carolina backcountry ignored the ban, dissatisfied with their political and economic status in

(10) the areas in which they lived.

When the American Revolution began in 1775, these residents supported the cause of independence from England. Realizing that they were not strong enough to defend their own territory against attack from either the British or hostile native tribes, the settlers appealed to the adjacent state of North Carolina within whose

(15) western claim they officially resided. Somewhat reluctantly North Carolina created Washington County to include almost all of present-day Tennessee. After the end of the war, North Carolina ceded its Tennessee territory to the new federal government in 1784, the same year that the new Congress passed an ordinance authorizing the possible formation of new states in the federal territories. As the former Washington

(20) County had just become one, the residents of the eastern part quickly organized a political entity named Franklin in honor of Benjamin Franklin. They adopted a constitution, elected a governor, and continued with their efforts to be admitted to the new nation as the 14th state.

For several years, starting in 1787, the "State of Franklin" maintained a precarious

(25) existence, characterized by continuing troubles with the Native American population, intrigues with the Spanish, who had been the first Europeans to explore the area two centuries prior, internal dissension, tensions with neighboring North Carolina, and ineffectual efforts to gain full recognition from the American Congress. Eventually Congress reorganized the whole Tennessee area into a new federal territory, familiarly

(30) known as the Southwest Territory. When the census of 1795 revealed that the population in the Southwest Territory had exceeded the required 60,000 residents, local politicians again petitioned for statehood. And in June of 1796, Tennessee was admitted to the Union as the 16th state.

Section Ⅰ Part A/B   Section Ⅰ Part C   Section 2   Section 3   総合模試   総合模試 解答・解説

40. What is the main topic of the passage?

(A) How territories become states

(B) The early history of Tennessee

(C) Tennessee's role in the Revolutionary War

(D) Why the State of Franklin failed

41. In paragraph 1, the author implies that the original European settlers were

(A) new arrivals from the European continent

(B) dissatisfied with their previous living conditions

(C) disinterested in the politics of revolutionary America

(D) supported by the government of North Carolina

42. In line 4, why does the author place "long hunters" in quotation marks?

(A) To make a comparison

(B) To suggest sarcasm

(C) To show a direct quotation

(D) To indicate a name

43. The word "adjacent" in line 14 is closest in meaning to

(A) adjoining

(B) isolated

(C) friendly

(D) aggressive

Go on to the next page ➡

44. The State of Franklin was troubled by all of the following EXCEPT

(A) friction with an adjacent state

(B) discord among its inhabitants

(C) conflicts with Native American tribes

(D) inadequate population growth

45. In paragraph 2, what action is NOT mentioned as a step residents took to gain statehood?

(A) Chose a governor

(B) Elected an assembly

(C) Approved a constitution

(D) Created a political body

46. According to the passage, the first group of non-Native Americans to discover the Tennessee region were the

(A) Spanish

(B) French

(C) Germans

(D) English

47. How many states were in the Union immediately prior to Tennessee's being granted statehood?

(A) Thirteen

(B) Fourteen

(C) Fifteen

(D) Sixteen

48. When did Tennessee finally achieve statehood?

(A) 1784

(B) 1787

(C) 1795

(D) 1796

49. The author organizes the discussion in the passage according to which principle?

(A) Chronology

(B) Classification

(C) Contrast

(D) Spatial Orientation

50. The paragraph immediately preceding this passage most likely discusses which of the following?

(A) The French and Indian War

(B) The life of Daniel Boone

(C) The British colonization of America

(D) Native American tribes in Tennessee

This is the end of the test.

総合模試　解答・解説

総合模試　正答一覧表

Listening

Part A

1	B
2	A
3	B
4	A
5	C
6	D
7	A
8	C
9	B
10	D
11	B
12	D
13	B
14	A
15	C
16	C
17	A
18	D
19	B
20	B
21	B
22	A
23	A
24	D
25	A
26	D
27	C
28	D
29	C
30	C

Part B

31	A
32	D
33	B
34	D
35	C
36	B
37	C
38	A

Part C

39	A
40	A
41	B
42	D
43	B
44	C
45	A
46	D
47	B
48	C
49	D
50	C

Structure and Written Expression

Structure

1	C
2	C
3	A
4	D
5	A
6	D
7	A
8	A
9	B
10	D
11	B
12	B
13	B
14	C
15	C

Written Expression

16	B
17	D
18	D
19	A
20	A
21	B
22	A
23	C
24	C
25	D
26	C
27	B
28	A
29	D
30	A
31	A
32	C
33	B
34	B
35	B
36	C
37	C
38	B
39	D
40	D

Reading

1	C
2	B
3	B
4	C
5	B
6	D
7	C
8	D
9	C
10	A
11	D
12	B
13	B
14	A
15	A
16	C
17	A
18	D
19	C
20	D
21	C
22	B
23	C
24	D
25	D
26	A
27	D
28	A
29	C
30	C
31	B
32	A
33	B
34	C
35	D
36	B
37	C
38	A
39	B
40	B
41	B
42	D
43	A
44	D
45	B
46	A
47	C
48	D
49	A
50	A

Answer Key **Section 1—Listening Comprehension**   Part A

1.   解答：B

◀)) 070　**M:** Are they going to be able to fix the printer?

　　W: I think so. But it would be a lot cheaper just to buy a new one.

　　　M:　プリンターは修理できるかな。

　　　W:　そう思うわ。でも，新しいのを買うほうがずっと安いかもしれないわね。

What can be inferred about the printer?　　プリンターについて何が推測できますか。

(A) It probably cannot be fixed.　　　　　(A) たぶん修理できない。

(B) It may be expensive to repair.　　　　(B) 修理は高くつくかもしれない。

(C) It was costly to purchase.　　　　　　(C) 購入は高くついた。

(D) It is difficult to replace.　　　　　　(D) 取り替えるのは難しい。

> **解法** 設問を先読みしてから会話を聞き，会話内でプリンターについて考えられることを聞き取る。推測に関する問題。女性は it would be a lot cheaper just to buy a new one と言っているので，修理は高くつくかもしれないことを示している。正解は (B)。
>
> **重要語**
> □ **costly** 「高価な，高くつく」

2.   解答：A

◀)) 071　**W:** Do you know what time the library opens on Sundays?

　　M: One, isn't it?

　　　W:　図書館は日曜日何時に開館するか知ってる？

　　　M:　1時じゃないかな。

What does the man mean?　　　　　　　　男性は何を言いたいのですか。

(A) The library probably opens at 1 o'clock.　(A) 図書館はたぶん1時に開く。

(B) There is only one library on campus.　　(B) キャンパスに図書館はひとつだけである。

(C) He has plans to go study by himself.　　(C) ひとりで勉強しにいくつもりである。

(D) The library is not open on Sundays.　　(D) 図書館は日曜日には開いていない。

> **解法** 設問を先読みしてから会話を聞き，会話内で男性が言いたいことを聞き取る。男性の発言の意図を問う問題。One, isn't it? から，開館時間はたぶん1時であると男性は述べている。正解は (A)。

3.

🔊 072 **M:** Isn't Bob majoring in both economics and art history?

W: He was. But he's dropped art history.

M: ボブは経済学と美術史の両方を専攻していたんじゃないの？

W: 以前の話よ。でも，美術史はやめたわよ。

What does the woman say about Bob?	女性はボブについて何と言っていますか。
(A) He wants to take a history class.	(A) 彼は歴史のクラスをとりたいと思っている。
(B) He no longer has a double major.	(B) 彼はもはや2分野を専攻していない。
(C) He has stopped studying economics.	(C) 彼は経済学の勉強をやめた。
(D) He has not decided yet on a major.	(D) 彼は専攻をまだ決めていない。

解法 設問を先読みしてから会話を聞き，会話内で女性がボブについて言っていることを聞き取る。会話の内容を問う問題。he's dropped art history から，ボブはもはや美術史を専攻していないことがわかる。正解は (B)。

重要語
□ **major** 「〜を専攻する」

4.

🔊 073 **W:** I don't like the sound of that cough. You really should see a physician over at health services.

M: Yes, I suppose you're right.

W: そのせきはよくないわね。医療施設で医師にちゃんと診てもらうべきだわ。

M: うん，そのとおりだと思うよ。

What does the woman want the man to do?	女性は男性に何をしてもらいたいのですか。
(A) Make a doctor's appointment	(A) 医師の診察予約を取る
(B) Sign up for a health class	(B) 保健の授業を取る
(C) Work out in the gym	(C) ジムで運動する
(D) Get an eye examination	(D) 目の検査を受ける

解法 設問を先読みしてから会話を聞き，会話内で女性が男性にしてもらいたいことを聞き取る。女性の発言の意図を問う問題。女性は You really should see a physician と言い，医師に診てもらうよう男性に勧めている。正解は (A)。

重要語
□ **cough** 「せき」
□ **physician** 「医師，内科医」

5.　　　　　　　　　　　　　　　　　　　　　　　　　　　　　　解答：C

◀) 074

M: Do you know what time the buses leave campus for the airport?

W: Why don't you check the schedule that's posted in the student center?

　　M:　空港行きのバスが何時に大学を出るか知ってる？

　　W:　学生会館に掲示されているスケジュールを確認してみたらどう？

What does the woman mean?

(A) She needs to leave for the airport soon.

(B) Mail is delivered directly to the student center.

(C) The man can look at the bus timetable himself.

(D) They do not have time in their schedule to go running.

女性は何を言いたいのですか。

(A) 彼女はまもなく空港へ向けて出発しなければならない。

(B) 郵便は直接学生会館に配達される。

(C) 男性はバスの時刻表を自分で見ることができる。

(D) 彼らはスケジュール上では走りに行く時間がない。

解法	設問を先読みしてから会話を聞き，会話内で女性が言いたいことを聞き取る。女性の発言の意図を問う問題。女性は，Why don't you check the schedule that's posted in the student center? と述べ，バスの時刻表を学生会館で見ることができると伝えている。正解は (C)。

【重要語】
□ **timetable**「時刻表」

6.　　　　　　　　　　　　　　　　　　　　　　　　　　　　　　解答：D

◀) 075

W: Wow, Bill. Are you still working on that essay? You must have revised it at least a dozen times.

M: Well, I feel like it. I was working on the essay day and night this week. In fact, I only rewrote it three or four times, though.

　　W:　ねえ，ビル。まだそのレポートに取り組んでいるの？　少なくとも10回余りは修正したみたいね。

　　M:　本当にそんなふうに思えるよね。今週は昼も夜もこのレポートにかかりきりだったから。でも，実際は3，4回書き直しただけだよ。

What does the man imply?

(A) He has yet to finish the report.

(B) He has to hand in the essay by three.

(C) He has written four different essays.

(D) He has worked hard on his paper.

男性は何を示唆していますか。

(A) 彼はまだレポートを仕上げていない。

(B) 彼は3時までにレポートを提出しなければならない。

(C) 彼は4つの異なるレポートを書いた。

(D) 彼はレポートに一生懸命取り組んだ。

解法	設問を先読みしてから会話を聞き，会話内で男性が示唆していることを聞き取る。男性の発言の意図を問う問題。男性は，I was working on the essay day and night this week. と述べ，エッセイに一生懸命取り組んだことを示唆している。正解は (D)。

【重要語】
□ **revise**「～を修正する，改訂する」
□ **dozen**「ダース，12，多数」

7.

🔊 076

M: Did you enjoy the orchestra concert last night?

W: Would you believe that even though my friend and I got there an hour before it started, all of the tickets had been sold out?

M: 昨夜のオーケストラのコンサートは楽しかった？

W: 友人と私は始まる1時間前に行ったのに，チケットが完売していたって信じられる？

What does the woman imply?	女性は何を示唆していますか。
(A) She did not get to hear the concert.	(A) 彼女はコンサートを聞くことができなかった。
(B) She sold her ticket to her friend.	(B) 彼女は友人に自分のチケットを売った。
(C) The concert was not as good as she expected.	(C) コンサートは期待していたほどよくなかった。
(D) The concert started an hour late.	(D) コンサートは1時間遅れで始まった。

解法 設問を先読みしてから会話を聞き，会話内で女性が示唆していることを聞き取る。女性の発言の意図を問う問題。女性は，自分たちが着く前にチケットが完売していたことが信じられないと言っているので，チケットを入手できずコンサートに入れなかったことがわかる。正解は (A)。

8.

🔊 077

W: I'm getting a group together to go to the football game on Saturday afternoon. You want to come?

M: Do I? Knowing how big of a fan I am, do you even have to ask me?

W: 土曜日の午後，フットボールの試合に行く仲間を募っているところなの。来る？

M: 僕が？　僕がすごいファンだと知っていて，わざわざ僕に聞くの？

What does the man imply?	男性は何を示唆していますか。
(A) He did not expect the woman to invite him.	(A) 女性が招待してくれるとは思わなかった。
(B) He already has plans for Saturday.	(B) 土曜日にはすでに予定がある。
(C) He definitely wants to go to the game.	(C) 絶対に試合に行きたい。
(D) He assumed the woman did not like football.	(D) 女性はフットボールを好きではないと思っていた。

解法 設問を先読みしてから会話を聞き，会話内で男性が示唆していることを聞き取る。男性の発言の意図を問う問題。「僕がすごいファンだと知っていて，わざわざ僕に聞くの？」との発言から，男性は当然試合に行きたいし，女性もそれをわかっていると思っていたのに，行くかと尋ねられて驚いていることがわかる。正解は (C)。

重要語
□ **definitely**「絶対に，断然」

9.

解答：B

🔊 078

M: I can't believe that the organic chemistry course is full. I really want to take it this semester.

W: Well, if it's any consolation, I took it last term and I hardly had a life outside of school.

M: 有機化学の科目がいっぱいだとは信じられないよ。今学期にぜひ取りたいんだ。

W: 慰めになるかどうかわからないけど，先学期その科目を取った結果，私に学外での生活はほとんどなかったわ。

What does the woman imply about the chemistry course?

女性は化学の科目について何を示唆していますか。

(A) It is often difficult to enroll in.
(B) It is extremely challenging.
(C) It is not being offered this term.
(D) It requires instructor permission.

(A) 登録するのが難しいことがある。
(B) 非常に難しい。
(C) 今学期は開講されない。
(D) 教員の許可が必要である。

解法 設問を先読みしてから会話を聞き，会話内で女性が化学の科目について示唆していることを聞き取る。女性の発言の意図を問う問題。女性は，先学期有機化学の科目を取った結果，hardly had a life outside of school であった。非常に難しい科目で勉強に集中しなければならず，学外のことに時間が取れなかったことを示しているので，正解は (B)。

重要語
□ **organic**「有機の」
□ **consolation**「慰め」

10.

解答：D

🔊 079

W: Hey, I'm glad I bumped into you. I was just going to call you and see if you wanted to grab some lunch.

M: Sounds great.

W: あら，思いがけず会えてよかったわ。電話して昼食を食べないか聞こうとしていたのよ。

M: いいね。

What will the man probably do?

男性はおそらく何をしますか。

(A) Telephone the woman soon
(B) Prepare a meal for the woman
(C) Help the woman pick up her books
(D) Eat lunch with the woman

(A) まもなく女性に電話する
(B) 女性のために食事を準備する
(C) 女性が本を買うのを手伝う
(D) 女性と食事をする

解法 設問を先読みしてから会話を聞き，会話内で男性がおそらく行うことを聞き取る。男性の行動を推測する問題。Sounds great. から，男性は女性の提案どおり，一緒に食事をすると考えられる。正解は (D)。

重要語
□ **bump into ...**「～に思いがけず会う」
□ **grab**「～をすばやく食べる，捕まえる」

11.

🔊 080

M: I can't believe classes have started again so quickly. By the way, how was your vacation at the beach over spring break?

W: Freezing. Who would have thought we could hardly go in the water?

M: こんなに早く授業が始まったなんて信じられないよ。ところで，春休みのビーチでの休暇はどうだった？

W: とても寒かったわ。水にほとんど入れないなんて思いもよらなかったわよ。

What does the woman imply?	女性は何を示唆していますか。
(A) They have not been served any water.	(A) 飲み水が出ていない。
(B) It was colder than she expected.	(B) 思ったより寒かった。
(C) There is now a water shortage.	(C) 水不足である。
(D) She was not able to take a break.	(D) 休暇を取れなかった。

解法 設問を先読みしてから会話を聞き，会話内で女性が示唆していることを聞き取る。女性の発言の意図を問う問題。「とても寒かったわ。水にほとんど入れないなんて思いもよらなかった」という発言は，寒くて水にほとんど入れないとは思っていなかったことを示唆している。正解は (B)。

重要語
- **freezing**
「とても寒い，凍るような」

12.

🔊 081

W: John, I don't think I've seen you for about a month. How is your senior research project coming along?

M: It couldn't be better. I've collected all of my data and am now analyzing the results.

W: ジョン，1 か月ぐらい会ってなかったわね。4 年次のリサーチプロジェクトはどんな具合なの？

M: 順調そのものだよ。データはすべて収集して，今結果を分析中だ。

What does the man say about his research project?	男性は自分のリサーチプロジェクトについて何と言っていますか。
(A) He lost some of the data he collected.	(A) 収集したデータの一部を失くした。
(B) He thought it would go better than it did.	(B) 実際よりはうまくやることができたのにと思った。
(C) It is producing unexpected results.	(C) 予期していなかった結果が出ている。
(D) It is proceeding smoothly.	(D) 順調に進んでいる。

解法 設問を先読みしてから会話を聞き，会話内で男性がリサーチプロジェクトについて言っていることを聞き取る。男性の発言の意図を問う問題。It couldn't be better. はとてもよい状態であることを表すので，男性のリサーチプロジェクトはうまく進んでいることがわかる。正解は (D)。

重要語
- **It couldn't be better.**
「最高である，上々である」
- **proceed**「進む」

13. 解答：B

M: Sally, why don't you come over to my place this afternoon and watch a movie?

W: Still putting off writing that essay for your English class, are you?

M: サリー，今日の午後僕のところに来て映画を見ない？

W: 英語のクラスのレポートを書くのをまだ延ばしているんでしょ？

What does the woman imply?	女性は何を示唆していますか。
(A) She does not like to watch foreign language films.	(A) 外国語の映画を見るのは好きではない。
(B) She thinks the man should focus on an assignment.	(B) 男性は課題に集中するべきだと考えている。
(C) She did not know that the man moved to a new place.	(C) 男性が新居に越したのを知らなかった。
(D) She has to go to her English class this afternoon.	(D) 今日の午後英語のクラスに行かなければならない。

解法 設問を先読みしてから会話を聞き，会話内で女性が示唆していることを聞き取る。女性の発言の意図を問う問題。女性は，男性が英語のクラスのレポートを書くのを先送りにしていることを指摘しているので，まず課題にとりかかるべきであると示唆している。正解は (B)。

重要語
□ **put off**「～を遅らせる」

14. 解答：A

W: This is taking forever. I've been standing in this line for half an hour!

M: Well, I'm sorry but you'll just have to wait your turn like everyone else.

W: いつになったら終わるの。30 分もこの列に並んでいるのよ！

M: ええと，申し訳ないのですが，他の人と同じように順番を待っていただかないと。

What does the man mean?	男性は何を言いたいのですか。
(A) The woman should be more patient.	(A) 女性はもう少し辛抱強くあるべきだ。
(B) He regrets she cannot sit down.	(B) 女性が座れないことを申し訳ないと思う。
(C) The woman should turn at the corner.	(C) 女性は角で曲がるべきだ。
(D) He will be done in about an hour.	(D) 自分は 1 時間くらいで終わる。

解法 設問を先読みしてから会話を聞き，会話内で男性が言いたいことを聞き取る。男性の発言の意図を問う問題。男性は女性に順番を待つように伝えているので，正解は (A)。

重要語
□ **stand in line**「列に並ぶ」

◀)） 084

M: Mary, I've been planning to contact you. When can we get together to plan for our group presentation?

W: Well, what's wrong with right now?

M: メアリー，連絡しようと思っていたんだ。グループ発表の予定を立てるのにいつ集まれるかな。

W: ええと，今じゃだめかしら。

What does the woman mean?	女性は何を言いたいのですか。
(A) She is really busy right now.	(A) 今とても忙しい。
(B) She thinks the man made a mistake.	(B) 男性は間違えたと思っている。
(C) She is available at the present time.	(C) 今都合がつく。
(D) She will be back in a moment.	(D) すぐに戻る。

解法 設問を先読みしてから会話を聞き，会話内で女性が言いたいことを聞き取る。女性の発言の意図を問う問題。女性は，what's wrong with right now? と述べ，今話し合うことを提案している。つまり今は彼女の都合がよいことを示しているので，正解は (C)。

重要語
□ **available**「都合がよい」

◀)） 085

W: Ever since I took up jogging, I sleep better and get more done during the day, too.

M: Amazing what a little exercise can do, isn't it?

W: ジョギングを始めてから，これまで以上によく眠れるし，日中もやることがはかどるわ。

M: ちょっとした運動がどんなに役立つか驚きだよね。

What does the man imply?	男性は何を示唆していますか。
(A) The woman should start exercising.	(A) 女性は運動を始めるべきだ。
(B) He needs to get some exercise himself.	(B) 自分は運動をする必要がある。
(C) Exercise is good for your health.	(C) 運動は健康によい。
(D) Sleeping too much can be bad for you.	(D) 睡眠を取りすぎるとよくないことがある。

解法 設問を先読みしてから会話を聞き，会話内で男性が示唆していることを聞き取る。男性の発言の意図を問う問題。男性の what a little exercise can do との発言から，運動が健康に役立つと考えていることがわかる。正解は (C)。

重要語
□ **take up ...**「～を始める」

17.

W: I just read an announcement on the university website that they're going to tear down Johnson Hall and build a new dorm.

M: And I thought that was just a rumor!

W: ジョンソン・ホールを取り壊して，新しい寮を建てるという告知を大学ホームページ上で読んだところよ。

M: 単なるうわさだと思っていたのに。

What had the man assumed?

(A) The information was not based upon fact.

(B) The university website was down.

(C) Everyone had already heard the announcement.

(D) He would not be eligible to stay in the dorm.

男性はどのように思っていましたか。

(A) 情報は事実に基づいていない。

(B) 大学のホームページはダウンしている。

(C) みんながすでに告知を聞いた。

(D) 自分は寮に留まる資格がない。

解法 設問を先読みしてから会話を聞き，会話内で男性が思っていたことを聞き取る。男性の発言の意図を問う問題。I thought that was just a rumor! から，男性は告知された内容は単なるうわさで，事実ではないと思っていたことがわかる。正解は(A)。

重要語
□ **tear down** ... 「～を取り壊す」
□ **rumor** 「うわさ」
□ **eligible** 「資格のある」

18.

W: I have an appointment to see Professor Wordsworth.

M: The meeting she's in should break up soon. Please have a seat and she'll be with you momentarily.

W: ワーズワース教授との面談の約束をいただいています。

M: 教授が出席中の会議はじきに終わるでしょう。どうぞお掛けください。教授はすぐにお会いしますので。

What does the man mean?

(A) The professor will have to cancel the appointment.

(B) The professor does not have much time to meet today.

(C) The woman should schedule another appointment.

(D) The woman should wait for the professor.

男性は何を言いたいのですか。

(A) 教授は約束をキャンセルしなければならないだろう。

(B) 教授は今日面談する時間があまりない。

(C) 女性は別の面談の約束を取るべきである。

(D) 女性は教授を待つべきである。

解法 設問を先読みしてから会話を聞き，会話内で男性が言いたいことを聞き取る。男性の発言の意図を問う問題。男性は，Please have a seat and she'll be with you momentarily. と述べ，女性に座って待つように伝えている。正解は (D)。

重要語
□ **break up** 「終わる，解散する」
□ **momentarily** 「すぐに」(= very soon)

19.

◀) 088

W: This headache is killing me. Do you have any aspirin I could take?

M: I'm afraid not. But there's an all-night pharmacy about a mile away on Mill Street. I'll drive over there right now and pick some up for you.

W: 頭が痛くて死にそうだわ。アスピリン持ってる？

M: 残念ながらないんだ。ミル通りを 1 マイルくらい行ったところに終夜営業の薬局がある。今すぐそこへ車で行って，買ってきてあげるよ。

What will the man probably do?	男性はおそらく何をしますか。
(A) Tell the woman how to get to the pharmacy	(A) 女性に薬局への行き方を教える
(B) Get some medicine for the woman	(B) 女性のために薬を買う
(C) Pick up the woman at the drugstore	(C) 薬局で女性を車に乗せる
(D) Offer the woman some of his aspirin	(D) 持っているアスピリンを女性に渡す

解法 設問を先読みしてから会話を聞き，会話内で男性がおそらく行うことを聞き取る。男性の行動を推測する問題。headache, aspirin, pharmacy, drive, pick some up などのキーワードから，女性が頭痛で困っていること，男性が薬局へ車で行ってアスピリンを買ってこようとしていることがわかる。正解は (B)。

重要語
□ **pharmacy** 「薬局」

20.

解答：B

089

W: The dean of students is proposing that all students be required to participate in volunteer activities in the community.

M: Really? I think we're in school to focus on our studies. Especially engineering students like us don't have so much free time for outside stuff.

W: 学生部長は，すべての学生が地域のボランティア活動に参加することを必修にすると提案しているわよ。

M: そうなの？　僕らは自分たちの学問に集中するために学校にいるのだと思うけどね。特に僕たちのような工学部の学生は，外のことに割ける自由な時間はそれほどないよ。

What does the man imply?　男性は何を示唆していますか。

(A) He wants to participate in a volunteer organization.
(B) He disagrees with the dean's proposal.
(C) He has more free time than he expected this term.
(D) He is thinking about changing his major.

(A) ボランティア組織に参加したい。
(B) 学生部長の提案に反対である。
(C) 今学期は予想していた以上に自由時間がある。
(D) 専攻を変更しようかと思っている。

解法 設問を先読みしてから会話を聞き，会話内で男性が示唆していることを聞き取る。男性の発言の意図を問う問題。男性は，学生の地域ボランティア活動について次のように述べ，学生部長には同意していない。また学生部長の意見に反対であることは，Really? 以下のイントネーションからも読み取ることができる。正解は (B)。

重要語
□ **dean of students**
「学生部長」
□ **engineering**「工学（部）」

》 I think we're in school to focus on our studies.
》 Especially engineering students like us don't have so much free time for outside stuff.

21.

解答：B

090

M: I'd like to request to pay my registration fees late this semester. I understand that in case of a genuine medical emergency it might be possible.

W: Yes, it is. You'll need to file a request along with a letter from a physician certifying the nature of your illness.

M: 今学期の登録料の支払い延期を申請したいのです。まさに健康面で非常事態だというときには可能だと思いますが。

W: ええ，できますよ。病気を証明する医師の手紙と一緒に申請書を提出していただく必要があります。

What does the man want to do?

(A) Pay his student health insurance premium
(B) Petition to pay his fees after the deadline
(C) Register for additional courses
(D) Make an appointment with a doctor

男性は何をしたいのですか。

(A) 学生健康保険の掛け金を支払う
(B) 期日以降に費用を支払う申請をする
(C) 追加科目を登録する
(D) 医師の診察予約を取る

解法 設問を先読みしてから会話を聞き，会話内で男性がしたいことを聞き取る。男性の希望に関する問題。pay，registration，late，file a request などの表現から，登録料の支払い延期の申請であることがわかる。正解は (B)。

重要語
- **registration fee**「登録料，授業料」
- **certify**「～を証明する」

22.　解答：A

◀) 091

M: You look like you're on cloud nine. Well, come on, tell me. What happened?

W: I just found out Professor Brosnahan gave me an A in my American literature class, and I thought I was close to failing.

M: うれしくてしょうがないみたいだね。ねえ，教えてよ。どうしたの？

W: アメリカ文学のクラスでブロズナハン教授が私に A をつけてくれたことがわかったの，私は落としそうだと思っていたけど。

How does the woman feel?

(A) Pleased
(B) Anxious
(C) Upset
(D) Disappointed

女性はどのように感じていますか。

(A) うれしい
(B) 心配している
(C) 取り乱している
(D) がっかりしている

解法 設問を先読みしてから会話を聞き，会話内で女性がどのように感じているかを聞き取る。女性の感情を問う問題。女性がアメリカ文学のクラスで A を取って喜んでいることは，発言内容だけでなくイントネーションからもわかる。You look like you're on cloud nine. がわからなくても，学生が A をもらえばうれしいことは推測できるだろう。正解は (A)。

重要語
- **on cloud nine**「非常に喜んで」（= on a cloud）
- **be close to** *doing*「～しそうである」

23.　解答：A

M: Are you interested in going to the glee club concert with me on Friday evening?

W: Wait a minute. You're going to a music concert? Now I've heard everything.

　M: 金曜日の夜にグリークラブのコンサートに一緒に行くのはどう？

　W: ちょっと待って。あなたが音楽会に行くの？　信じられないわ。

What had the woman assumed about the man?　女性は男性についてどのように思っていましたか。

(A) He would not attend the glee club concert.　(A) 彼はグリークラブのコンサートに行かない。

(B) He would not be able to join the glee club.　(B) 彼はグリークラブに入ることはできない。

(C) He was going to the concert with someone else.　(C) 彼は別の人とコンサートに行く。

(D) He did not know where the concert was being held.　(D) 彼はコンサートがどこで行われるか知らない。

解法 設問を先読みしてから会話を聞き，会話内で女性が思っていたことを聞き取る。女性の発言の意図を問う問題。女性は男性からグリークラブのコンサートに行くと聞き，そのようなことをしない人だと思っていたため意外に感じている。この意外さは女性のイントネーションにも現れている。正解は (A)。

重要語
□ **glee club**
「グリークラブ，（男声）合唱団」
□ **Now I've heard everything.**
「これは驚いた」

24.　解答：D

M: I'm really sorry I'm late, Judy.

W: Well, Patrick, it's not like this is the first time. I'm beginning to wonder whether this study group is really something you're interested in being part of.

　M: 遅れて本当にごめん，ジュディ。

　W: そうね，パトリック，初めての遅刻というわけじゃないしね。この学習グループはあなたが参加したいと思うようなものなのか，疑問に思えてきたわ。

What does the woman imply about the man and the study group?　女性は男性と学習グループについて何を示唆していますか。

(A) He should have attended the first meeting.　(A) 彼は最初のミーティングに参加すべきだった。

(B) He will probably enjoy taking part in it.　(B) 彼はおそらく参加して楽しむだろう。

(C) He has been making a big contribution to it.　(C) 彼はグループに大きな貢献をしてきた。

(D) He ought to be more punctual in attending it.　(D) 彼は参加する際はもっと時間を守るべきだ。

解法 設問を先読みしてから会話を聞き，会話内で女性が示唆していることを聞き取る。女性の発言の言外の意味を問う問題。late, study group などから，男性が学習グループに遅刻してきたことがわかる。正解は (D)。女性の皮肉まじりの口調もヒントになる。

重要語
□ **punctual**
「時間を守るような」

M: I just found out I got the scholarship I applied for. I'm thrilled. No more working 40 hours a week just to make ends meet.

W: That's wonderful. I know for quite a while you've wanted to be able to concentrate more on your studies.

M: 申請していた奨学金をもらえたことがわかったところなんだ。とてもうれしいよ。これからは，やりくりするのに週40時間も働かなくてもすむよ。

W: それはすごいわね。あなたがもっと勉強に集中したがっていたのは，ずいぶん前からわかっていたわ。

What can be inferred about the man from this conversation?

この会話から男性について何が推測できますか。

(A) He will reduce the number of hours he works.
(B) He will apply for another scholarship.
(C) He will request permission to take extra classes.
(D) He will meet his advisor later in the week.

(A) 彼は労働時間を減らすだろう。
(B) 彼は別の奨学金を申し込むだろう。
(C) 彼は追加の科目を取る許可を求めるだろう。
(D) 彼は今週の後半に指導教官と面談するだろう。

解法 設問を先読みしてから会話を聞き，会話内で男性についてわかることを聞き取る。推測に関する問題。scholarship，No more working 40 hours a week などから，男性は奨学金を受けることになり，週40時間も働く必要がなくなったことがわかる。つまり，今後労働時間を減らすことが推測できる。正解は (A)。

重要語
- □ **scholarship**「奨学金」
- □ **apply for ...**「〜を申請する」
- □ **make ends meet**「やりくりする」

26.

🔊 095

M: Roxanne, there's a dance in the student union tonight. You wouldn't by any chance be interested in going?

W: There's nothing I would rather do, but I'm afraid I've got to finish a 10-page research paper by tomorrow morning. I've been putting this essay off for about a month, and now I don't have much choice. I guess it's my own fault.

M: ロクサン，今夜学生会館でダンスがあるけど。ひょっとして興味がないかな。

W: それ以上やりたいことはないくらいだけど，明日の朝までに研究レポート10枚を終わらせなければならないの。このレポートを1か月近くもやらないで延ばしてきたから，もう選択の余地はないのよ。自分のせいだけどね。

What do we learn about the woman from this conversation?

(A) She does not like to dance.
(B) She enjoys writing research papers.
(C) She started her essay about a month before.
(D) She regrets not doing the assignment earlier.

この会話から女性について何がわかりますか。

(A) 彼女は踊るのが好きではない。
(B) 彼女は研究レポートを書くことを楽しんでいる。
(C) 彼女は1か月ほど前にレポートを書き始めた。
(D) 彼女はもっと早く課題をやらなかったことを後悔している。

解法 設問を先読みしてから会話を聞き，会話内で女性についてわかることを聞き取る。女性の発言の意図を問う問題。女性の問題点は，レポートを1か月もやらずに延ばしてきたことである。イントネーションや，I guess it's my own fault.「自分のせいだ」という発言からも，彼女が後悔していることがわかる。正解は (D)。

重要語
□ **by any chance**
「ひょっとして，万一」

27.

🔊 096

M: I'm having a hard time studying in my dorm room. The lounge is right across the hall and some of the guys keep the TV turned up really high.

W: That doesn't sound good. Well, I guess you don't have any other choice but to try the library.

M: 寮の部屋でなかなか勉強できないんだ。ラウンジが廊下の向こう側にあるんだけど，何人かがテレビを大音量で見ているんだよね。

W: それはよくないわね。図書館に行ってみるしかないでしょうね。

What is the man's problem?　　　　　　　　男性の問題は何ですか。

(A) The television in the dorm is not working.　　(A) 寮のテレビが故障している。

(B) He was not able to go to the library to study.　(B) 勉強をするために図書館へ行けなかった。

(C) The dorm is too noisy for him to concentrate.　(C) 寮はうるさすぎて集中できない。

(D) He missed the TV program he wanted to see.　(D) 見たかったテレビ番組を見逃した。

> **解法** 設問を先読みしてから会話を聞き，会話内で男性の問題点を聞き取る。hard time studying, TV turned up really high などのキーワードを聞き取れば，男性はテレビの音量が大きくて勉強できずに困っていることがわかる。正解は (C)。

28.

🔊 097

W: Vern, I haven't seen you since you graduated. Are you back on campus for the job fair?

M: Yes. Now I'm working for the personnel department of a bank and my job is recruitment. That's why my boss sent me here to answer any questions that students may have about the bank I work for.

W: ヴァーン，卒業以来顔を見なかったわね。就職フェアでキャンパスに戻ってきたの？

M: そうだよ。今銀行の人事部で働いていて，新人採用の仕事をしているんだ。勤務している銀行について学生からの質問に答えるために，上司が僕をここによこしたわけだよ。

What do we learn about the man from this conversation?　　この会話から男性について何がわかりますか。

(A) He was unable to graduate on time.　　(A) 彼は予定どおり卒業できなかった。

(B) He will conduct a survey with his boss.　(B) 彼は上司と調査を行うだろう。

(C) He is looking for a new place to work.　(C) 彼は新しい職場を探している。

(D) He is recruiting new bank employees.　(D) 彼は銀行で働く新人を採用している。

> **解法** 設問を先読みしてから会話を聞き，会話内で男性についてわかることを聞き取る。会話内の情報を問う問題。I'm working for the personnel department of a bank and my job is recruitment から，男性は銀行の新人採用の仕事をしていることがわかる。正解は (D)。
>
> **重要語**
> □ **personnel department**
> 「人事部」

29.　　　　　　　　　　　　　　　　　　　　　　　　　　　　解答：C

098

W: Oh, my! How am I ever going to get all this reading done? Professor Rodgers is making us read three whole chapters by Friday.

M: Wait a minute. You've known about these reading assignments since the beginning of the semester, right? They're all written on the syllabus, aren't they?

W: これはたいへん！　どうやって全部を読み終えればいいのよ。ロジャーズ教授は金曜日までに3章分を全部読めと言うのよ。

M: ちょっと待って。この読書課題のことは学期の始めからわかっていただろう？　教授細目に全部書いてあるよね。

What is the woman's problem?　　　　　　　　女性の問題は何ですか。

(A) She has not attended class very often.　(A) 彼女はそれほど授業に出席していなかった。
(B) She lost her copy of the syllabus.　　　(B) 彼女は教授細目をなくした。
(C) She put off doing her required reading.　(C) 彼女はやらなければならない読書を行わず延ばしてきた。
(D) She does not understand the class assignment.　(D) 彼女は課題を理解していない。

解法　設問を先読みしてから会話を聞き，会話内で女性の問題点を聞き取る。女性は金曜日までに読書課題をこなすのが難しいと感じているが，読書課題は学期の始めからわかっていたことを男性に指摘されている。つまり彼女の問題点は知っていながら読まずにいたことになるので，正解は (C)。

重要語

□ **reading assignment**
「読書課題」
□ **syllabus**「シラバス，教授細目」

30.　　　　　　　　　　　　　　　　　　　　　　　　　　　　解答：C

099

M: Hi, Janet, I was just heading over to the cafeteria. I know it's a bit noisy, but what do you say to catching a bite to eat together?

W: Oh, Bob, it's been a long and busy day. That's the last place I want to go.

M: やあ，ジャネット。カフェテリアに行くところなんだ。ちょっとうるさいけど，一緒に軽く食べない？

W: あら，ボブ，長くて忙しい一日だったわ。あそこは一番行きたくないところね。

What does the woman imply?　　　　　　　　女性は何を示唆していますか。

(A) She would prefer to go to the cafeteria later.　(A) カフェテリアには後で行きたい。
(B) She was just at the cafeteria.　　　　　(B) さっきまでカフェテリアにいた。
(C) She does not want to go to the cafeteria.　(C) カフェテリアには行きたくない。
(D) She has not been at the cafeteria for a long time.　(D) カフェテリアには長い間行っていない。

解法　設問を先読みしてから会話を聞き，会話内で女性が示唆していることを聞き取る。イントネーションなど言い方がポイントになる問題。女性の最後の発言 Oh, Bob, it's been a long and busy day. That's the last place I want to go. のうち，the last place は強調され，本当に行きたくないという気持ちが表れた言い方になっている。正解は (C)。

重要語
□ **catch a bite**「軽く食べる」

Questions 31-34

🔊 101 Listen to the following conversation between two students at school.

W: It's hard to believe that Professor Conrad is retiring at the end of this term.

M: I know. He's been teaching biology here for 30 years, I've heard, and he seems almost a permanent part of the university.

W: What I most admire is that he's never lost his enthusiasm for teaching. He's just as excited about teaching Introduction to Biology as he probably was the first time he taught the class.

M: You can say that again. Even though I'm a political science major and don't really like science very much, I have to admit that his course was one of the best I've taken here.

W: I wish we could do something for him. I mean, besides the official university reception.

M: Now there's an idea. Why don't we throw a going-away party for him? You know, talk to some of the biology majors and some of his advisees, and have our own gathering. I'm sure he'd really appreciate it.

W: Why not? I bet we could even reserve one of the big labs to hold it in. Wouldn't that be great? A farewell gathering in the same place where he's conducted so many experiments and collected so many specimens.

学校で2人の学生が交わす次の会話を聞きなさい。

W: コンラッド教授が今学期の終わりに退官するなんて信じられないわ。

M: そうだね。教授はここで30年間生物学を教えてきて，もう大学の一部のような存在だって聞いたよ。

W: 何より敬服したのが，人を教える情熱をまったく失っていないということよ。おそらく初めて授業をしたときと同じくらい熱心に「生物学概論」を教えているわ。

M: そのとおり。僕は政治学の専攻で，科学はあまり好きではないけれど，教授の授業はここで受けた最もすばらしい授業のひとつだと認めざるを得ないね。

W: 教授に何かしてあげられるといいわね。つまり，大学の公式な歓送会とは別にね。

M: いい考えがある。お別れパーティーを開いたらどうだろう。生物学専攻の学生や教授の指導学生に声をかけて，自分たちの集まりをするのさ。きっと教授も喜ぶよ。

W: そうね。きっと会場として大きな実験室も押さえられるわ。すばらしいじゃない。教授がたくさんの実験をして，多くの標本を集めた場所でお別れパーティーだなんて。

◈ 設問を素早く先読みしてから会話を聞き，次の点を聞き取る。

31. 学生が教授について話している理由，　　**33.** 授業に関する学生の意見，

32. 教授の専門分野，　　　　　　　　　　　**34.** パーティーの場所

31.

◀》102

Why are the two students discussing Professor Conrad?

(A) He is retiring.

(B) He just won an award.

(C) He was recently promoted.

(D) He suffers from poor health.

学生2人はなぜコンラッド教授について話しているのですか。

(A) 退官するから。

(B) 賞をもらったから。

(C) 最近昇進したから。

(D) 体調を崩しているから。

解法 学生が教授について話している理由を問う問題。女性が冒頭で「コンラッド教授が退官するなんて信じられない」と言い，そこから教授の思い出話とお別れパーティーについて会話が進んでいる。正解は (A)。

》It's hard to believe that Professor Conrad is retiring at the end of this term.

32.

◀》102

What field does Professor Conrad teach?

(A) Geography

(B) Ecology

(C) Chemistry

(D) Biology

コンラッド教授はどの分野を教えていますか。

(A) 地理学

(B) 生態学

(C) 化学

(D) 生物学

解法 教授の専門分野を問う問題。次からわかるように，コンラッド教授は生物学を教えている。正解は (D)。

》He's been teaching biology here for 30 years

》He's just as excited about teaching Introduction to Biology

》talk to some of the biology majors

33.

🔊 102 | What do the students say about Professor Conrad's class? | 学生たちはコンラッド教授の授業について何と言っていますか。
|---|---|
| (A) It required a lot of work. | (A) たくさん勉強しなくてはならなかった。 |
| (B) It was unusually stimulating. | (B) 非常に刺激的なものだった。 |
| (C) It mainly attracted science majors. | (C) 主として科学専攻の学生に人気があった。 |
| (D) It focused on original research. | (D) 独自の研究に焦点を合わせた。 |

解法 教授の授業に対する評価を問う問題。コンラッド教授は人を教える情熱を失わず，彼の授業はすばらしいと学生たちは評価している。正解は (B)。

》 What I most admire is that he's never lost his enthusiasm for teaching. He's just as excited about teaching Introduction to Biology as he probably was the first time he taught the class.

》 I have to admit that his course was one of the best I've taken here.

34.

🔊 102 | Where do the students plan to hold the party? | 学生たちはどこでパーティーを開くつもりですか。 |
|---|---|
| (A) In a lecture hall | (A) 大教室で |
| (B) In a hotel | (B) ホテルで |
| (C) In a conference center | (C) 会議センターで |
| (D) In a laboratory | (D) 実験室で |

解法 パーティの場所を問う問題。次のように，パーティーの場所は実験室を予定している。正解は (D)。

》 I bet we could even reserve one of the big labs to hold it in.

》 A farewell gathering in the same place where he's conducted so many experiments and collected so many specimens.

重要語
- □ **political science** 「政治学」
- □ **going-away party** 「お別れパーティー」
- □ **advisee** 「指導学生」
- □ **I bet ...** 「きっと〜」
- □ **specimen** 「標本」

Questions 35-38

🔊 103 Listen to the following conversation between a professor and a student.

W: Hi, Professor Brown. I really need your signature on my course registration form.

M: Hi, Margaret. Come on in and let me see it, and then I'll tell you whether as your advisor I can approve your selections. First, some questions. You're a junior now, right?

W: That's right. I've taken all of my general education courses, and I took two composition courses when I was a freshman. So, basically I'm concentrating on my major now.

M: All right. That sounds reasonable. What classes do you have in mind?

W: I'd like to take Professor Dobson's seminar on Southern writers—I've heard it's a great course. I'd also like to take a course on 20th-century British women writers, because I don't know much about them. The third course I'm looking at is World Literature—I haven't read much African or Asian literature. And I'd like to expand my horizons. My fourth course is going to be French. I still have one more semester left until I fulfill my foreign language requirement.

M: That sounds really good, Margaret. I have only one concern. You've really loaded up on literature courses—that's a huge amount of reading to do. Most of those courses require one book a week; that means you have to handle three complete books a week, plus all the papers you'll have to write. Don't you think you should try to balance your courses a little more?

W: What do you have in mind?

M: It's just an example. But you might take an art history or music course. Even something that relates to your literature studies—the arts are really connected in the 19th and 20th centuries, as you know—but a course that doesn't focus on such long texts such as novels.

W: I can see what you're saying, and I'd like to think about it.

M: Why don't you do that? You've still got a week before registration. Take a closer look at the course offerings for next term and the college catalog, and come back and see me with some additional ideas.

教授と学生が交わす次の会話を聞きなさい。

W: こんにちは，ブラウン教授。履修登録申請書にサインをしていただきたいのですが。

M: やあ，マーガレット。中に入って見せてください。それから指導教官としてあなたの選択を承認できるかどうか話しましょう。まずいくつか質問をします。あなたは今3年生ですね。

W: そうです。一般教養科目はすべて取り終えて，1年生のときにはライティングの授業を2つ取りました。それで基本的に今は自分の専攻に専念しています。

M: よろしい，適切ですね。どんな授業を考えていますか。

W: 私はドブソン教授の南部作家に関するゼミを取りたいと思っています。すばらしい授業だと聞きました。それから20世紀のイギリス女流作家の授業も，私はあまり知識がないので受けたいと思います。3つめに私が考えている科目は世界文学です。アフリカやアジアの文学をあま

り読んだことがないのです。自分の視野を広げたいと思っています。4つめの科目はフランス語です。外国語の必修科目を終えるまでにまだ1学期残っていますので。

M: とてもいいと思いますよ、マーガレット。ひとつだけ気がかりなことがあります。あなたは文学の科目をずいぶん入れています。大量に読まなければならないわけです。これらの科目のほとんどは週に1冊読まなければなりません。つまり、あなたは週に3冊の本を読み終え、レポートも書かなくてはいけないわけです。もう少し調整するほうがよいとは思いませんか。

W: どのようにお考えですか。

M: ひとつの例ですが、美術史や音楽の科目を取ることもできます。何かあなたの文学研究に関係のあること—19世紀、20世紀は芸術同士が密接に結びついていますからね、小説のように多くの文章量に力を注がなくてよいものを選ぶこともできます。

W: おっしゃることはわかりますので、考えてみたいと思います。

M: そうしてみたらいいですね。登録までにはまだ1週間あります。来学期の授業要項と大学便覧によく目を通して、ほかにも案を考えてまた来てください。

◇ 設問を素早く先読みしてから会話を聞き、次の点を聞き取る。
　35. 女性が教授を訪ねている理由，　　**37.** 教授が気にかけていること，
　36. 女性の研究分野，　　　　　　　　**38.** 教授のアドバイス

35.　　　　　　　　　　　　　　　　　　　　　　　　　　　　　　　　　解答：C

🔊 104　Why is the woman visiting the professor?　　　女性はなぜ教授を訪ねているのですか。

(A) To apply for a research assistantship　　　(A) 研究助手の仕事に応募するため

(B) To register for his literature course　　　(B) 教授の文学の授業に履修登録するため

(C) To get his approval for course registration　　(C) 履修登録を承認してもらうため

(D) To discuss the possibility of changing majors　(D) 専攻を変更する可能性を話し合うため

> **解法** 女性の行動の目的を問う問題。教授を訪ねた理由は履修登録申請書にサインをもらうためであり，冒頭で女性は次のように言っている。正解は (C)。
> 》I really need your signature on my course registration form.

36.　　　　　　　　　　　　　　　　　　　　　　　　　　　　　　　　　解答：B

🔊 104　What is the woman's area of study?　　　女性の研究分野は何ですか。

(A) Art　　　(A) 美術

(B) Literature　　　(B) 文学

(C) Music　　　(C) 音楽

(D) Women's Studies　　　(D) 女性学

> **解法** 女性の研究分野を問う問題。女性の履修科目について会話が進むが，文学の科目について次のように繰り返し語られていることから，研究分野は文学だとわかる。正解は (B)。
> 》I'd like to take Professor Dobson's seminar on Southern writers
> 》I'd also like to take a course on 20th-century British women writers
> 》The third course I'm looking at is World Literature

37.

🔊 104　What is the professor concerned about?

(A) The woman was absent from too many classes.

(B) The woman has not completed her required courses.

(C) The woman's plan of study may be too demanding.

(D) The woman missed the deadline for registration.

教授は何を気にかけていますか。

(A) 女性は授業の欠席が多すぎた。

(B) 女性は必修科目を終えていない。

(C) 女性の学習計画はきつすぎるかもしれない。

(D) 女性は登録期限に間に合わなかった。

> **解法**　教授の気がかりな点を問う問題。教授は女性が文学の科目をずいぶん入れていて学習がきつくなることを気にかけている。正解は (C)。
>
> 》 I have only one concern. You've really loaded up on literature courses—that's a huge amount of reading to do. Most of those courses require one book a week; that means you have to handle three complete books a week, plus all the papers you'll have to write. Don't you think you should try to balance your courses a little more?

38.

🔊 104　What advice does the professor give the woman?

(A) She should take a greater variety of courses.

(B) She should concentrate more on her major.

(C) She should consider taking an extra course.

(D) She should take a foreign language.

教授は女性にどのようなアドバイスをしていますか。

(A) 幅広い科目を履修するべきである。

(B) 専攻分野にもっと力を注ぐべきである。

(C) 追加科目を取ることを考えるべきである。

(D) 外国語の授業を取るべきである。

> **解法**　教授の提案を問う問題。教授は女性の読書量が多くなりすぎることを懸念して，美術史や音楽など，文学の研究に関係する別の科目を取ることを提案している。正解は (A)。
>
> 》 Don't you think you should try to balance your courses a little more?
>
> 》 But you might take an art history or music course. Even something that relates to your literature studies

> **重要語**
> □ **signature**「サイン」
> □ **junior**「3年生」
> □ **freshman**「1年生」
> □ **horizon**「視野，(知識の) 範囲」
> □ **load up**「～を詰め込む，積み込む」

Questions 39-42

🔊 106   Listen to the following lecture given in an astronomy class.

1   Good morning, students. Today, we're going to turn our attention to the largest planet in the Solar System: Jupiter. It's enormous. Believe it or not, Jupiter is bigger than all of the other planets combined.

2   Next, as for energy, particularly in the form of heat, Jupiter gives off nearly twice as much energy as it receives from the Sun. Partly as a result of this heat and its composition, Jupiter has no solid surface, only layers of gaseous clouds.

3   Yet another interesting characteristic of Jupiter is its high reflectivity, which is related to its cloud cover. Jupiter is typically the brightest heavenly object in the sky because its clouds reflect the Sun's light so effectively.

4   One last point. Jupiter's moons are just as interesting as Jupiter itself. Its four largest satellites were the first objects in the Solar System to be discovered through the use of a telescope—Galileo first glimpsed them in 1610. OK, now, let me take any questions and comments you have about Jupiter, and, after I address these, in the last part of class, I'm going to talk about its amazing moons.

天文学のクラスでの次の講義を聞きなさい。

1   おはようございます，みなさん。今日は太陽系最大の惑星である木星に目を向けましょう。それは巨大です。信じられないかもしれませんが，木星はその他すべての惑星を合わせたよりも巨大です。

2   次に，エネルギー，特に熱という点に関してですが，木星は太陽から受ける量の倍近くのエネルギーを放出しています。この熱と星の組成が一因となって，木星には固体の地表がなく，ガス状の雲の層があるだけとなっています。

3   そして，もうひとつ木星の興味深い特徴はその高い反射性で，これは木星が雲に覆われていることに関係があります。木星の雲は太陽光をとてもよく反射するため，通常は天空で最も明るい天体です。

4   最後に一点お話します。木星の衛星は木星と同じほど興味深いものです。木星の大きなものから数えて４つの衛星は，望遠鏡で発見された太陽系の最初の天体でした。1610年にガリレオがそれらを最初に見つけました。はい，では皆さんから木星について質問や意見を聞きましょう。それらについて話してから，授業の最後に，木星の驚くべき衛星について話をします。

◆ 設問を素早く先読みしてからトークを聞き，次の点を聞き取る。

39. 木星の大きさ，　**40.** 木星の特徴，　**41.** 木星の視認性，　**42.** 教授の次の行動

39.

🔊 **107**

According to the professor, how large is Jupiter?

(A) Larger than all of the other planets combined

(B) Eleven times as large as all of its moons

(C) Ten times as large as the Earth

(D) Half as large as the Sun

教授によれば，木星はどのくらいの大きさですか。

(A) 他の全惑星を合わせたより大きい

(B) 木星の全衛星の 11 倍

(C) 地球の 10 倍

(D) 太陽の半分

> **解法** 木星はその他すべての惑星を合わせたよりも巨大なので，正解は (A)。
>
> 》Jupiter is bigger than all of the other planets combined. **❶**

40.

🔊 **107**

According to the lecture, which of the following is a noteworthy feature of Jupiter?

(A) It gives off heat.

(B) It has few clouds.

(C) Its magnetic fields are reversed.

(D) Its surface is very dense.

講義によれば，木星の注目すべき特徴は次のどれですか。

(A) 熱を放出する。

(B) 雲がほとんどない。

(C) 磁場が逆転している。

(D) 地表は高密度である。

> **解法** 次の部分から正解は (A)。列挙の表現 Next，Yet another，One last point をヒントにして整理しながら聞き取りをしよう。
>
> 》as for energy, particularly in the form of heat, Jupiter gives off nearly twice as much energy as it receives from the Sun. **❷**

41.

🔊 **107**

What does the professor say about Jupiter's visibility?

(A) It can typically be seen just after sunset.

(B) It is usually the brightest object in the sky.

(C) It increases when the planet approaches the Sun.

(D) It varies depending upon atmospheric conditions.

木星の視認性について教授は何と言っていますか。

(A) 日没後によく見られる。

(B) 通常，天空で最も明るい。

(C) 太陽に近づくとよく見えるようになる。

(D) 大気の状態により異なる。

> **解法** 木星は通常，天空で最も明るい天体と述べている。正解は (B)。
>
> 》Jupiter is typically the brightest heavenly object in the sky **❸**

42. 　　　　　　　　　　　　　　　　　　　　　　　　　　　　解答：**D**

◀)) 107　What will the professor do next?　　　　　　教授は次に何をしますか。

(A) Show slides of Jupiter　　　　　　　　　(A) 木星のスライドを見せる

(B) Talk about Jupiter's moons　　　　　　　(B) 木星の衛星について話す

(C) Conclude the class　　　　　　　　　　　(C) 授業をまとめる

(D) Answer questions　　　　　　　　　　　　(D) 質問に答える

解法　教授は次に学生から木星についての質問や意見を聞くつもりなので，正解は (D)。

　　》OK, now, let me take any questions and comments you have about Jupiter （**4**）

重要語　□ **Solar System**「太陽系」　　　　　□ **gaseous**「ガス状の」
　　　　　□ **give off** ...「～を放出する」　　　□ **reflectivity**「反射性」
　　　　　□ **layer**「層」

Questions 43-46

🔊 108　Listen to the following lecture in an art history class.

1　To introduce you to an important school of early 20th-century painters, the so-called Ashcan School, I'd like to remind you of my own philosophy of art. Put simply, it's this: Artists in all of the arts make discoveries about the wonders of nature and the dignity of human beings. They give these an order or form which enables us to see and understand life with greater depth. Now, beauty often results from this artistic ordering, but not always. In other words, beauty is a by-product of art, not its primary aim. Therefore, not all works of art are beautiful.

2　This especially applies to American artists from the Ashcan School who came into prominence from about 1910 to 1940 and who painted stark scenes of urban and industrial subjects like railroad tracks, factories, and tenement houses. During this time, these pictures of city life were considered ugly and offensive, and many art critics and art lovers refused to accept their work. Yet these painters discovered in such subjects much that was poignant, powerful, and moving, and that now, ironically, is in some ways considered attractive.

3　Edward Hopper is a good example. Hopper used bright colors to paint ordinary scenes from everyday life. Despite these colors, his paintings conveyed a somber, melancholy mood, such as through the eerie light of an all-night diner that revealed how isolated and lonely the customers were. Like other artists of the Ashcan School, Hopper's most popular paintings were commonplace scenes from city life. His subjects included city streets, roadside lunch counters, and barren apartments. One of the strongest qualities of Hopper's paintings, however, was a sense of calmness—a great existential solitude that is easily interpretable as the loneliness of modern life.

美術史のクラスでの次の講義を聞きなさい。

1　皆さんに 20 世紀初頭の画家の重要な流派，いわゆるアッシュカン派を紹介するにあたって，私の美術哲学を思い出してもらいたいと思います。単純にこうです。すべての芸術分野の芸術家は自然の驚異と人間の尊厳についての発見をするものだ，ということです。芸術家はこれらの発見に何らかの秩序や様式を与え，私たちが人生をより深く見つめ，理解できるようにするのです。さて，美はこうした芸術の秩序化からしばしば生まれますが，常にそういうわけではありません。言い換えると，美は芸術の副産物であって，第一の目的ではないのです。ですから，すべての芸術作品が美しいわけではありません。

2　このことは 1910 年から 1940 年ごろに台頭した，線路や工場，安アパートといった都市的，工業的な荒涼とした風景を描いたアッシュカン派というアメリカの芸術家集団に特に当てはまります。この時期，こうした都市生活の絵画は醜悪で不快なものと見られており，多くの美術批評家や

美術愛好家は彼らの作品を拒絶しました。ですが，これらの画家は，そうした素材が大いに心を打ち，力強く，感動を呼ぶことを見出しており，皮肉なことに今日ではそれらはある意味魅力的だと思われているのです。

3 　エドワード・ホッパーはよい例です。ホッパーは鮮やかな色遣いで日常生活の何気ない風景を描きました。こうした色合いにもかかわらず，彼の作品は陰気で重たい雰囲気を醸し出しており，たとえば終夜営業の食堂で気味の悪い明かりのもと，客がいかに孤立して孤独であるかが描かれているといった具合でした。アッシュカン派の他の芸術家と同様に，ホッパーの最も人気のある絵は都市生活の平凡な風景でした。彼の採り上げた題材には，街なかの通り，道端のランチカウンター，さびれたアパートなどがありました。しかし，ホッパーの絵の最もすぐれた点のひとつは静寂でした。つまりそれは，現代生活の寂しさと容易に解釈される大きな実存的な孤独のことです。

◆ 設問を素早く先読みしてからトークを聞き，次の点を聞き取る。

43. アッシュカン派の画家の活動時期，　**45.** 美術鑑賞者に拒絶された理由，
44. 芸術の本質，　　　　　　　　　　**46.** ホッパーが表現したこと

43. 　　　　　　　　　　　　　　　　　　　　　　　　　　　　解答：B

🔊 **109** When did the painters of the Ashcan School create their art? | アッシュカン派の画家たちは，いつ彼らの芸術を作り出しましたか。

(A) The late 19th century
(B) The early 20th century
(C) The mid-20th century
(D) The late 20th century

(A) 19世紀後半
(B) 20世紀初頭
(C) 20世紀中頃
(D) 20世紀後半

> **解法** 講義の冒頭で「皆さんに20世紀初頭の画家の重要な流派，いわゆるアッシュカン派を紹介するにあたって〜」と述べているので，正解は (B)。
> 》 To introduce you to an important school of early 20th-century painters, the so-called Ashcan School, I'd like to remind you of my own philosophy of art. **1**

44. 　　　　　　　　　　　　　　　　　　　　　　　　　　　　解答：C

🔊 **109** What does the professor say about the nature of art? | 芸術の本質について教授は何と言っていますか。

(A) Beauty is the basis of all art.
(B) Most artists strive to create beauty.
(C) Not all art is beautiful.
(D) Beauty is created by artistic truth.

(A) 美がすべての芸術の根本である。
(B) ほとんどの芸術家は美の創造に奮闘する。
(C) すべての芸術が美しいわけではない。
(D) 美は芸術的真実から作られる。

> **解法** 教授によると，美は芸術の副産物であって，第一の目標ではないので，すべての芸術作品が美しいわけではない。正解は (C)。
> 》 In other words, beauty is a by-product of art, not its primary aim. Therefore, not all works of art are beautiful. **1**

45.

解答：A

🔊 109 Why were the Ashcan painters initially rejected by many viewers of art?

(A) They chose to paint barren scenes from city life.

(B) They depicted unrecognizable objects.

(C) Their painting technique was crude.

(D) The colors they used were extremely bright.

アッシュカン派の画家たちは，はじめなぜ多くの美術鑑賞者に拒絶されたのですか。

(A) 都市生活の不毛な風景を描くことを選んだから。

(B) 認識不可能なものを描いたから。

(C) 描写技術が未熟だったから。

(D) 彼らの使った色がきわめて明るかったから。

> **解法** アッシュカン派の特徴として，都市的，工業的な荒涼とした風景を描いたこと，都市生活の絵画は醜悪で不快なものと見られて拒絶されたことを述べている。正解は (A)。
> 》 During this time, these pictures of city life were considered ugly and offensive, and many art critics and art lovers refused to accept their work. (**2**)

46.

解答：D

🔊 109 According to the lecture, what feeling did Edward Hopper's paintings often express?

(A) Excitement

(B) Elegance

(C) Poverty

(D) Loneliness

講義によれば，エドワード・ホッパーの絵画がしばしば表現した感覚は何でしたか。

(A) 興奮

(B) 優雅

(C) 貧困

(D) 孤独

> **解法** 講義の中で barren，calmness，solitude，loneliness などの語句で繰り返し述べているように，ホッパーの作品が表現したのは殺風景，静寂，孤独，寂しさである。正解は (D)。
> 》 One of the strongest qualities of Hopper's paintings, however, was a sense of calmness—a great existential solitude that is easily interpretable as the loneliness of modern life. (**3**)

> **重要語**
> □ **by-product**「副産物」
> □ **come into prominence**「台頭する」
> □ **stark**「荒涼とした」
> □ **tenement**「住宅，(安い) アパート」
> □ **offensive**「不快な，攻撃的な」
> □ **poignant**「心を打つ，辛辣な」
> □ **somber**「陰うつな」
> □ **eerie**「不気味な」
> □ **barren**「殺風景な，不毛の」

Questions 47-50

Listen to the following lecture in a geology class.

1   Today, class, I'd like to move our discussion from forces within the Earth—the volcanic and seismic energies we've been discussing in the last few classes—to the atmospheric and surface forces that shape the Earth's surface. One obvious example of these forces is wind—since wind can cause terrific erosion, especially in areas where the topsoil has been directly exposed. The Dust Bowl of the 1930s is a good example of this. Harmful farming practices in the Midwest removed a great deal of the natural prairie cover, and when drought struck and the winds picked up, a lot of soil was removed in huge sandstorms.

2   In addition to atmospheric forces, there are also surface ones. One of them is water, especially as it moves across the face of the Earth in streams and rivers. One particularly notable landmark or physical feature caused by water is the Grand Canyon in Arizona. It's amazing how the Colorado River cut this incredible valley through the rock. When I saw it, I was overwhelmed by the sheer drop down to the water.

3   While the Grand Canyon is probably the single most famous example in North America, all of us have stood on the bank of a river, even the Mississippi for example, and noticed how the surrounding land is much higher than the river. This illustrates the power of erosion. And basically, these two great shapers of the planet's surface—wind and water—are the two forces that sculpt the entire planet's surface. Over time, they will erode even the hardest rocks.

地学のクラスでの次の講義を聞きなさい。

1   みなさん，今日はこれまで数回の授業で話し合ってきた火山や地震エネルギーといった地中の力から，地球の表面の形を変える大気や地上の力に話を移したいと思います。こうした力でひとつのわかりやすい例は風です。風は，特に表土が直接さらされている場所では大きな浸食を引き起こすからです。1930年代の黄塵（こうじん）地帯はこのよい例です。中西部で行われた有害な農法により天然の大草原保護層が大幅に失われ，そして干ばつが襲い，風が吹き荒れたときに大量の表土が巨大な砂嵐で姿を消しました。

2   大気の力に加えて，地上の力も存在しています。そのひとつは水，特に水が河川となって地表を流れるときのことです。水によって作られた地形や物理的特徴として特に注目すべきもののひとつにアリゾナのグランドキャニオンがあります。コロラド川がこの信じられないような谷をいかに岩から切り出したのかを考えると，驚きです。あれを見たときに私は，水面までの切り立った急斜面に圧倒されました。

3   グランドキャニオンはおそらく北米で最も有名な例でしょうが，川岸，たとえばミシシッピ川の岸に立って，川に比べて周囲の陸地がずっと高いということに，だれもが気づいたことがあるでしょう。これは浸食の力を示しています。そして，基本的に地表を形成する2つの大きな要素である風と水は，地表全体を変化させる2つの力でもあります。時がたつにつれて，それらは最も固い岩でさえも浸食するでしょう。

◈ 設問を素早く先読みしてからトークを聞き，次の点を聞き取る。

47. これまでの授業内容，　　**49.** 黄塵地帯の原因となる活動，

48. この講義が扱う過程，　　**50.** 水によって作られた地形の例

47.

解答：B

🔊 **111**

Which of the following were the students probably discussing in previous classes?

(A) Meteors

(B) Volcanoes

(C) Hurricanes

(D) Tides

次のうち，以前のクラスで学生が話し合っていたと思われるのはどれですか。

(A) 隕石

(B) 火山

(C) ハリケーン

(D) 潮の干満

> **解法** 冒頭に述べられているように，これまでの授業の話題は，火山や地震エネルギーといった地中の力であった。正解は (B)。
>
> 》 Today, class, I'd like to move our discussion from forces within the Earth—the volcanic and seismic energies we've been discussing in the last few classes—to the atmospheric and surface forces （**1**）

48.

解答：C

🔊 **111**

What process is this lecture mainly about?

(A) Rock formation

(B) Storm creation

(C) Erosion

(D) Extinction

この講義は主として何の過程についてですか。

(A) 岩の形成

(B) 嵐の発生

(C) 浸食

(D) 絶滅

> **解法** 次のように風と水による浸食について述べられているので，正解は (C)。
>
> 》 wind can cause terrific erosion （**1**）
>
> 》 This illustrates the power of erosion. （**3**）
>
> 》 Over time, they will erode even the hardest rocks. （**3**）

49.　解答：D

🔊 **111** According to the professor, what human activity caused the Dust Bowl of the 1930s?

(A) The cutting of forests
(B) The damming of rivers
(C) Inadequate irrigation
(D) Poor farming practices

教授によれば，どんな人間の活動が1930年代の黄塵（こうじん）地帯の原因になりましたか。

(A) 森林伐採
(B) 川のダム建築
(C) 不十分な灌漑
(D) 劣った農法

解法 害を及ぼす農法により天然の大草原保護層が大幅に失われ，砂嵐で大量の表土がなくなったので，正解は (D)。

》Harmful farming practices in the Midwest removed a great deal of the natural prairie cover (**1**)

50.　解答：C

🔊 **111** What example of a dramatic land feature created by water is mentioned by the professor?

(A) The Great Lakes
(B) Death Valley
(C) The Grand Canyon
(D) The Missouri River

水によって作られた劇的な地形の例として何が教授によって言及されましたか。

(A) 五大湖
(B) 死の谷
(C) グランドキャニオン
(D) ミズーリ川

解法 水によって作られた地形の例として，教授はグランドキャニオンを挙げている。正解は (C)。

》One particularly notable landmark or physical feature caused by water is the Grand Canyon in Arizona. (**2**)

》While the Grand Canyon is probably the single most famous example in North America, (**3**)

重要語
□ **seismic**「地震の」
□ **erosion**「浸食」（動詞：erode）
□ **the Dust Bowl**「黄塵（こうじん）地帯」
　＊砂嵐のよく起こる米国中南部の乾燥平原地帯
□ **prairie**「大平原，プレイリー」
□ **overwhelm**「〜を圧倒する」
□ **sheer**「切り立った」

Answer Key **Section 2—Structure and Written Expression**

Structure

1.

解答：C

Sociology is the study of human interaction within a society, along with the rules and processes that both unite and separate people as members of associations, groups, and institutions.

> **訳** 社会学は，団体，集団，組織の構成員として人々を結びつけたり，分けたりする規範や過程を研究するとともに，社会の中での人々の相互作用を研究する学問である。

> **解法** 冒頭の空所に主語と動詞が必要であるから (C) Sociology is the を用いる。

> **重要語** □ **sociology**「社会学」　　　□ **interaction**「相互作用，相互影響」

2.

解答：C

A powerful hurricane can inflict massive damage and widespread loss of life with its high winds, **heavy rains**, and storm surges.

> **訳** 強風，大雨，高潮によって，大型ハリケーンは大きな被害と広範囲にわたる生活上の損失を与えることがある。

> **解法** 名詞 high winds, storm surges と並列させて (C) heavy rains を用いる。

> **重要語** □ **inflict**「〜を与える，負わせる」　　　□ **surge**「高潮」

3.

解答：A

The Erie Canal, **built from 1817 to 1825,** was an engineering marvel of the 19th century that connected the Hudson River to Lake Erie through a system of 57 locks.

> **訳** エリー運河は 1817 年から 1825 年に作られたが，57 の閘門（こうもん）のシステムを通じてハドソン川とエリー湖をつないだものとして，19 世紀の工学上の驚異であった。

> **解法** The Erie Canal を説明して「それは 1817 年から 1825 年に作られたが」と同格で表すのは，which was が省略された形の (A) built from 1817 to 1825 である。

> **重要語** □ **canal**「運河」　　　□ **locks**「閘門（こうもん）」＊水面に高低差のある場所で，水面を昇降させて船を行き来させるための装置
> 　　　　　□ **marvel**「驚異的なもの」

4.

In upper Wisconsin, the northern pike and the walleyed pike are the two most popular game fish among anglers, **the third being** the large-mouth bass.

> **訳** 北部ウィスコンシンでは，カワカマス (northern pike) とウォールアイドパイク (walleyed pike) が釣り師に最も人気のある対象魚であり，3番目はオオクチバス (large-mouth bass) である。

> **解法** カンマの前と後の部分を接続詞を使わずにつなぐには分詞を用いるので，「3番目は～」を表すのは (D) the third being である。

> > **重要語** □ **game fish**「釣りの対象魚」　　□ **angler**「釣り師」

5.

About 70 percent of all adults report **having suffered** from back pain at some point in their lives.

> **訳** 約70%の成人は，人生のどこかの時点で腰痛に苦しんだことがあると報告している。

> **解法** 動詞 report の後は動名詞や wh- で始まる節を用いる。ここでは動名詞を用いることを考えると正解は (A) か (B) になるが，過去の事柄を表す《have + 過去分詞形》を用いた (A) having suffered が正解である。

> > **重要語** □ **suffer**「～をこうむる，経験する」

6.

In 1865, Robert E. Lee and Ulysses S. Grant **signed** a treaty at Appomattox Courthouse ending the War Between the States.

> **訳** 1865年，ロバート・E・リーとユリシーズ・S・グラントはアポマトックス・コートハウスで南北戦争終結の協定に調印した。

> **解法** 設問文には述語動詞が欠けている。1865年のことなので，空所には動詞の過去形 (D) signed を入れる。

> > **重要語** □ **treaty**「協定」　　□ **the War Between the States**「南北戦争」

7.

In mammals, **the larger** the brain is in proportion to total body weight, the greater the intelligence of the animal.

> **訳** 哺乳動物においては，総体重に比べて脳が大きければ大きいほど知能は高い。

> **解法** 比較級を用いた重要構文のひとつに《the + 比較級～, the + 比較級 ...》「～すればするほど…」がある。カンマ後の the greater に合わせて，空所には (A) the larger が入る。

8.　　　　　　　　　　　　　　　　　　　　　　　　　　　　　　　　　解答：A

Although the tomato is popularly regarded as a vegetable, it is biologically classified as a fruit.

> **訳**　トマトは一般に野菜とみなされているが，生物学的には果物に分類されている。

> **解法**　「野菜とみなされている」ことと「果物に分類されている」ことは対照を表すので，接続詞は (A) Although を用いる。(B) In spite of は群前置詞で後に句をとるため，空所に入れることはできない。

> > **重要語**　□ **popularly**「一般に」　　　　□ **biologically**「生物学的に」

9.　　　　　　　　　　　　　　　　　　　　　　　　　　　　　　　　　解答：B

Ocean ridges are **mountain ranges** on the floor of the ocean where tectonic plates meet and magma rises to the surface of the seabed.

> **訳**　海嶺（かいれい）は海底山脈であって，地殻構造プレート同士がぶつかり，マグマが海底面まで上昇している。

> **解法**　設問文で述べているのは一般的な（海底）山脈なので，定冠詞 the を付けない。複数形 (B) mountain ranges を用いる。

> > **重要語**　□ **mountain range**「山脈」　　□ **tectonic plate**「地殻構造プレート」
> > 　　　　　　　　　　　　　　　　　　　　　　＊地球最表層を構成している岩板

10.　　　　　　　　　　　　　　　　　　　　　　　　　　　　　　　　解答：D

Anne Marbury Hutchinson, **an early leader** of the Massachusetts Bay Colony, was known for her sharp intellect and forceful personality.

> **訳**　アン・マーベリー・ハッチンソンはマサチューセッツ湾入植地の初期の指導者で，鋭い知性と激しい気性で知られていた。

> **解法**　主語 Anne Marbury Hutchinson と述語動詞 was known の間のカンマで区切られた部分には，主語と同格の語句が入る。この同格部分は主語も動詞も不要。(D) の《冠詞 (an) ＋形容詞 (early) ＋名詞 (leader)》が適切である。

> > **重要語**　□ **forceful**「激しい」

11.　　　　　　　　　　　　　　　　　　　　　　　　　　　　　　　　解答：B

Being higher in nutrients but **lower in fat**, the milk of goats may be better for human consumption than that of cows.

> **訳**　栄養価が高く脂肪分が低いので，人間が飲むには牛乳よりヤギのミルクのほうがよいかもしれない。

> **解法**　文頭の比較級がヒントとなる。higher in nutrients と並列させるには，比較級を含み同じ構造の (B) lower in fat を選ぶ。

> > **重要語**　□ **nutrient**「栄養になるもの」

12.

In geology, **a drainage basin consists** of one principal river and its tributaries.

訳 地質学では，流域はひとつの本流とその支流からなる。

解法 空所以外の部分には主語と述語動詞が欠けている。主語は a drainage basin，動詞は consists なので (B) が正解。

> **重要語** ☐ **drainage basin**「流域，集水域」　　☐ **tributary**「支流」

13.

Being the part of the brain which coordinates muscular movements and balance, the cerebellum is rather large in birds since flight requires such precise coordination.

訳 小脳は筋肉の動きや平衡を調節する脳の部位であるが，飛行のためにきわめて正確な調整を必要とするため鳥類のそれはかなり大きい。

解法 設問文はカンマ後に主語も述語動詞もそろっている。空所に (B) の Being the part of を入れて分詞構文にすると，カンマ以前の部分が副詞句となり正しい文構造となる。

> **重要語** ☐ **muscular**「筋肉の」　　☐ **coordination**「調整」
> ☐ **cerebellum**「小脳」

14.

A catchment area, originally an area from which water is collected by a river, now also refers to the area **from which** a school draws its students.

訳 集水域とは，もともとは水が川によって集められた地域のことだが，現在では学校が学生を集める区域のことも指す。

解法 関係代名詞の問題。先行詞である area「から」学校が学生を集めるので，目的格の関係代名詞 which の前に前置詞 from を置く必要がある。正解は (C)。

15.

Only if a society has abundant resources and a well-developed infrastructure **can it support** a rapid rise in population.

訳 社会に豊富な資源とよく整備された社会基盤がそろっている場合に限り，人口の急増に対処できる。

解法 否定語の場合と同様，「〜のみ」という意味の only が文頭にくると，主節の語順は《助動詞＋主語＋動詞》か《動詞＋主語》になる。ここでは前者の語順の (C) can it support が正解。

> **重要語** ☐ **abundant**「豊富な」　　☐ **infrastructure**「社会基盤」

Written Expression

16.

解答：B　**causes** を **cause** にする

Two eco-systems are considered interdependent if alterations in one **cause** changes in the other.

訳　一方の生態系の変化が他方の生態系に変化をもたらすなら，2つの生態系は相互依存の関係にあると考えられる。

解法　if 節の主語 alterations in one は複数形なので，一致させる動詞形は causes ではなく cause になる。空所直前の one に惑わされないように注意する。

重要語　□ **eco-system**「生態系」　　□ **alteration**「変化」
□ **interdependent**「相互依存の」

17.

解答：D　**their** を **its** にする

The raptor, comprising a large number of keen-sighted birds, hunts for food while in flight and catches **its** prey live.

訳　猛禽（きん）類は多くのすぐれた視力の鳥を含んでおり，飛行しながら狩りをして，生きたままの獲物を捕える。

解法　主語の raptor は単数形なので，所有格の代名詞も一致させて their ではなく単数形 its を用いる。

重要語　□ **raptor**「猛禽（きん）類」　　□ **comprise**「～を含む，構成する」

18.

解答：D　**large** を **largest** にする

Lake Michigan, the only Great Lake located entirely within the United States, is the fifth **largest** freshwater body of water in the world.

訳　ミシガン湖は五大湖の中でアメリカ合衆国内にのみ位置している唯一の湖であり，世界で5番目に大きい淡水湖である。

解法　「世界で5番目に大きい」を表すには，the fifth large ではなく，最上級を用いて the fifth largest にする必要がある。

重要語　□ **the Great Lakes**「五大湖」　　□ **freshwater**「淡水の」
＊北米大陸の Superior, Michigan,
Huron, Erie, Ontario の5湖

19.

Much volcanic activity occurs in places where the Earth's tectonic plates meet, such as in the Ring of Fire that borders the Pacific Ocean.

> **訳**　多くの火山活動は，例えば太平洋の環太平洋火山帯のような地球の構造プレートが出会う場所で起こる。

> **解法**　activity には不可算名詞と可算名詞がある。ここでは不可算名詞の activity が用いられているため，可算名詞を修飾する形容詞 many ではなく，不可算名詞を修飾する形容詞 much を使う必要がある。
>
> > **重要語**　□ **the Ring of Fire**「環太平洋火山帯」

20.

The 31st president Herbert C. Hoover, **whose** economic policies were considered pro-business, was later blamed for the Great Depression.

> **訳**　ハーバート・C・フーバー第31代大統領は，その経済政策は企業寄りと考えられたが，後に大恐慌をもたらしたと非難された。

> **解法**　関係詞節には主語 economic policies，述語動詞 were considered，補語 pro-business がそろっているので，主格，目的格として機能する関係代名詞 who は誤り。economic policies を修飾する所有格 whose を用いる。
>
> > **重要語**　□ **pro-business**「企業寄りの」　　□ **the Great Depression**「大恐慌」

21.

Although the first color **film was marketed** in 1935, color photography did not become widely affordable until the 1960s.

> **訳**　最初のカラー映画は1935年に市場に登場したが，カラー撮影は1960年代までは一般的に手の届く範囲の価格ではなかった。

> **解法**　「映画は市場取引された」ので，受動態の《be 動詞＋過去分詞形》を用いる。脱落している was を加えて was marketed とする。
>
> > **重要語**　□ **market**「〜を市場で取引する」　　□ **affordable**「（値段などが）手の届く範囲の」
> > □ **photography**「撮影，写真」

22.　　　　　　　　　　　　解答：A　　falling decrease を decrease にする

A decrease in the purchasing power of a currency is the most immediate indication of inflation.

訳　通貨の購買力の低下は最もインフレに直結する指標である。

解法　decrease「低下」に falling の意味が含まれているため，falling decrease とすると重複になる。ここでは falling は不要である。

　　　　重要語　□ **currency**「通貨」

23.　　　　　　　　　　　　　　　解答：C　　a を an にする

In addition to pain, swelling around a joint is an obvious sign of injury.

訳　痛みに加えて，関節付近の腫れは明らかな損傷の兆候である。

解法　obvious の前の不定冠詞は a ではなく an が適切である。

　　　　重要語　□ **swelling**「腫れ」　　　　　□ **obvious**「明らかな」
　　　　　　　　　□ **joint**「関節」

24.　　　　　　　　　　　　　　　解答：C　　sharp を sharply にする

When people experience emotional stress, their respiration and heart rate rise sharply, providing them for a short time with increased strength and stamina.

訳　人は感情的なストレスを経験すると，呼吸と心拍数が著しく上昇し，短期的に強さとスタミナが増す。

解法　動詞 rise を修飾するのは形容詞 sharp ではなく，副詞 sharply である。

　　　　重要語　□ **respiration**「呼吸」　　　　　□ **heart rate**「心拍数」

25.　　　　　　　　　　　　　　　解答：D　　humid を humidity にする

The altitude displayed on an aircraft's altimeter is really a measurement of air pressure, and therefore can also be influenced by such factors as temperature and humidity.

訳　飛行機の高度計に示される高度は，実際は気圧を測定したものなので，温度や湿度などの要素に影響されることがある。

解法　名詞 temperature と並列されるのは，形容詞の humid ではなく名詞の humidity である。

　　　　重要語　□ **altitude**「高度」　　　　　□ **humidity**「湿度」
　　　　　　　　　□ **altimeter**「高度計」

317

26.

International Falls, Minnesota, is widely considered the coldest **city** in the entire continental United States.

訳 ミネソタ州インターナショナル・フォールズは米国本土内で最も寒い都市であると広く考えられている。

解法 主語の International Falls は，続く be 動詞が is であることからもわかるように単数扱いなので，対応する補語の (C) cities も city とする必要がある。

重要語 □ **continental**「大陸の」

27.

An affidavit is a **legal** document used in court proceedings in which a person swears that certain facts are true.

訳 宣誓供述書とは司法審理で用いる法律文書で，そこでは人はある事柄が真実であることを誓う。

解法 (B) legally は副詞なので名詞 document を修飾できない。形容詞 legal を用いれば正しい修飾関係となる。

重要語 □ **affidavit**「宣誓供述書」　　□ **swear**「宣誓する」
　　　　　□ **legal**「法的な」

28.

The dugong, perhaps **the** gentlest of large, sea-dwelling mammals, is now in danger of extinction due to human encroachment on its natural habitat.

訳 ジュゴンはおそらく海に生息する大型哺乳動物の中で最も穏やかだが，人間に自然の生息地を侵害され，現在絶滅の危機に瀕している。

解法 形容詞の最上級の前には不定冠詞 a は付かない。(A) a を定冠詞 the とする。

重要語 □ **dwell**「住む」　　　　　□ **encroachment**「侵害」
　　　　　□ **mammal**「哺乳動物」　　□ **habitat**「生息地」

29.

Although a rise in temperature can sometimes be caused by severe stress or strenuous exercise, fever is **most often** a sign of infection.

訳 体温の上昇は厳しいストレスや激しい運動で起こることもあるが，発熱は感染の兆候であることが最も多い。

解法 (D) often most は語順が誤り。副詞 most は副詞 often を修飾するのだからその前に置く。

重要語 □ **strenuous**「激しい」　　□ **infection**「感染（症）」

30.　　　　　　　　　　　　　　　　　　　　　　　　解答：A　　initial を削除する

Vermont was the **first** state to be permitted to join the union in 1791, thus gaining admittance to the newly formed nation.

> **訳**　バーモントは1791年に連邦への加盟を認められた最初の州であり，新国家への加盟許可を得た。

> **解法**　first と initial は同意語で重複している。initial を削除すると正しい文になる。

> > **重要語**　□ **union**「連邦，アメリカ合衆国」　　□ **admittance**「加盟許可」

31.　　　　　　　　　　　　　　　　　　　　　　解答：A　　researches を research にする

The early **research** in behavioral psychology aimed at identifying measurable stimuli and responses.

> **訳**　行動心理学の初期の研究は，測定可能な刺激と反応を明らかにすることを目的とした。

> **解法**　この文で (A) researches は具体的な個々の研究を指しているわけではないため，単数形が適切。research にする。

> > **重要語**　□ **measurable**「測定可能な」　　□ **stimuli**「刺激」（単数形：stimulus）

32.　　　　　　　　　　　　　　　　　　　　　　　解答：C　　herself を her にする

Ida Tarbell was an American journalist whose articles on corruption made **her** one of the most prominent newspaper writers of her time.

> **訳**　アイダ・ターベルはアメリカ人ジャーナリストで，汚職に関する記事を書いてその時代の最も著名な新聞記者のひとりとなった。

> **解法**　made の主語は articles なので，再帰代名詞 herself を目的語にとることはできない。単に目的格の her とすれば正しい文となる。

> > **重要語**　□ **corruption**「汚職」　　□ **prominent**「著名な」

33.　　　　　　　　　　　　　　　　　　　　　　解答：B　　includes を include にする

The main industries of Waco, Texas, **include** aircraft parts, glass, cement, tires, and textiles.

> **訳**　テキサス州ワコの主要産業には航空機部品，ガラス，セメント，タイヤ，繊維が含まれる。

> **解法**　主語 industries が複数形なので，それに合わせて (B) の動詞 includes を include に変える。

> > **重要語**　□ **textile**「繊維」

34.　　　　　　　　　　　　　　　　　　　　解答：B　　are を入れて onions are all とする

Asparagus, tulips, and green **onions are all** plants included in the lily family.

> **訳**　アスパラガス，チューリップ，グリーンオニオンはすべてユリ科に含まれる植物である。

> **解法**　主語は Asparagus, tulips, and green onions だが，述語動詞が欠落している。onions のあとに be 動詞の are を入れる必要がある。

35. 　　　　　　　　　　　　　　　　　　　　　　　　　　　　解答：A　　about を削除する

Considering its size, South Dakota is one of the least populated of all of the fifty states.

訳　面積を考えれば，サウスダコタ州は全 50 州のうち最も人口の少ない州のひとつである。

解法　文頭の considering は「～を考えれば」という前置詞であり，about は不要。(A) about を削除する。ちなみに動詞 consider も他動詞のため，前置詞を必要としない。

36. 　　　　　　　　　　　　　　　　　　　　　　　　　　　　解答：C　　and を or にする

The Heisenberg uncertainty principle proposes that it is possible to accurately specify either the position or the momentum of a particle, but not both at the same time.

訳　ハイゼンベルクの不確定性原理は，粒子の位置と運動量のどちらか一方を正確に特定することは可能だが，同時に両方はできないと主張している。

解法　「同時に両方はできない」と述べているので，接続詞は (C) and ではなく or にする。either は or とセットで either *A* or *B*「A または B」と覚えてしまうとよい。

　　　　　　重要語　□ **momentum**「運動量」　　□ **particle**「粒子」

37. 　　　　　　　　　　　　　　　　　　　　　　　解答：A　　that を those または ones にする

Renewable resources are those [ones] which can be replaced naturally over time, such as forests or fishing grounds.

訳　再生可能な資源とは，森林や漁場のように時がたてば自然と元通りになる資源をいう。

解法　主語 renewable resources は複数形なので，それを受ける代名詞は (A) that ではなく those または ones を用いる。

　　　　　　重要語　□ **renewable**「再生可能な」

38. 　　　　　　　　　　　　　　　　　　　　　　　　　　　　解答：B　　she を削除する

Louisa May Alcott, a novelist, lived in Boston and served as a nurse with the Union Army during the Civil War.

訳　小説家ルイーザ・メイ・オルコットはボストンに住み，南北戦争中は北軍の看護婦を務めた。

解法　問題文の主語は Louisa May Alcott，述語動詞は lived である。(B) she は主語として重複しているので，これを削除する。

　　　　　　重要語　□ **the Union Army**「北軍」

39.

The mosaic is one of the oldest and most durable forms of artistic **decoration**.

訳　モザイクは最も古く，最も耐久性のある芸術的装飾様式のひとつである。

解法　形容詞 artistic は動詞 decorate を修飾できない。(D) を名詞 decoration とする。

重要語　□ **durable**「耐久性のある」

40.

Kinship forms the basis for most human societies and for such social groupings as the family, clan, or **tribe**.

訳　血縁関係は，ほとんどの人間社会や，家族，一族，部族といった社会集団の基礎を形成している。

解法　(D) tribal は「部族の」という意味の形容詞である。名詞 family，clan と並列させるために名詞 tribe にする。

重要語　□ **kinship**「血縁関係」　　　□ **clan**「一族」

Answer Key **Section 3—Reading Comprehension**

Questions 1-10

(パラグラフ 1)　There are two major types of deserts in the world: deserts of dryness and deserts of cold. The former, what most people have in mind when they speak of the "desert," comprises areas with an arid climate, sparse or no vegetation, angular landforms, abundant sand, and an absence of full-flowing rivers. The latter type
(5) of desert can be found on the polar fringes of the continents of the Northern Hemisphere and the ice-covered wastelands of Greenland and Antarctica.

(パラグラフ 2)　Deserts of dryness cover about 18 percent of the Earth's surface and deserts of cold cover 16 percent. All deserts, regardless of type, share two common attributes: any precipitation, whether in the form of rain or snow, is both meager
(10) and uncertain.

(パラグラフ 3)　Any attempt to measure rainfall in the desert is almost meaningless, because the amount of precipitation does not necessarily correspond with the amount of water absorbed by the soil. At times, clouds form and one can see rain beginning to fall from them, only to be re-evaporated before it reaches the
(15) ground. Further, the small amount of rain that does reach the ground is subject to great variation from year to year. Finally, months or even years may pass between rains.

(パラグラフ 4)　Water, therefore, is not the main agent of erosion as it is in other types of terrain where more precipitation falls. In humid lands with full-flowing streams,
(20) water sweeps away accumulated rock fragments. In the desert, though, only the wind and intermittent streams can transport them. Wind moves only the finest of dust, and streams seldom reach beyond the desert. Hence, little of the weathered rock material is removed. The result is an abundance of sharp, angular weathered landforms.

(パラグラフ1)　世界の砂漠には主に2つの種類がある。乾燥砂漠と寒冷砂漠である。前者は、ほとんどの人が「砂漠」と言うときに思い浮かべるものであり、気候は乾燥し、草木はまばらか皆無、地形はごつごつして、豊富な砂があり、常に流れている川のない地域のことである。後者のタイプの砂漠は、北半球にある大陸の北極寄りの辺地や、グリーンランドや南極の氷で覆われた荒れ地に見られる。

(パラグラフ2)　乾燥砂漠は地表の約18%、寒冷砂漠は16%を占めている。種類にかかわらず、すべての砂漠には2つの共通点がある。雨にせよ雪にせよ、降水量は少なく、そして不確実であるということである。

(パラグラフ3)　砂漠の降水量を測ろうとする試みは、降水量と地面に吸収される水量が必ずしも同じではないため、ほとんど意味がない。時には、雲ができて、そこから雨が降ってくるのが見えても、地面に届く前に再び蒸発してしまうこともある。さらに、地面に到達するわずかな雨は、年によって量が大きく変わりやすい。最後に、雨が去り次の雨が来るまでに、数か月もしくは数年たつこともある。

パラグラフ4 それゆえ，主として浸食を行うのは，もっと降水量の多い地域とは異なり，水ではない。一年中流れている川があるような湿度の高い土地では，水が堆積した岩石の破片を押し流す。しかしながら，砂漠では，風と断続的に流れる川だけがそれらを運ぶことができる。風は微小の塵しか運ばず，川はめったに砂漠を越えて流れない。そのため，風化された岩石はほとんど移動せず，その結果，鋭いごつごつした風化した地形が多いのである。

1.

解答：C

What does the passage mainly discuss?	パッセージは主に何を論じていますか。
(A) Northern deserts	(A) 北部の砂漠
(B) Rainfall in the desert	(B) 砂漠における降雨
(C) Characteristics of deserts	(C) 砂漠の特徴
(D) The origin of deserts	(D) 砂漠の起源

解法 パッセージの主要なポイントを問う問題。次のように砂漠の特徴を述べており，(C) が正解。

》 All deserts, regardless of type, share two common attributes: ... (パラグラフ2)

》 Hence, little of the weathered rock material is removed. The result is an abundance of sharp, angular weathered landforms. (パラグラフ4)

2.

解答：B

The word "arid" in line 3 is closest in meaning to	3行目の arid という語に最も意味が近い語はどれですか。
(A) severe	
(B) dry	(A) 厳しい
(C) scorching	(B) 乾燥した
(D) erratic	(C) 焼けつくような
	(D) 不規則な

解法 語彙問題。arid は「乾燥した」を意味する。arid の意味がわからなくても，この文は乾燥砂漠の特徴を述べていることがわかれば，答えを推測できる。正解は (B)。

3.

The phrase "The latter type" in lines 4 refers to	4行目の The latter type は何を指していますか。
(A) deserts of dryness	(A) 乾燥砂漠
(B) deserts of cold	(B) 寒冷砂漠
(C) areas	(C) 地域
(D) angular landforms	(D) ごつごつした地形

> **解法** 語句が指す対象を問う語法問題。「世界の砂漠には主に2つの種類がある。乾燥砂漠と寒冷砂漠である。前者は～，後者のタイプの砂漠は～」との記述から，後者は寒冷砂漠を指していることがわかる。正解は (B)。
>
> 》 There are two major types of deserts in the world: deserts of dryness and deserts of cold. The former, ... The latter type of desert ...

4.

Which of the following qualities of a dry desert is NOT mentioned in the passage?	次の乾燥砂漠の特徴のうち，パッセージの中で述べられていないものはどれですか。
(A) A shortage or absence of plants	(A) 草木はまばらか，まったくない
(B) A lack of year-round rivers	(B) 常に流れている川がない
(C) Frigid temperatures	(C) 極寒の気温
(D) Ample sand	(D) 豊富な砂

> **解法** 記述されていない情報を問う問題。パラグラフ1で乾燥砂漠の特徴を次のように述べており，含まれていない (C) が正解。
>
> 》 areas with an arid climate, sparse or no vegetation, angular landforms, abundant sand, and an absence of full-flowing rivers

---

5.

Paragraph 3 mentions all of the follow limitations of measuring rainfall in the desert EXCEPT	砂漠の降水量を測ることの限界について，パラグラフ3で述べられていないことはどれですか。
(A) failure of the soil to absorb water	(A) 地面が水を吸収しないこと
(B) lack of precise instruments	(B) 正確な機器が不足していること
(C) great variation in amounts of rainfall	(C) 降雨量が大きく変動すること
(D) long periods with no precipitation	(D) 長い間降雨がないこと

> **解法** 記述されていない情報を問う問題。(A) は本文中では「雨が地面に届く前に再び蒸発してしまうこと」，(C) は「雨は年によって量が大きく変わりやすいこと」，(D) は「雨と雨の間隔がときには数か月や数年であること」と説明されているので，正解は (B)。
>
> 》 Any attempt to measure rainfall in the desert is ... At times, clouds form and one can see rain beginning to fall from them, only to be re-evaporated before it reaches the ground. Further, the small amount of rain that does reach the ground is subject to great variation from year to year. Finally, months or even years may pass between rains.

6.
解答：D

The word "agent" in line 18 is closest in meaning to

(A) representative
(B) solution
(C) resource
(D) cause

18行目の agent という語に最も意味が近い語はどれですか。

(A) 代表
(B) 解決策
(C) 資源
(D) 原因

> **解法** 語彙問題。Water, therefore, is not the main agent of erosion は「それゆえ，主として浸食を行うのは水ではない」を意味する。agent は「行為者，張本人，動因」を表す。agent を知らなくても，水と浸食の関係を考えれば答えを推測することができる。正解は (D)。

7.
解答：C

Paragraph 4 suggests that in non-desert terrain

(A) there is less wind than there is in desert regions
(B) precipitation is more sporadic than it is in the desert
(C) water is the main cause of changes in the shape of landforms
(D) streams tend to be intermittent depending on the season

パラグラフ4では，砂漠以外の地域はどうであると示唆していますか。

(A) 砂漠地帯よりも風が少ない
(B) 砂漠よりも降水が散発的である
(C) 地形変化の主な原因は水である
(D) 季節によって川が流れたり流れなかったりする

> **解法** 推測に関する問題。パラグラフ4では，降水量の多い地域と異なり，砂漠では水は浸食の張本人ではないと述べている。降水量の多い地域とは砂漠以外の地域のことであり，そこでは浸食，すなわち地形変化の原因は水であることが示唆されている。正解は (C)。
> 》 Water, therefore, is not the main agent of erosion as it is in other types of terrain where more precipitation falls.

8.
解答：D

In line 21, the word "them" refers to

(A) other types of terrain
(B) humid lands
(C) full-flowing streams
(D) rock fragments

21行目の them は何を指していますか。

(A) 他のタイプの地域
(B) 湿度の高い土地
(C) 一年中流れている川
(D) 岩石の破片

> **解法** 代名詞が指す対象を問う語法問題。「風と断続的に流れる川だけがそれらを運ぶことができる」の「それら」に当たる目的語は，その前の文の「堆積した岩石の破片」である。them と同様に目的語を見つけだすことが必要である。正解は (D)。
> 》 ... water sweeps away accumulated rock fragments. In the desert, though, only the wind and intermittent streams can transport them.

9.

Where in the passage does the author give a specific example of how evaporation can exceed precipitation?	パッセージのどこで著者は蒸発量が降雨量を超えることがあるという具体例を述べていますか。
(A) Paragraph 1	(A) パラグラフ 1
(B) Paragraph 2	(B) パラグラフ 2
(C) Paragraph 3	(C) パラグラフ 3
(D) Paragraph 4	(D) パラグラフ 4

解法 指定された内容を表すパラグラフを選ぶ問題。evaporation, precipitation, rain をキーワードとして探し出す。At times, clouds form and one can see rain beginning to fall from them, only to be re-evaporated before it reaches the ground.「時には，雲ができてそこから雨が降ってくるのが見えても，地面に届く前に再び蒸発してしまうこともある」との部分が答えであり，正解は (C)。

10.

解答：A

Where would this text most likely appear?	この文章はおそらくどこに掲載されていますか。
(A) A geography textbook	(A) 地学の教科書
(B) A research report	(B) 研究報告
(C) A college bulletin	(C) 大学要覧
(D) A conference summary	(D) 学会の概要報告

解法 文章のタイプに関する問題。この文章は，砂漠の特徴や種類を一般的に解説している。選択肢のなかでは「地学の教科書」に掲載されていると思われるので，正解は (A)。

重要語
- □ **arid**「乾燥した，不毛の」
- □ **sparse**「まばらな，点在する」
- □ **vegetation**「植物，草木」
- □ **angular**「角のある，角張った」
- □ **polar fringe**「極の周辺地域」
- □ **hemisphere**「半球」
- □ **Antarctica**「南極大陸」
- □ **precipitation**「降水（量）」
- □ **meager**「やせた，貧弱な」
- □ **absorb**「〜を吸収する」
- □ **be subject to ...**「〜しやすい，〜になりやすい」
- □ **terrain**「地域，地形」
- □ **accumulate**「堆積する，蓄積する」

Questions 11-20

パラグラフ1　It's easy to forget that human technology is not new but in fact has evolved over about two-and-a-half million years since the first stone implements were used to extend and amplify human muscle and dexterity.

パラグラフ2　The first and most important jump occurred between 50,000 and 100,000 (5) years ago and is closely linked to physical changes in the human body. It was during this time that anatomical changes led to fully vocalized speech and modern brain function, which in turn led to the development of more specialized bone tools, single-purpose stone implements such as meat scrapers, and compound tools such as spears with shafts and axes with handles. Like all (10) technology, these better tools extended the reach and effectiveness of human activity and ingenuity, in this case, hunting and food preparation.

パラグラフ3　The second jump occurred 13,000 years ago in some parts of the world and still has not yet occurred in other parts of the world. It concerns, of course, the invention of agriculture. The growing of food, rather than the gathering and (15) hunting of it, revolutionized human societies since it required that humans remain in one place to care for fields and orchards, rather than migrating with the animals and the seasons. This transformed their societies, since it led to such practices as division of labor.

パラグラフ4　It is impossible to overestimate the effects of this shift which influenced (20) human society far more than the telephone, the TV, or the computer combined. When people settled down, it meant that they were able to amass non-transportable possessions and to further develop tools—that is, technology—eventually leading to the machine. Hunter-gatherers were limited to technology that could be carried with them, such as spears, stakes, ropes, and drinking (25) gourds. However, when people remained in one place, they could build permanent houses (and develop all of the technology needed to construct and maintain them effectively), fire pottery to store water and cook food, and spend their free time developing more technology which could be passed on to the next generation. Beyond its effect on humans' material lives, the shift from (30) hunting and gathering to specialized food-production—specifically to farming and to the raising of livestock—completely revised how humans conceived of themselves and led to new stories, myths, and religions.

パラグラフ1　忘れてしまいがちだが，人間のテクノロジーは新しいものではなく，最初の石器が使われて人間の筋肉と器用さを発展増強させて以来，およそ250万年以上にわたって実際には進化してきた。

パラグラフ 2 まず何よりも重要な飛躍は 5 万年から 10 万年前に起こったが，これは人体の肉体的変化と密接な関わりがある。この時期に人体に構造上の変化が起こり，完全な発話と現代的な脳機能を人間は得た。それによって，さらに目的の特化した骨の道具，肉をこそぎ取る道具のような単一目的の石器，柄の付いた槍や握りの付いた斧などの複合的な道具が作られた。あらゆるテクノロジーと同様に，これらのより優れた道具により，人間の行動および工夫—この場合には狩りや食料調達—の範囲が広がり，効率がよくなった。

パラグラフ 3 2 番目の飛躍は 1 万 3,000 年前に世界の数か所で起こったが，他の地域では今もまだ始まっていない。これはもちろん農業の発明である。採取や狩猟で食料を手に入れるのではなく，食物を栽培するということは，人間の社会に変革をもたらした。栽培のためには，季節に応じて動物と移動するのではなく，畑や果樹園の面倒を見るために定住しなければならなかったからである。これにより分業などの仕組みが生まれたため，食物の栽培は社会を変化させたと言える。

パラグラフ 4 電話，テレビ，コンピュータを合わせたよりも，はるかに人間社会に大きな影響を与えたこの転換の効果は，いくら評価してもし過ぎることはないのである。人は定住することで，持ち運びのできない財産を蓄積し，テクノロジーである道具を発展させ，さらには機械にまで進化させることができた。狩猟や採取を行う人々にとって，テクノロジーは，やり，棒，ロープ，水飲み用ヒョウタンのような携帯できるものに限られていた。しかし，定住することで，人々は耐久性のある家を建て（また，それを効率よく建設し，維持するために必要なテクノロジーを発展させ），水を溜めて料理をするための陶器を作り，自由な時間に次世代に受け継がれるテクノロジーをさらに開発することができた。狩猟と採取から分業化した食料生産，特に農業と畜産への転換は，人間の物質的な生活に影響を与えただけでなく，人間の自己認識を完全に変えてしまい，新たな物語や神話，宗教を生み出した。

---

11. 解答：D

What is the author's main point?	著者が述べている主題は何ですか。

(A) The pace of technological change is very fast today.

(B) Humans have always been creative by nature.

(C) Technology continually improves human life.

(D) Some important technologies were invented long ago.

(A) 現在では技術変革の速度がとても速い。

(B) 人間は本来，創造性に富んでいる。

(C) テクノロジーは人間の生活を改善し続ける。

(D) 一部の重要なテクノロジーははるか昔に発明された。

解法 パッセージの主要なポイントを問う問題。冒頭で「テクノロジーは新しいものではない」とまず主張したうえで，著者はさらにパラグラフ 2 で「最も重要なテクノロジーの飛躍は 5 万年から 10 万年前に起こった」と述べ，続いてその内容を詳述している。正解は (D)。

》 The first and most important jump occurred between 50,000 and 100,000 years ago ...

12. 解答：B

Which of the following does the author mention as the first technological invention?

(A) Weapons
(B) Tools
(C) Fire
(D) Pots

次のうち，最初のテクノロジーの発明として著者が述べているのはどれですか。

(A) 兵器
(B) 道具
(C) 火
(D) つぼ

> **解法** 記述されている情報を問う問題。パラグラフ1の以下の部分で述べているように，最初の発明は原始的な石器である。正解は (B)。
>
> 》 It's easy to forget that human technology is not new but in fact has evolved over about two-and-a-half million years since the first stone implements were used ...

13. 解答：B

According to the author, when did the most significant advance in technology occur?

(A) Two-and-a-half million years ago
(B) Between fifty and one hundred thousand years ago
(C) Around thirteen thousand years ago
(D) In the 20th century

著者によれば，テクノロジーに最も重要な進歩があったのはいつですか。

(A) 250万年前
(B) 5万年から10万年前
(C) 1万3,000年ほど前
(D) 20世紀

> **解法** 記述されている情報を問う問題。パラグラフ2に次の記述があるように，最も重要な飛躍は5万年から10万年前に起こった。設問のキーワード the most significant advance をカギに，同意表現を探すとよい。正解は (B)。
>
> 》 The first and most important jump occurred between 50,000 and 100,000 years ago ...

14. 解答：A

The word "amplify" in line 3 is closest in meaning to

(A) increase
(B) generate
(C) condense
(D) replace

3行目の amplify という語に最も意味が近い語はどれですか。

(A) ～を増やす
(B) ～を作り出す
(C) ～を圧縮する
(D) ～を置き換える

> **解法** 語彙問題。to extend and amplify human muscle and dexterity は「人間の筋肉と器用さを発展増強する」を表し，amplify は「～を増幅する，拡充する」を意味する。正解は (A)。

15.

In paragraph 2, the author implies that	パラグラフ2で著者は何を示唆していますか。
(A) human technology and physiology evolved together	(A) 人間のテクノロジーと生理機能はともに発展した
(B) the earliest humans were unusually inventive	(B) 初期の人類は非常に創意に富んでいた
(C) the first technology extended human life spans	(C) 最初のテクノロジーは人間の寿命を延ばした
(D) some technologies spread rapidly among early societies	(D) 一部のテクノロジーは古代社会で急速に広がった

解法 推測に関する問題。パラグラフ2で，テクノロジーの発展と，人類の肉体的変化，すなわち完全な発話と現代的な脳機能のような肉体的な進歩とは密接な関わりがあるという次の2文から，テクノロジーと生理機能はともに発展したと示唆している。正解は (A)。

 》 The first and most important jump occurred between 50,000 and 100,000 years ago and is closely linked to physical changes in the human body.

 》 anatomical changes led to fully vocalized speech and modern brain function, which in turn led to the development of more specialized bone tools, ...

16.

According to the passage, which of the following is probably the most significant result of the rise of agriculture?	パッセージによれば，次のうち，農業の出現がもたらした最も重要な結果と思われるのはどれですか。
(A) Humans were able to increase their populations.	(A) 人間は人口を増やすことができた。
(B) Villages began to trade with each other.	(B) 村落が互いに通商を始めた。
(C) People accumulated possessions and passed on knowledge.	(C) 人間は財産を蓄積し，知識を次に伝えた。
(D) Families could construct safer and larger dwellings.	(D) 家族はより安全で大きな住居を造ることができた。

解法 記述されている情報を問う問題。農業の影響についてはパラグラフ3と4に記述されている。パラグラフ4で次の2文がポイントとなる。正解は (C)。

 》 they were able to amass non-transportable possessions ...

 》 spend their free time developing more technology which could be passed on to the next generation

17.

解答：A

The word "livestock" in line 31 is closest in meaning to	31 行目の livestock という語に最も意味が近い語はどれですか。
(A) farm animals	(A) 農場の動物
(B) cultivated plants	(B) 栽培された作物
(C) staples	(C) 特産物
(D) fruits	(D) 果物

解法 語彙問題。the shift from hunting and gathering to specialized food-production—specifically to farming and to the raising of livestock は「狩猟と採取から分業化した食料生産，特に農業と畜産への転換」を表し，the raising of livestock は「家畜を育てること」を意味する。正解は (A)。

18.

解答：D

Which of the following statements best describes the organization of paragraph 4?	パラグラフ4の構成を最もよく表しているのは次のどれですか。
(A) An extended definition	(A) 詳細な定義
(B) A comparison of viewpoints	(B) 視点の比較
(C) A series of types	(C) タイプの列挙
(D) A claim followed by supporting points	(D) ある主張とそれを支えるポイント

解法 パラグラフの構成に関する問題。パラグラフ3で「食物を栽培することは人間の社会に変革を起こした」と述べ，パラグラフ4で「食物栽培は社会に大きな影響を与えた」と主張している。その主張を支えるために具体的に挙げられている影響とは，財産の蓄積，道具の発展，耐久性のある家の建築，陶器作り，次世代に受け継がれるテクノロジー開発，自己認識の変革，物語，神話，宗教の創出である。正解は (D)。

19.

解答：C

With which of the following statements would the author most likely agree?	次のうち，著者が最も賛成しそうな意見はどれですか。
(A) Modern societies will continue to change radically.	(A) 現代社会は抜本的な変化を続けるだろう。
(B) Many technologies can harm or even destroy their makers.	(B) 多くのテクノロジーは作り手に害を与え，滅ぼしてしまうことさえある。
(C) The invention of agriculture has had the greatest effect on culture.	(C) 農業の発明は文化に最も大きな影響を与えた。
(D) Humans have remained fundamentally the same for thousands of years.	(D) 人間は数千年も根本的に変わっていない。

解法 推測に関する問題。パラグラフ4で農業が与えた影響の大きさに関する記述がある。次の部分を理解することが重要である。正解は (C)。

》 It is impossible to overestimate the effects of this shift which influenced human society far more than the telephone, the TV, or the computer combined.

In which paragraph does the author refer to the relationship between technology and how people view themselves?	テクノロジーと人間の自己認識との関係を著者が述べているのは，どのパラグラフですか。
(A) Paragraph 1	(A) パラグラフ 1
(B) Paragraph 2	(B) パラグラフ 2
(C) Paragraph 3	(C) パラグラフ 3
(D) Paragraph 4	(D) パラグラフ 4

解法 指定された内容を表すパラグラフを選ぶ問題。テクノロジーと人間の自己認識との関係は，パラグラフ 4 の次の部分で述べている。設問の how people view themselves は，パラグラフ 4 の how humans conceived of themselves に対応している。正解は (D)。

》 the shift from hunting and gathering to specialized food-production—specifically to farming and to the raising of livestock—completely revised how humans conceived of themselves ...

重要語
- □ **evolve**「進化する，発展する」
- □ **implement**「道具，器具」
- □ **dexterity**「器用さ，機敏さ」
- □ **anatomical**「解剖の，解剖学（上）の」
- □ **vocalized speech**「発話」
- □ **ingenuity**「工夫，発明の才」
- □ **migrate**「移住する」
- □ **division of labor**「分業」
- □ **amass**「～を蓄積する，ため込む」
- □ **livestock**「家畜」
- □ **myth**「神話」

Questions 21-29

(パラグラフ 1) One group of Native Americans who migrated much later to the Southwest than other tribes was the Navajo. While the ancestors of the Navajo likely crossed the land bridge between Asia and Canada some 20,000 years ago, archaeological evidence suggests that they first came to their present home (5) approximately five centuries ago. Navajo folklore tells of emerging into this world from earlier worlds, which can be interpreted as a tale of migrations.

(パラグラフ 2) Although they have always lived in an extremely dry, harsh, and relatively remote desert of the Southwest, the Navajo have never been fully isolated from their neighbors. In fact, it is clear that they adopted many agricultural practices (10) from the Pueblos who lived in the region prior to them. It was probably this association which contributed both to their economic development and to their sedentary tendencies. In general, the Navajo have been a far less nomadic people than has been portrayed in the popular literature, content to eke out an existence by farming land which is virtually barren.

(パラグラフ 3) In addition to borrowing from other cultures, the Navajo often staged raids on adjacent peoples, making them feared by other tribes and Europeans alike. However, it is misleading to think of the Navajo as a single tribe, at least until the arrival of the European Americans in the late 1840s. While united loosely by language and cultural tradition, the Navajo certainly were not one political (20) body and never functioned as a single unit. A battle waged by one group would not necessarily be condoned or even known about by another. Moreover, an agreement made by one group would not bind all Navajo.

(パラグラフ 4) This changed with the introduction of the reservation system in the two decades after the American military occupied New Mexico in 1846 during the war (25) between the United States and Mexico. Discovering to their dismay the reality of the dispersed Navajo population while attempting to exert their control over the region, the American authorities came into direct conflict with the Navajo and skirmishes were common for many years. It was decided in the middle of the 1860s that the Navajo must be converted to Christianity and forcibly moved to (30) a reservation located some 300 miles to the east of their homeland. More than 2,000 Navajo died, but as a result of this experience the Navajo banded together politically and pressured the United States government to allow them to return home. The government finally relented and in 1868 the Navajo were ceded a huge tract of their original homeland straddling the three states of Arizona, Utah, and (35) New Mexico, an area which serves as their primary reservation now. Today the Navajo population is second to none among all Native American tribes.

アメリカ先住民のなかで，他の部族よりはるかに遅れて南西部に移住した集団のひとつがナバホ族であった。ナバホ族の祖先はアジアとカナダの横断陸路を約2万年前に渡ってきたと思われるが，現在の場所に初めてやって来たのは500年ほど前であると考古学的証拠が示している。ナバホ族の伝承では旧世界から新世界へ移ってきた様子が語られており，これは移住の話だと解釈することができる。

パラグラフ2 ナバホ族は，南西部のきわめて乾燥して厳しい比較的遠隔の砂漠地帯にずっと住んできたが，近隣の部族から完全に孤立してはいなかった。実際は，彼らの前にその地域に住んでいたプエブロ族から多くの農業技術を取り入れたことは明らかである。彼らの経済発展と定住傾向は，どちらもおそらくこの交流が根底にあった。一般的にナバホ族は大衆文学に描かれていたような遊牧民族とはほど遠く，実際はやせている土地を耕すことで何とか生計を立てて満足してきた。

パラグラフ3 ナバホ族は，他の文化からの借用に加えて，しばしば近くの部族を急襲したため，他の部族やヨーロッパ人から恐れられていた。しかし，ナバホ族を一種族と考えるのは誤解である。少なくとも1840年代後半にヨーロッパ系アメリカ人が現れるまでは，そうであった。ことばや文化的伝統でゆるやかに結びついていたものの，ナバホ族は単一の政治体ではなく，決してひとつの集団として機能していなかった。あるグループによって行われた戦いを，別のグループは必ずしも許容したり承知したりしてはいなかった。そのうえ，ひとつのグループが結んだ協定は，ナバホ族全体に拘束力を持つわけではなかった。

パラグラフ4 アメリカ・メキシコ間の戦争時の1846年，アメリカ軍がニューメキシコを占領し，その後20年間で特別保留地制度が導入されると，この状態は変わった。アメリカ政府は，その地域を支配しようとするうちにナバホ族が散在しているという驚くべき実態を知り，ナバホ族に直接戦いを仕掛け，小競り合いが長年続いた。1860年代半ばに決められたのは，ナバホ族をキリスト教に改宗させ，彼らの土地から300マイルも東に離れた保留地に強制的に移住させることだった。2,000人以上のナバホ族が死んだが，この出来事により，ナバホ族は政治的に結束し，自分たちの土地へ帰る許可を出すよう合衆国政府に圧力をかけた。政府は最終的に折れ，1868年にナバホ族は，アリゾナ，ユタ，ニューメキシコの3州にまたがる，もともと自分たちのものであった広大な土地を譲り受けた。現在そこが彼らの主要な特別保留地である。今日ナバホ族の人口は，すべてのアメリカ先住民の中で最も多い。

21. 解答：C

With what topic is this passage mainly concerned? このパッセージは主として何のトピックを取り扱っていますか。

(A) The history of Native Americans
(B) The struggle of Native Americans in the Southwest
(C) The story of the Navajo peoples
(D) The new Navajo reservation

(A) アメリカ先住民の歴史
(B) 南西部のアメリカ先住民の闘争
(C) ナバホ族の人々の話
(D) ナバホ族の新たな特別保留地

解法 パッセージの主要なポイントを問う問題。パッセージでは，ナバホ族は南西部の砂漠地帯の乾燥した地域にずっと住んできたこと，他の文化からの借用に加えて，しばしば近くの部族を急襲してきたこと，ナバホ族が散在していることなど，ナバホ族の人々の話についてであるので，正解は(C)。

22.

解答：B

According to the author, how many years ago did the Navajo first appear in the American Southwest?	著者によれば，アメリカ南西部に初めてナバホ族が現れたのは何年前ですか。
(A) 250 years	(A) 250 年
(B) 500 years	(B) 500 年
(C) 5,000 years	(C) 5,000 年
(D) 20,000 years	(D) 2 万年

解法 記述されている情報を問う問題。パラグラフ 1 にナバホ族が現在の場所すなわち南西部に初めてやって来たのは approximately five centuries ago「500 年ほど前」とあるので，正解は (B)。

23.

解答：C

In line 2, the word "ancestors" could best be replaced with which of the following?	2 行目の ancestors という語は次のどの語と最も適切に入れ換えることができますか。
(A) Citizens	(A) 市民
(B) Descendants	(B) 子孫
(C) Forebearers	(C) 先祖
(D) Rulers	(D) 統治者

解法 語彙問題。ancestor は forebearer「先祖」を意味する。正解は (C)。fore- は「先〜，前もって〜」という意味の接頭辞。

24.

解答：D

Paragraph 3 implies that prior to the arrival of the European Americans in the late 1840s the Navajo were	1840 年代後半にヨーロッパ系アメリカ人が現れるまで，ナバホ族はどうだったとパラグラフ 3 で示唆されていますか。
(A) little concerned with agriculture	(A) 農業にほとんど関心がなかった
(B) hostile towards outsiders	(B) 外部の人々と敵対していた
(C) linguistically diverse	(C) 言語的に多様だった
(D) politically fragmented	(D) 政治的に分裂していた

解法 記述されている情報を問う問題。the Navajo certainly were not one political body and never functioned as a single unit「ナバホ族は単一の政治体ではなく，決してひとつの集団として機能していなかった」の一文から，正解は (D)。

25.

The word "waged" in line 20 is closest in meaning to	20行目のwagedという語に最も意味が近い語はどれですか。
(A) finished	(A) 終えられた
(B) reported	(B) 報告された
(C) planned	(C) 計画された
(D) conducted	(D) 行われた

解法 語彙問題。パラグラフ3のwageは「(闘争などを)行う」を意味する。この語は，battle「戦い」を修飾していることに注意する。正解は(D)。

26.

The Navajo homeland can be described as all of the following EXCEPT	ナバホ族本来の土地についての描写として当てはまらないのは次のどれですか。
(A) fertile	(A) 肥沃な
(B) vast	(B) 広大な
(C) rugged	(C) 厳しい
(D) remote	(D) 遠隔の

解法 記述されていない情報を問う問題。(B)はパラグラフ4のa huge tract of their original homeland「もともと自分たちのものであった広大な土地」，(C)と(D)はパラグラフ2のan extremely dry, harsh, and relatively remote desert「きわめて乾燥して厳しい比較的遠隔の砂漠地帯」にそれぞれ示されている。パラグラフ2にfarming land which is virtually barren「実際はやせている土地」とあるので，「肥沃な」はあてはまらない。正解は(A)。

27.

The word "their" in line 25 refers to	25行目のtheirは何を指していますか。
(A) American military	(A) アメリカ軍
(B) United States	(B) アメリカ合衆国
(C) dispersed Navajo population	(C) 散在しているナバホ族
(D) American authorities	(D) アメリカ政府

解法 代名詞が指す対象を問う語法問題。theirを含む文は分詞構文になっており，これは主節のthe American authorities「アメリカ政府」を指している。代名詞が指している対象が代名詞の後に置かれている点に注意。正解は(D)。

28.　　　　　　　　　　　　　　　　　　解答：**A**

What aspect of Navajo experience does the last paragraph mainly discuss?	最後のパラグラフはナバホ族の体験のどのような点を主に論じていますか。
(A) Physical relocation	(A) 物理的移住
(B) Cultural origins	(B) 文化的起源
(C) Agricultural practices	(C) 農作業
(D) Population growth	(D) 人口増加

解法 パラグラフの主要なポイントを問う問題。パラグラフ4は "the introduction of the reservation system" "forcibly moved to a reservation" など，特別保留地制度の導入，保留地への強制移住などについて論じている。正解は (A)。

29.　　　　　　　　　　　　　　　　　　解答：**C**

It can be concluded from the passage that the Navajo	ナバホ族について，パッセージでどのように締めくくられていますか。
(A) taught farming techniques to their neighbors	(A) 近隣の人々に農業技術を教えた
(B) are essentially a tribe of nomads	(B) 本質的には遊牧民族である
(C) constitute the largest Native American tribe	(C) 最大のアメリカ先住民族である
(D) have a higher level of education than other tribes	(D) 他の部族より教育水準が高い

解法 記述されている情報を問う問題。パラグラフ4は Today the Navajo population is second to none among all Native American tribes.「今日ナバホ族の人口は，すべてのアメリカ先住民の中で最も多い」と述べている。正解は (C)。

重要語
- **folklore**「民間伝承，民俗」
- **interpret**「～を解釈する，説明する」
- **harsh**「厳しい」
- **sedentary**「定住性の，固着した」
- **nomadic**「遊牧民の」
- **eke out**「何とか生計を立てる」
- **barren**「不毛の」
- **raid**「急襲」
- **wage**「(闘争などを) 行う」
- **condone**「～を大目に見る，容赦する」
- **reservation**「特別保留地，政府指定保留地」
- **dismay**「ろうばい，落胆」
- **disperse**「散在する」
- **exert**「～を行使する，働かせる」
- **skirmish**「小競り合い」
- **forcibly**「無理強いして，強制的に」
- **relent**「やさしくなる，和らぐ」
- **tract**「広い地域」
- **straddle**「またがる」
- **second to none**「だれ [何もの] にも劣らない」

337

パラグラフ1 Drugs have traditionally been prescribed according to the estimated dose needed and the optimal period between doses. However, it is well-known that the human body's daily cycle, known as the circadian rhythm, has a significant influence on the body's physical state as well as its receptivity to drugs. Focusing on this day-night

(5) cycle, scientists have come up with the following hypothesis: If some diseases also follow cyclical patterns during the course of a single day and night, it may be possible both to pinpoint the most effective times of the day for administering drugs and to take advantage of the rhythms to minimize their undesirable side effects.

パラグラフ2 In general, body temperature and blood pressure start to increase after people

(10) wake up and they start to decline from early to late evening. This general cycle helps to promote activity during the daytime while allowing the body to rest at night. However, there are individual differences in circadian rhythm—not everyone runs according to the same exact biological cycle—and as a result, some people are more energetic in the daytime while others are more energetic at night. Scientists and

(15) doctors know that irregular lifestyles, such as working the night shift every third week, jet lag after a long trip, and even surgery can affect the circadian cycle. One interesting physiological discovery is that the body's circadian rhythm is regulated by a particular part of the brain known as the "biological clock." When some diseases occur, this inner clock not only affects a patient's activity levels but also affects the

(20) state of the disease during the course of the day.

パラグラフ3 Among the significant influences of the biological clock on those suffering from particular medical syndromes is that strokes and heart attacks tend to occur in the morning since they are typically associated with an increase in blood pressure. By contrast, bronchial asthma attacks occur mainly between the evening and the

(25) early morning due to changes in the rhythm of the respiratory system during that period. Already a treatment has been devised for bronchial asthma sufferers: they take special drugs before going to bed, and these drugs are slowly released into the patient's system so that they are effective during the patient's most vulnerable hours.

パラグラフ4 In the future, it is likely that medicines currently labeled with instructions such as

(30) "To be taken three times a day after meals" will instead read "To be taken according to your particular biological clock."

パラグラフ1 薬は従来，必要とされる服用量と最適の服用周期に従って処方されてきた。しかし，人体の一日周期，いわゆる概日リズムが薬に対する感応性と同様，体調に大きな影響を与えることはよく知られている。科学者はこの昼夜の周期に注目し，次の仮説を立てた。すなわち，もし病気も一昼夜の周期パターンと同期するのであれば，最も効果的な投薬時間を特定したり，望ましくない副作用を最小限に抑えるためにそのリズムを利用したりすることが可能かもしれないという仮説である。

パラグラフ**2**　一般的に体温と血圧は起床後に上昇し，夕方から夜にかけて下降し始める。この一般的な周期のため，昼間の活動は促進され，夜間に体を休めるようになっている。ただし概日リズムには個人差があり，全員が同じ生物学的周期に従っているわけではない。その結果，昼間のほうが精力的な人もいれば，夜のほうが精力的な人もいる。科学者や医師は，3週おきにある夜勤，長旅後の時差ぼけ，手術など，変則的な生活スタイルが概日リズムに影響を与えることを知っている。ひとつ生理学的に興味深い発見は，人体の概日リズムが「体内時計」として知られる脳の特定の部位によって統御されているということである。何らかの病気が発生すると，この体内時計は，患者の活動レベルを左右するだけでなく，一日の流れにおいてその病状にまで影響するのである。

パラグラフ**3**　体内時計が特定の医学的症候群を持つ人々に与える重大な影響のひとつとして，卒中や心臓発作は一般的に血圧の上昇と関わるため，朝に起こりやすいという点がある。逆に，気管支喘息の発作は，夕方から早朝にかけて呼吸器系のリズムが変わるため，そのころに主に起こる。気管支喘息の患者のためにはすでに治療法が考案されており，患者が寝る前に特別な薬を飲むと，その薬が患者の呼吸器系にゆっくりと広がり，最も患者が発作を起こしやすい時間帯に薬が効くという仕組みである。

パラグラフ**4**　「一日3回食後にお飲みください」というような現在の薬の服用指示は，将来はその代わりに「あなた自身の体内時計に合わせてお飲みください」となりそうである。

30.　　　　　　　　　　　　　　　　　　　　　　　　　　　　　　　解答：**C**

What topic does the passage mainly discuss?　パッセージは主に何のトピックを論じていますか。

(A) Scientists' discovery of circadian rhythms　(A) 科学者による概日リズムの発見

(B) Drugs that work better at night　(B) 夜間により効き目のある薬

(C) How body rhythms influence medicine　(C) 体のリズムがいかに薬に影響するか

(D) Resetting the biological clock　(D) 体内時計のリセット

解法　パッセージの主要なポイントを問う問題。パッセージでは体内時計，投薬，病気の関連について述べられているので，正解は(C)。最後の文「将来はその代わりに『あなた自身の体内時計に合わせてお飲みください』となりそうである」にも注意する。

31.　　　　　　　　　　　　　　　　　　　　　　　　　　　　　　　解答：**B**

How long does the circadian rhythm last?　概日リズムはどれくらい続きますか。

(A) 12 hours　(A) 12時間

(B) 24 hours　(B) 24時間

(C) During the daylight hours　(C) 明るい時間帯

(D) For the duration of one night　(D) 一晩

解法　記述されている情報を問う問題。circadian rhythm を文中に探すと，パラグラフ1に the human body's daily cycle, known as the circadian rhythm「人体の一日周期，いわゆる概日リズム」とあるので，正解は(B)。

32. 解答：A

The word "optimal" in line 2 is closest in meaning to

2行目の optimal という語に最も意味が近い語はどれですか。

(A) ideal

(B) extended

(C) fixed

(D) assumed

(A) 理想的な

(B) 延長された

(C) 固定された

(D) 想定された

> **解法** 語彙問題。Drugs have traditionally been prescribed according to the estimated dose needed and the optimal period between doses.「薬は従来，必要とされる服用量と最適の服用周期に従って処方されてきた」のなかの optimal は「最適の，最善の」を意味する。ideal「理想的な，申し分のない」が最も意味が近い。正解は (A)。

33. 解答：B

In line 8, the word "their" refers to

8行目の their は何を指していますか。

(A) some diseases

(B) drugs

(C) rhythms

(D) cyclical patterns

(A) いくつかの病気

(B) 薬

(C) リズム

(D) 周期パターン

> **解法** 代名詞が指す対象を問う語法問題。for administering drugs and to take advantage of the rhythms to minimize their undesirable side effects において「それらの望ましくない副作用」の「それら」とはその前の drugs を指しているので，正解は (B)。

34. 解答：C

According to the passage, what happens to blood pressure in the evening?

パッセージによれば，夕方に血圧はどうなりますか。

(A) It is stable.

(B) It rises.

(C) It falls.

(D) It rises then falls.

(A) 安定している。

(B) 上昇する。

(C) 下降する。

(D) 上昇して下降する。

> **解法** 記述されている情報を問う問題。パラグラフ2の冒頭に body temperature and blood pressure ... and they start to decline from early to late evening とあるので，血圧は夕方から下降し始めることがわかる。正解は (C)。

35.　　　　　　　　　　　　　　　　　　　　　　　　解答：D

What part of the human body appears to regulate the circadian rhythm?

(A) The heart
(B) The optic nerves
(C) The glandular system
(D) The brain

人体のどの部分が概日リズムを統御していると考えられますか。

(A) 心臓
(B) 視神経
(C) 腺の系統
(D) 脳

解法　記述されている情報を問う問題。パラグラフ 2 では the body's circadian rhythm is regulated by a particular part of the brain known as the "biological clock"「人体の概日リズムが『体内時計』として知られる脳の特定の部位によって統御されている」と述べているので，正解は (D)。

36.　　　　　　　　　　　　　　　　　　　　　　　　解答：B

It can be inferred from paragraph 2 that

(A) regular working hours may be harmful to health
(B) not all people have the same circadian rhythm
(C) most people experience higher bodily temperature in the evening
(D) morning is seldom the best time for physical activity

パラグラフ 2 から何が推測できますか。

(A) 規則的な就業時間は健康に悪影響を及ぼすかもしれない
(B) すべての人が同じ概日リズムを持っているわけではない
(C) ほとんどの人は夕方に体温が上がる
(D) 体を動かすのに朝が最適だということはほとんどない

解法　推測に関する問題。パラグラフ 2 で there are individual differences in circadian rhythm「概日リズムには個人差がある」と述べているので，正解は (B)。

37.　　　　　　　　　　　　　　　　　　　　　　　　解答：C

The word "syndromes" in line 22 could best be replaced by which of the following?

(A) Accelerations
(B) Adaptations
(C) Afflictions
(D) Aggravations

22 行目の syndromes という語は次のどの語と最も適切に入れ換えることができますか。

(A) 加速
(B) 適合
(C) 病気
(D) 悪化

解法　語彙問題。particular medical syndromes のうち syndromes は「症候群，いくつかの症候で形成されるまとまった病態」を意味するので，「病気，苦痛（の種）」を表す (C) Afflictions が正解。

With which of the following statements would the author probably agree?	次のうち，著者がおそらく賛成する意見はどれですか。
(A) In the future, the administration of medication may be carefully timed.	(A) 将来，投薬は注意深く時間設定されるかもしれない。
(B) All diseases have a specific relationship to the body's biological clock.	(B) すべての病気は体内時計に特定の関わりがある。
(C) Drugs should be prescribed only as a last resort for serious illness.	(C) 重病の場合，薬は最後の手段として処方されるべきだ。
(D) The instructions for taking prescriptive medicines are highly inaccurate.	(D) 処方薬の飲み方の説明書はたいへん不正確である。

解法 推測に関する問題。パラグラフ4に薬について次の記述があり，体内時計に合わせた飲み方になるかもしれないと述べているので，正解は (A)。なお，「体内時計が特定の医学的症候群を持つ人々に与える影響」について言及しているので，「すべての病気」について述べている (B) は正解ではない。

》 In the future, it is likely that medicines currently labeled with instructions such as "To be taken three times a day after meals" will instead read "To be taken according to your particular biological clock."

Which of the following best describes the author's tone in the passage?	次のうち，パッセージにおける著者の論調を最もよく表しているのはどれですか。
(A) Skeptical	(A) 懐疑的な
(B) Optimistic	(B) 楽観的な
(C) Sarcastic	(C) 皮肉っぽい
(D) Outspoken	(D) 遠慮のない

解法 著者の立場に関する問題。パラグラフ1で it may be possible both to pinpoint the most effective times of the day ... と述べるなど，パッセージには将来の投薬治療に対する著者の楽観的な論調が見てとれる。正解は (B)。

重要語
- □ **prescribe**「～を処方する」
- □ **dose**「(薬の) 1回分の服用量」
- □ **optimal**「最適の」
- □ **circadian rhythm**「概日リズム」
- □ **come up with ...**「～を提供する，考え出す」
- □ **hypothesis**「仮説，仮定」
- □ **administer**「～を投与する」
- □ **take advantage of ...**「～を利用する」
- □ **side effect**「副作用」
- □ **biological**「生物学 (上) の」
- □ **jet lag**「時差ぼけ」
- □ **surgery**「手術，外科」
- □ **physiological**「生理学上の」
- □ **syndrome**「症候群」
- □ **stroke**「卒中，発作」
- □ **bronchial asthma**「気管支喘息」
- □ **respiratory system**「呼吸器系」
- □ **devise**「～を考案する，発明する」
- □ **vulnerable**「脆弱な，傷つきやすい」
- □ **instructions**「指示，使用説明書」

Questions 40-50

パラグラフ1　The Treaty of Paris in 1763 concluded the French and Indian War and ended any direct French influence in what was to become the United States, thus assuring British title to the area south of the Ohio River comprising Kentucky and Tennessee. Soon, the so-called "long hunters," including the legendary Daniel Boone, returned
(5) from expeditions to Tennessee with glowing reports about the richness of the land and the opportunities present there. Despite the fact that the British government formally barred any settlement west of the Appalachian Mountains, hundreds of English, Scotch-Irish, and German inhabitants of the Virginia and North Carolina backcountry ignored the ban, dissatisfied with their political and economic status in
(10) the areas in which they lived.

パラグラフ2　When the American Revolution began in 1775, these residents supported the cause of independence from England. Realizing that they were not strong enough to defend their own territory against attack from either the British or hostile native tribes, the settlers appealed to the adjacent state of North Carolina within whose
(15) western claim they officially resided. Somewhat reluctantly North Carolina created Washington County to include almost all of present-day Tennessee. After the end of the war, North Carolina ceded its Tennessee territory to the new federal government in 1784, the same year that the new Congress passed an ordinance authorizing the possible formation of new states in the federal territories. As the former Washington
(20) County had just become one, the residents of the eastern part quickly organized a political entity named Franklin in honor of Benjamin Franklin. They adopted a constitution, elected a governor, and continued with their efforts to be admitted to the new nation as the 14th state.

パラグラフ3　For several years, starting in 1787, the "State of Franklin" maintained a precarious
(25) existence, characterized by continuing troubles with the Native American population, intrigues with the Spanish, who had been the first Europeans to explore the area two centuries prior, internal dissension, tensions with neighboring North Carolina, and ineffectual efforts to gain full recognition from the American Congress. Eventually Congress reorganized the whole Tennessee area into a new federal territory, familiarly
(30) known as the Southwest Territory. When the census of 1795 revealed that the population in the Southwest Territory had exceeded the required 60,000 residents, local politicians again petitioned for statehood. And in June of 1796, Tennessee was admitted to the Union as the 16th state.

パラグラフ1　1763 年のパリ条約でフレンチ・インディアン戦争に終止符が打たれ，後に合衆国となる地域におけるフランスの直接支配権はなくなり，ケンタッキーとテネシーを含むオハイオ川以南の地域にイギリスの権利が保証された。まもなく，伝説的なダニエル・ブーンを含むいわゆる「ロング・ハンター」が，土地の豊かさとそこに存在する機会に関する熱のこもった報告を手に，テネシー

Section Ⅰ Part A/B　Section Ⅰ Part C　Section 2　Section 3　総合模試　総合模試 解答・解説

遠征から戻ってきた。イギリス政府がアパラチア山脈以西の植民を公式に禁じたにもかかわらず，バージニアやノースカロライナの未開拓地に住んでいた数百人のイギリス人，スコットランド系アイルランド人，ドイツ人は，住んでいる地域での自分たちの政治的，経済的状況に満足できず，その禁止令を無視した。

パラグラフ2 1775 年にアメリカ独立革命が始まると，これらの住人たちはイギリスからの独立の大義を支持した。移住者たちは，イギリスや敵対的な先住民の攻撃から自分たちの領土を守るだけの力がないことをわかっていたため，隣のノースカロライナ州に訴えた。彼らは公にはそこの西部に居住していることになっていたからだ。ノースカロライナはやや不承不承ながらも現在のテネシー州のほぼ全域を含む「ワシントン郡」を作った。終戦後 1784 年に，ノースカロライナはテネシーの領土を新連邦政府に割譲した。それは，新連邦議会が，連邦領土に新たな州作りを認める法律を通過させた年でもあった。前ワシントン郡がちょうど連邦領土のひとつになったとき，東部の住民はすぐにベンジャミン・フランクリンに敬意を表してフランクリンと名付けられた政治体を作った。彼らは法律を作り，知事選挙を行い，14 番目の州として新国家に加入できるよう努力を続けた。

パラグラフ3 1787 年からの数年間，「フランクリン州」は不安定な状態だった。そこでは，先住民との間に絶えないトラブル，2 世紀前にヨーロッパ人として最初にこの地を探索したスペイン人との陰謀，内部紛争，隣接するノースカロライナ州との緊張関係が見られ，連邦議会から全面的な承認を得ようとするも効果が上がらなかった。最終的に連邦議会は，テネシー地域を新たな連邦領土に再構成し，この地方は南西準州として知られた。1795 年の調査で南西準州の人口が規定の 6 万人を超えたことが明らかになり，地元の政治家は再び州への昇格を請願した。そして 1796 年 6 月，テネシーは 16 番目の州として連邦に加盟した。

40.　　　　　　　　　　　　　　　　　　　　　　　　　　　　　　　　解答：B

What is the main topic of the passage?	このパッセージの主なトピックは何ですか。
(A) How territories become states	(A) 準州がどのように州になるか
(B) The early history of Tennessee	(B) テネシーの初期の歴史
(C) Tennessee's role in the Revolutionary War	(C) 革命戦争でのテネシーの役割
(D) Why the State of Franklin failed	(D) なぜフランクリン州が失敗したか

解法 パッセージの主要なポイントを問う問題。パッセージでは次のように，植民地時代からテネシーが州になるまでの歴史を述べている。正解は (B)。

》Soon, the so-called "long hunters," including the legendary Daniel Boone, returned from expeditions to Tennessee ...（パラグラフ 1）

》North Carolina ceded its Tennessee territory to the new federal government in 1784, ...（パラグラフ 2）

》Eventually Congress reorganized the whole Tennessee area into a new federal territory, ...（パラグラフ 3）

》And in June of 1796, Tennessee was admitted to the Union as the 16th state.（パラグラフ 3）

41. 解答：B

In paragraph 1, the author implies that the original European settlers were	パラグラフ 1 で，ヨーロッパ系住民はどうであったと著者は示唆していますか。
(A) new arrivals from the European continent	(A) ヨーロッパ大陸から新たにやって来た人々だった
(B) dissatisfied with their previous living conditions	(B) 以前の生活状況に不満だった
(C) disinterested in the politics of revolutionary America	(C) アメリカ独立革命の政治情勢には興味がなかった
(D) supported by the government of North Carolina	(D) ノースカロライナ政府に支援されていた

解法 記述されている情報を問う問題。パラグラフ 1 の最後で，ヨーロッパ系住民が政治的，経済的に不満を持っていたことを述べている。正解は (B)。

》 ... hundreds of English, Scotch-Irish, and German inhabitants of the Virginia and North Carolina backcountry ignored the ban, dissatisfied with their political and economic status in the areas in which they lived.

42. 解答：D

In line 4, why does the author place "long hunters" in quotation marks?	4 行目で，著者はなぜ「ロング・ハンター」に引用符を使ったのですか。
(A) To make a comparison	(A) 比較するため
(B) To suggest sarcasm	(B) 皮肉を表すため
(C) To show a direct quotation	(C) 直接的な引用を示すため
(D) To indicate a name	(D) ある名称を示すため

解法 引用符の用法に関する問題。long hunters は本文にあるような遠征に行った人を一般的に呼んだ名称であり，それを示すために引用符が使われている。long hunters 直前の so-called は「いわゆる」を意味しているが，ここからも世間一般で用いる名称であることがわかる。正解は (D)。

》 Soon, the so-called "long hunters," including the legendary Daniel Boone, returned from expeditions to Tennessee ...

43. 解答：A

The word "adjacent" in line 14 is closest in meaning to	14 行目の adjacent という語に最も意味が近い語はどれですか。
(A) adjoining	(A) 隣接した
(B) isolated	(B) 孤立した
(C) friendly	(C) 親しみのある
(D) aggressive	(D) 攻撃的な

解法 語彙問題。adjacent は「隣接した，近隣の」を意味するので，(A) adjoining が正解。

The State of Franklin was troubled by all of the following EXCEPT

(A) friction with an adjacent state

(B) discord among its inhabitants

(C) conflicts with Native American tribes

(D) inadequate population growth

次のうち，フランクリン州が抱えた問題に含まれないものはどれですか。

(A) 隣の州との衝突

(B) 住民同士の不和

(C) 先住民族との争い

(D) 不十分な人口増加

解法 記述されていない情報を問う問題。パラグラフ3で問題が列挙されている。

》continuing troubles with the Native American population …… (C)

》internal dissension …… (B)

》tensions with neighboring North Carolina …… (A)

(D) の人口については，1795年の調査で規定の6万人を超え州への昇格を請願したと述べるに留まっている。正解は (D)。

In paragraph 2, what action is NOT mentioned as a step residents took to gain statehood?

(A) Chose a governor

(B) Elected an assembly

(C) Approved a constitution

(D) Created a political body

パラグラフ2で，州になるために住民がしなかったことはどれですか。

(A) 知事を選出した

(B) 議会を選出した

(C) 法律を認めた

(D) 政治体を組織した

解法 記述されていない情報を問う問題。住民は政治体を組織し，法律を作り，知事選挙を行った。正解は (B)。

》... the residents of the eastern part quickly organized a political entity ...

》They adopted a constitution, elected a governor, and continued with their efforts to be admitted to the new nation as the 14th state.

According to the passage, the first group of non-Native Americans to discover the Tennessee region were the

(A) Spanish

(B) French

(C) Germans

(D) English

パッセージによれば，アメリカ先住民以外で最初にテネシー地域を発見したのはだれですか。

(A) スペイン人

(B) フランス人

(C) ドイツ人

(D) イギリス人

解法 記述されている情報を問う問題。パラグラフ3で intrigues with the Spanish, who had been the first Europeans to explore the area two centuries prior「2世紀前にヨーロッパ人として最初にこの地を探索したスペイン人との陰謀」と述べているので，正解は (A)。

47. 解答：C

How many states were in the Union immediately prior to Tennessee's being granted statehood?	テネシーが州として認められる直前に連邦にはいくつの州がありましたか。
(A) Thirteen	(A) 13
(B) Fourteen	(B) 14
(C) Fifteen	(C) 15
(D) Sixteen	(D) 16

解法 数字情報に関する問題。最後の一文から，テネシーが州として認められる前に 15 州あったことがわかる。正解は (C)。

》 Tennessee was admitted to the Union as the 16th state. （パラグラフ 3）

48. 解答：D

When did Tennessee finally achieve statehood?	テネシーがついに州になったのはいつですか。
(A) 1784	(A) 1784 年
(B) 1787	(B) 1787 年
(C) 1795	(C) 1795 年
(D) 1796	(D) 1796 年

解法 数字情報に関する問題。最後の文に，テネシーが州になったのは 1796 年と記述されている。正解は (D)。

》 And in June of 1796, Tennessee was admitted to the Union as the 16th state.

49. 解答：A

The author organizes the discussion in the passage according to which principle?	著者はどの原則に従ってパッセージの論述を組み立てていますか。
(A) Chronology	(A) 年代順
(B) Classification	(B) 分類
(C) Contrast	(C) 対比
(D) Spatial Orientation	(D) 空間的配置

解法 パッセージの構成に関する問題。1763 年から 1796 年まで年代順に初期のテネシーについて述べている。正解は (A)。

Section 1 Part A/B　Section 1 Part C　Section 2　Section 3　総合模試　総合模試 解答・解説

The paragraph immediately preceding this passage most likely discusses which of the following?	次のうち，このパッセージの直前のパラグラフで最も述べていそうなことはどれですか。
(A) The French and Indian War	(A) フレンチ・インディアン戦争
(B) The life of Daniel Boone	(B) ダニエル・ブーンの生涯
(C) The British colonization of America	(C) アメリカのイギリス植民地化
(D) Native American tribes in Tennessee	(D) テネシーの先住民部族

> **解法** 前パラグラフの内容を推測する問題。最初に「1763 年のパリ条約でフレンチ・インディアン戦争に終止符が打たれ」とあるため，直前ではそれに関係ある事柄を述べていると推測できる。正解は (A)。

重要語

- **treaty**「条約，協定」
- **title**「所有権」
- **expedition**「遠征（隊）」
- **glowing**「熱のこもった，賞賛に満ちた」
- **bar**「～を禁じる」
- **ban**「禁止（令）」
- **cause**「理由，大義」
- **claim**「主張，主張した領土」
- **reside**「住む」

- **cede**「～を割譲する」
- **ordinance**「法令，布告，条例」
- **precarious**「不安定な，危険な」
- **intrigue**「陰謀，策略」
- **dissension**「紛争」
- **tension**「緊張（状態）」
- **census**「国勢調査」
- **petition**「請願する」

SECTION 1

#					#					#				
1	Ⓐ	Ⓑ	Ⓒ	Ⓓ	21	Ⓐ	Ⓑ	Ⓒ	Ⓓ	41	Ⓐ	Ⓑ	Ⓒ	Ⓓ
2	Ⓐ	Ⓑ	Ⓒ	Ⓓ	22	Ⓐ	Ⓑ	Ⓒ	Ⓓ	42	Ⓐ	Ⓑ	Ⓒ	Ⓓ
3	Ⓐ	Ⓑ	Ⓒ	Ⓓ	23	Ⓐ	Ⓑ	Ⓒ	Ⓓ	43	Ⓐ	Ⓑ	Ⓒ	Ⓓ
4	Ⓐ	Ⓑ	Ⓒ	Ⓓ	24	Ⓐ	Ⓑ	Ⓒ	Ⓓ	44	Ⓐ	Ⓑ	Ⓒ	Ⓓ
5	Ⓐ	Ⓑ	Ⓒ	Ⓓ	25	Ⓐ	Ⓑ	Ⓒ	Ⓓ	45	Ⓐ	Ⓑ	Ⓒ	Ⓓ
6	Ⓐ	Ⓑ	Ⓒ	Ⓓ	26	Ⓐ	Ⓑ	Ⓒ	Ⓓ	46	Ⓐ	Ⓑ	Ⓒ	Ⓓ
7	Ⓐ	Ⓑ	Ⓒ	Ⓓ	27	Ⓐ	Ⓑ	Ⓒ	Ⓓ	47	Ⓐ	Ⓑ	Ⓒ	Ⓓ
8	Ⓐ	Ⓑ	Ⓒ	Ⓓ	28	Ⓐ	Ⓑ	Ⓒ	Ⓓ	48	Ⓐ	Ⓑ	Ⓒ	Ⓓ
9	Ⓐ	Ⓑ	Ⓒ	Ⓓ	29	Ⓐ	Ⓑ	Ⓒ	Ⓓ	49	Ⓐ	Ⓑ	Ⓒ	Ⓓ
10	Ⓐ	Ⓑ	Ⓒ	Ⓓ	30	Ⓐ	Ⓑ	Ⓒ	Ⓓ	50	Ⓐ	Ⓑ	Ⓒ	Ⓓ
11	Ⓐ	Ⓑ	Ⓒ	Ⓓ	31	Ⓐ	Ⓑ	Ⓒ	Ⓓ					
12	Ⓐ	Ⓑ	Ⓒ	Ⓓ	32	Ⓐ	Ⓑ	Ⓒ	Ⓓ					
13	Ⓐ	Ⓑ	Ⓒ	Ⓓ	33	Ⓐ	Ⓑ	Ⓒ	Ⓓ					
14	Ⓐ	Ⓑ	Ⓒ	Ⓓ	34	Ⓐ	Ⓑ	Ⓒ	Ⓓ					
15	Ⓐ	Ⓑ	Ⓒ	Ⓓ	35	Ⓐ	Ⓑ	Ⓒ	Ⓓ					
16	Ⓐ	Ⓑ	Ⓒ	Ⓓ	36	Ⓐ	Ⓑ	Ⓒ	Ⓓ					
17	Ⓐ	Ⓑ	Ⓒ	Ⓓ	37	Ⓐ	Ⓑ	Ⓒ	Ⓓ					
18	Ⓐ	Ⓑ	Ⓒ	Ⓓ	38	Ⓐ	Ⓑ	Ⓒ	Ⓓ					
19	Ⓐ	Ⓑ	Ⓒ	Ⓓ	39	Ⓐ	Ⓑ	Ⓒ	Ⓓ					
20	Ⓐ	Ⓑ	Ⓒ	Ⓓ	40	Ⓐ	Ⓑ	Ⓒ	Ⓓ					

SECTION 2

#					#				
1	Ⓐ	Ⓑ	Ⓒ	Ⓓ	21	Ⓐ	Ⓑ	Ⓒ	Ⓓ
2	Ⓐ	Ⓑ	Ⓒ	Ⓓ	22	Ⓐ	Ⓑ	Ⓒ	Ⓓ
3	Ⓐ	Ⓑ	Ⓒ	Ⓓ	23	Ⓐ	Ⓑ	Ⓒ	Ⓓ
4	Ⓐ	Ⓑ	Ⓒ	Ⓓ	24	Ⓐ	Ⓑ	Ⓒ	Ⓓ
5	Ⓐ	Ⓑ	Ⓒ	Ⓓ	25	Ⓐ	Ⓑ	Ⓒ	Ⓓ
6	Ⓐ	Ⓑ	Ⓒ	Ⓓ	26	Ⓐ	Ⓑ	Ⓒ	Ⓓ
7	Ⓐ	Ⓑ	Ⓒ	Ⓓ	27	Ⓐ	Ⓑ	Ⓒ	Ⓓ
8	Ⓐ	Ⓑ	Ⓒ	Ⓓ	28	Ⓐ	Ⓑ	Ⓒ	Ⓓ
9	Ⓐ	Ⓑ	Ⓒ	Ⓓ	29	Ⓐ	Ⓑ	Ⓒ	Ⓓ
10	Ⓐ	Ⓑ	Ⓒ	Ⓓ	30	Ⓐ	Ⓑ	Ⓒ	Ⓓ
11	Ⓐ	Ⓑ	Ⓒ	Ⓓ	31	Ⓐ	Ⓑ	Ⓒ	Ⓓ
12	Ⓐ	Ⓑ	Ⓒ	Ⓓ	32	Ⓐ	Ⓑ	Ⓒ	Ⓓ
13	Ⓐ	Ⓑ	Ⓒ	Ⓓ	33	Ⓐ	Ⓑ	Ⓒ	Ⓓ
14	Ⓐ	Ⓑ	Ⓒ	Ⓓ	34	Ⓐ	Ⓑ	Ⓒ	Ⓓ
15	Ⓐ	Ⓑ	Ⓒ	Ⓓ	35	Ⓐ	Ⓑ	Ⓒ	Ⓓ
16	Ⓐ	Ⓑ	Ⓒ	Ⓓ	36	Ⓐ	Ⓑ	Ⓒ	Ⓓ
17	Ⓐ	Ⓑ	Ⓒ	Ⓓ	37	Ⓐ	Ⓑ	Ⓒ	Ⓓ
18	Ⓐ	Ⓑ	Ⓒ	Ⓓ	38	Ⓐ	Ⓑ	Ⓒ	Ⓓ
19	Ⓐ	Ⓑ	Ⓒ	Ⓓ	39	Ⓐ	Ⓑ	Ⓒ	Ⓓ
20	Ⓐ	Ⓑ	Ⓒ	Ⓓ	40	Ⓐ	Ⓑ	Ⓒ	Ⓓ

SECTION 3

#					#					#				
1	Ⓐ	Ⓑ	Ⓒ	Ⓓ	21	Ⓐ	Ⓑ	Ⓒ	Ⓓ	41	Ⓐ	Ⓑ	Ⓒ	Ⓓ
2	Ⓐ	Ⓑ	Ⓒ	Ⓓ	22	Ⓐ	Ⓑ	Ⓒ	Ⓓ	42	Ⓐ	Ⓑ	Ⓒ	Ⓓ
3	Ⓐ	Ⓑ	Ⓒ	Ⓓ	23	Ⓐ	Ⓑ	Ⓒ	Ⓓ	43	Ⓐ	Ⓑ	Ⓒ	Ⓓ
4	Ⓐ	Ⓑ	Ⓒ	Ⓓ	24	Ⓐ	Ⓑ	Ⓒ	Ⓓ	44	Ⓐ	Ⓑ	Ⓒ	Ⓓ
5	Ⓐ	Ⓑ	Ⓒ	Ⓓ	25	Ⓐ	Ⓑ	Ⓒ	Ⓓ	45	Ⓐ	Ⓑ	Ⓒ	Ⓓ
6	Ⓐ	Ⓑ	Ⓒ	Ⓓ	26	Ⓐ	Ⓑ	Ⓒ	Ⓓ	46	Ⓐ	Ⓑ	Ⓒ	Ⓓ
7	Ⓐ	Ⓑ	Ⓒ	Ⓓ	27	Ⓐ	Ⓑ	Ⓒ	Ⓓ	47	Ⓐ	Ⓑ	Ⓒ	Ⓓ
8	Ⓐ	Ⓑ	Ⓒ	Ⓓ	28	Ⓐ	Ⓑ	Ⓒ	Ⓓ	48	Ⓐ	Ⓑ	Ⓒ	Ⓓ
9	Ⓐ	Ⓑ	Ⓒ	Ⓓ	29	Ⓐ	Ⓑ	Ⓒ	Ⓓ	49	Ⓐ	Ⓑ	Ⓒ	Ⓓ
10	Ⓐ	Ⓑ	Ⓒ	Ⓓ	30	Ⓐ	Ⓑ	Ⓒ	Ⓓ	50	Ⓐ	Ⓑ	Ⓒ	Ⓓ
11	Ⓐ	Ⓑ	Ⓒ	Ⓓ	31	Ⓐ	Ⓑ	Ⓒ	Ⓓ					
12	Ⓐ	Ⓑ	Ⓒ	Ⓓ	32	Ⓐ	Ⓑ	Ⓒ	Ⓓ					
13	Ⓐ	Ⓑ	Ⓒ	Ⓓ	33	Ⓐ	Ⓑ	Ⓒ	Ⓓ					
14	Ⓐ	Ⓑ	Ⓒ	Ⓓ	34	Ⓐ	Ⓑ	Ⓒ	Ⓓ					
15	Ⓐ	Ⓑ	Ⓒ	Ⓓ	35	Ⓐ	Ⓑ	Ⓒ	Ⓓ					
16	Ⓐ	Ⓑ	Ⓒ	Ⓓ	36	Ⓐ	Ⓑ	Ⓒ	Ⓓ					
17	Ⓐ	Ⓑ	Ⓒ	Ⓓ	37	Ⓐ	Ⓑ	Ⓒ	Ⓓ					
18	Ⓐ	Ⓑ	Ⓒ	Ⓓ	38	Ⓐ	Ⓑ	Ⓒ	Ⓓ					
19	Ⓐ	Ⓑ	Ⓒ	Ⓓ	39	Ⓐ	Ⓑ	Ⓒ	Ⓓ					
20	Ⓐ	Ⓑ	Ⓒ	Ⓓ	40	Ⓐ	Ⓑ	Ⓒ	Ⓓ					

SECTION 1

#					#					#				
1	Ⓐ	Ⓑ	Ⓒ	Ⓓ	21	Ⓐ	Ⓑ	Ⓒ	Ⓓ	41	Ⓐ	Ⓑ	Ⓒ	Ⓓ
2	Ⓐ	Ⓑ	Ⓒ	Ⓓ	22	Ⓐ	Ⓑ	Ⓒ	Ⓓ	42	Ⓐ	Ⓑ	Ⓒ	Ⓓ
3	Ⓐ	Ⓑ	Ⓒ	Ⓓ	23	Ⓐ	Ⓑ	Ⓒ	Ⓓ	43	Ⓐ	Ⓑ	Ⓒ	Ⓓ
4	Ⓐ	Ⓑ	Ⓒ	Ⓓ	24	Ⓐ	Ⓑ	Ⓒ	Ⓓ	44	Ⓐ	Ⓑ	Ⓒ	Ⓓ
5	Ⓐ	Ⓑ	Ⓒ	Ⓓ	25	Ⓐ	Ⓑ	Ⓒ	Ⓓ	45	Ⓐ	Ⓑ	Ⓒ	Ⓓ
6	Ⓐ	Ⓑ	Ⓒ	Ⓓ	26	Ⓐ	Ⓑ	Ⓒ	Ⓓ	46	Ⓐ	Ⓑ	Ⓒ	Ⓓ
7	Ⓐ	Ⓑ	Ⓒ	Ⓓ	27	Ⓐ	Ⓑ	Ⓒ	Ⓓ	47	Ⓐ	Ⓑ	Ⓒ	Ⓓ
8	Ⓐ	Ⓑ	Ⓒ	Ⓓ	28	Ⓐ	Ⓑ	Ⓒ	Ⓓ	48	Ⓐ	Ⓑ	Ⓒ	Ⓓ
9	Ⓐ	Ⓑ	Ⓒ	Ⓓ	29	Ⓐ	Ⓑ	Ⓒ	Ⓓ	49	Ⓐ	Ⓑ	Ⓒ	Ⓓ
10	Ⓐ	Ⓑ	Ⓒ	Ⓓ	30	Ⓐ	Ⓑ	Ⓒ	Ⓓ	50	Ⓐ	Ⓑ	Ⓒ	Ⓓ
11	Ⓐ	Ⓑ	Ⓒ	Ⓓ	31	Ⓐ	Ⓑ	Ⓒ	Ⓓ					
12	Ⓐ	Ⓑ	Ⓒ	Ⓓ	32	Ⓐ	Ⓑ	Ⓒ	Ⓓ					
13	Ⓐ	Ⓑ	Ⓒ	Ⓓ	33	Ⓐ	Ⓑ	Ⓒ	Ⓓ					
14	Ⓐ	Ⓑ	Ⓒ	Ⓓ	34	Ⓐ	Ⓑ	Ⓒ	Ⓓ					
15	Ⓐ	Ⓑ	Ⓒ	Ⓓ	35	Ⓐ	Ⓑ	Ⓒ	Ⓓ					
16	Ⓐ	Ⓑ	Ⓒ	Ⓓ	36	Ⓐ	Ⓑ	Ⓒ	Ⓓ					
17	Ⓐ	Ⓑ	Ⓒ	Ⓓ	37	Ⓐ	Ⓑ	Ⓒ	Ⓓ					
18	Ⓐ	Ⓑ	Ⓒ	Ⓓ	38	Ⓐ	Ⓑ	Ⓒ	Ⓓ					
19	Ⓐ	Ⓑ	Ⓒ	Ⓓ	39	Ⓐ	Ⓑ	Ⓒ	Ⓓ					
20	Ⓐ	Ⓑ	Ⓒ	Ⓓ	40	Ⓐ	Ⓑ	Ⓒ	Ⓓ					

SECTION 2

#					#				
1	Ⓐ	Ⓑ	Ⓒ	Ⓓ	21	Ⓐ	Ⓑ	Ⓒ	Ⓓ
2	Ⓐ	Ⓑ	Ⓒ	Ⓓ	22	Ⓐ	Ⓑ	Ⓒ	Ⓓ
3	Ⓐ	Ⓑ	Ⓒ	Ⓓ	23	Ⓐ	Ⓑ	Ⓒ	Ⓓ
4	Ⓐ	Ⓑ	Ⓒ	Ⓓ	24	Ⓐ	Ⓑ	Ⓒ	Ⓓ
5	Ⓐ	Ⓑ	Ⓒ	Ⓓ	25	Ⓐ	Ⓑ	Ⓒ	Ⓓ
6	Ⓐ	Ⓑ	Ⓒ	Ⓓ	26	Ⓐ	Ⓑ	Ⓒ	Ⓓ
7	Ⓐ	Ⓑ	Ⓒ	Ⓓ	27	Ⓐ	Ⓑ	Ⓒ	Ⓓ
8	Ⓐ	Ⓑ	Ⓒ	Ⓓ	28	Ⓐ	Ⓑ	Ⓒ	Ⓓ
9	Ⓐ	Ⓑ	Ⓒ	Ⓓ	29	Ⓐ	Ⓑ	Ⓒ	Ⓓ
10	Ⓐ	Ⓑ	Ⓒ	Ⓓ	30	Ⓐ	Ⓑ	Ⓒ	Ⓓ
11	Ⓐ	Ⓑ	Ⓒ	Ⓓ	31	Ⓐ	Ⓑ	Ⓒ	Ⓓ
12	Ⓐ	Ⓑ	Ⓒ	Ⓓ	32	Ⓐ	Ⓑ	Ⓒ	Ⓓ
13	Ⓐ	Ⓑ	Ⓒ	Ⓓ	33	Ⓐ	Ⓑ	Ⓒ	Ⓓ
14	Ⓐ	Ⓑ	Ⓒ	Ⓓ	34	Ⓐ	Ⓑ	Ⓒ	Ⓓ
15	Ⓐ	Ⓑ	Ⓒ	Ⓓ	35	Ⓐ	Ⓑ	Ⓒ	Ⓓ
16	Ⓐ	Ⓑ	Ⓒ	Ⓓ	36	Ⓐ	Ⓑ	Ⓒ	Ⓓ
17	Ⓐ	Ⓑ	Ⓒ	Ⓓ	37	Ⓐ	Ⓑ	Ⓒ	Ⓓ
18	Ⓐ	Ⓑ	Ⓒ	Ⓓ	38	Ⓐ	Ⓑ	Ⓒ	Ⓓ
19	Ⓐ	Ⓑ	Ⓒ	Ⓓ	39	Ⓐ	Ⓑ	Ⓒ	Ⓓ
20	Ⓐ	Ⓑ	Ⓒ	Ⓓ	40	Ⓐ	Ⓑ	Ⓒ	Ⓓ

SECTION 3

#					#					#				
1	Ⓐ	Ⓑ	Ⓒ	Ⓓ	21	Ⓐ	Ⓑ	Ⓒ	Ⓓ	41	Ⓐ	Ⓑ	Ⓒ	Ⓓ
2	Ⓐ	Ⓑ	Ⓒ	Ⓓ	22	Ⓐ	Ⓑ	Ⓒ	Ⓓ	42	Ⓐ	Ⓑ	Ⓒ	Ⓓ
3	Ⓐ	Ⓑ	Ⓒ	Ⓓ	23	Ⓐ	Ⓑ	Ⓒ	Ⓓ	43	Ⓐ	Ⓑ	Ⓒ	Ⓓ
4	Ⓐ	Ⓑ	Ⓒ	Ⓓ	24	Ⓐ	Ⓑ	Ⓒ	Ⓓ	44	Ⓐ	Ⓑ	Ⓒ	Ⓓ
5	Ⓐ	Ⓑ	Ⓒ	Ⓓ	25	Ⓐ	Ⓑ	Ⓒ	Ⓓ	45	Ⓐ	Ⓑ	Ⓒ	Ⓓ
6	Ⓐ	Ⓑ	Ⓒ	Ⓓ	26	Ⓐ	Ⓑ	Ⓒ	Ⓓ	46	Ⓐ	Ⓑ	Ⓒ	Ⓓ
7	Ⓐ	Ⓑ	Ⓒ	Ⓓ	27	Ⓐ	Ⓑ	Ⓒ	Ⓓ	47	Ⓐ	Ⓑ	Ⓒ	Ⓓ
8	Ⓐ	Ⓑ	Ⓒ	Ⓓ	28	Ⓐ	Ⓑ	Ⓒ	Ⓓ	48	Ⓐ	Ⓑ	Ⓒ	Ⓓ
9	Ⓐ	Ⓑ	Ⓒ	Ⓓ	29	Ⓐ	Ⓑ	Ⓒ	Ⓓ	49	Ⓐ	Ⓑ	Ⓒ	Ⓓ
10	Ⓐ	Ⓑ	Ⓒ	Ⓓ	30	Ⓐ	Ⓑ	Ⓒ	Ⓓ	50	Ⓐ	Ⓑ	Ⓒ	Ⓓ
11	Ⓐ	Ⓑ	Ⓒ	Ⓓ	31	Ⓐ	Ⓑ	Ⓒ	Ⓓ					
12	Ⓐ	Ⓑ	Ⓒ	Ⓓ	32	Ⓐ	Ⓑ	Ⓒ	Ⓓ					
13	Ⓐ	Ⓑ	Ⓒ	Ⓓ	33	Ⓐ	Ⓑ	Ⓒ	Ⓓ					
14	Ⓐ	Ⓑ	Ⓒ	Ⓓ	34	Ⓐ	Ⓑ	Ⓒ	Ⓓ					
15	Ⓐ	Ⓑ	Ⓒ	Ⓓ	35	Ⓐ	Ⓑ	Ⓒ	Ⓓ					
16	Ⓐ	Ⓑ	Ⓒ	Ⓓ	36	Ⓐ	Ⓑ	Ⓒ	Ⓓ					
17	Ⓐ	Ⓑ	Ⓒ	Ⓓ	37	Ⓐ	Ⓑ	Ⓒ	Ⓓ					
18	Ⓐ	Ⓑ	Ⓒ	Ⓓ	38	Ⓐ	Ⓑ	Ⓒ	Ⓓ					
19	Ⓐ	Ⓑ	Ⓒ	Ⓓ	39	Ⓐ	Ⓑ	Ⓒ	Ⓓ					
20	Ⓐ	Ⓑ	Ⓒ	Ⓓ	40	Ⓐ	Ⓑ	Ⓒ	Ⓓ					

島崎 美登里（しまざき・みどり）

　コロンビア大学大学院（英語教育学）修士課程修了。埼玉県立大学名誉教授。著書に『英語教育を変えよう』（共著）など，論文に Developing Vocabulary in a University Reading Class: Autonomous Learning and Multiple Exposures in Context,『第二言語によるコミュニケーションに関わる学習者の情意要因』などがある。

Paul Wadden, Ph.D.（ポール・ワーデン）

　順天堂大学国際教養学部教授。ヴァーモント大学大学院修了（修辞学）。イリノイ州立大学大学院修了（英米文学博士）。

　著述家・文学者。ニューヨーク・タイムズ，ウォールストリート・ジャーナル，ワシントン・ポストなど，多数の新聞および雑誌に執筆。著書に *A Handbook for Teaching English at Japanese Colleges and Universities*（Oxford University Press），*Teaching English at Japanese Universities: A New Handbook*（Routledge），TESOL Quarterly, College Composition, College Literature に掲載の言語教育に関する論文，70 冊を超える TOEFL TEST, TOEIC TEST 対策教材など多数。

Robert A. Hilke（ロバート・A・ヒルキ）

　（株）リンクグローバルソリューション　プリンシパル。（株）ヒルキ コミュニケーションズ代表取締役社長。

　トヨタ，キヤノン，松下電器産業などで異文化間コミュニケーションのコンサルタントとして活躍。カリフォルニア大学サンディエゴ校大学院（言語学）修士課程修了。元国際基督教大学専任講師。

　異文化コミュニケーションおよび言語能力テストのスペシャリストで，TOEIC, TOEFL, GRE 対策教材などの著書多数。いずれのテストも繰り返し受験し，その傾向，特徴を詳細に把握したうえでの模擬問題の執筆と受験指導で定評がある。ほかに，『国際ビジネス感覚養成講座』など，語学教育に関する著書や論文多数。

© Midori Shimazaki; Paul Wadden; Robert A. Hilke, 2023, Printed in Japan

はじめて受ける TOEFL ITP® TEST 総合対策【改訂版】

2010年3月31日	初版第1刷発行
2023年2月25日	改訂初版第1刷発行
2024年11月5日	第2刷発行

著　者	島崎美登里／Paul Wadden／Robert A. Hilke
制　作	ツディブックス株式会社
発行者	田中 稔
発行所	株式会社 語研
	〒101－0064
	東京都千代田区神田猿楽町2－7－17
	電　　話　03－3291－3986
	ファクス　03－3291－6749
組　版	ツディブックス株式会社
印刷・製本	シナノ書籍印刷株式会社

ISBN978-4-87615-368-8 C0082

書名　　ハジメテウケル トーフルアイティーピーテスト ソウゴウタイサク カイテイバン
著者　　シマザキ ミドリ／ポール・ワーデン／ロバート・ヒルキ

本書の感想はスマホから↓

株式会社 語研
語研ホームページ https://www.goken-net.co.jp/